SHIPS OF HEAVEN

www.penguin.co.uk

SHIPS OF HEAVEN

The Private Life of Britain's Cathedrals

Christopher Somerville

doubleday

TRANSWORLD PUBLISHERS
61–63 Uxbridge Road, London W5 5SA
www.penguin.co.uk

Transworld is part of the Penguin Random House group of companies
whose addresses can be found at global.penguinrandomhouse.com

Penguin
Random House
UK

First published in Great Britain in 2019 by Doubleday
an imprint of Transworld Publishers

A CIP catalogue record for this book
is available from the British Library.

ISBNs 9780857523648 (hb)
9780857523655 (tpb)

Typeset in 11.5/15.5pt Minion Pro by Jouve (UK), Milton Keynes
Printed and bound in Great Britain by Clays Ltd, Elcograf S.p.A.

Penguin Random House is committed to a sustainable
future for our business, our readers and our planet. This book
is made from Forest Stewardship Council® certified paper.

MIX
Paper from
responsible sources
FSC® C018179

13 5 7 9 10 8 6 4 2

To the Holy Dusters of Salisbury Cathedral, and all the cathedral volunteers up and down the land, without whose generosity and hard work the Ships of Heaven would very soon run aground.

Contents

CONTENTS

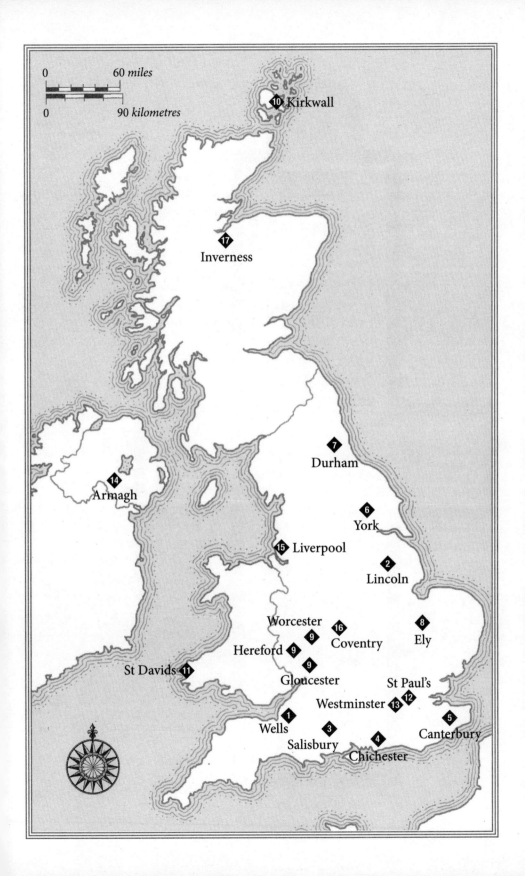

0   60 *miles*

0   90 *kilometres*

10 Kirkwall

17 Inverness

7
Durham

14
Armagh

6
York

15 Liverpool

2
Lincoln

Worcester **16**
9 Coventry
Hereford **9**

8
Ely

St Davids **11**

9
Gloucester

St Paul's

Westminster **13** **12**

1
Wells

3
Salisbury

4
Chichester

5
Canterbury

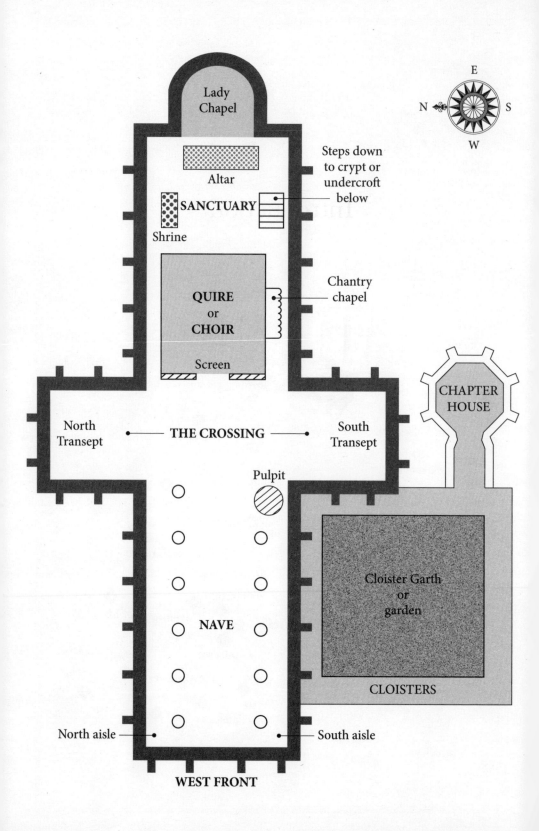

Introduction

I'M SIX YEARS OLD – six or seven, maybe. Small, anyhow. I'm standing on Cathedral Green in the tiny Somerset city of Wells, my head tilted back as far as my neck will crane. Up in the air it's blowing a gale, driving the clouds from west to east. In front of me, filling all earth and sky, is the biggest thing I've ever seen. It's bigger than a ship, but it looks just like one. There are people all over it, stone people, sitting very still. There are towers and battlements like a fighting warship in a storybook. And it looks as though it's moving towards me, steadily and mightily. It's going to roll right over me.

I see it coming, surging through the blue water of Heaven, the sky full of clouds like white horses, blown by the west wind, streaming away behind it. Inside my head there's a rushing and a toppling. The giant square prow full of stern stone faces presses forward till it looms sky-high over my head, and suddenly the grass behind me tilts up to thump the back of my skull. I have fallen flat on my back, run down and sunk by the great ship of Wells Cathedral.

This early memory has fixed in my head forever the idea of cathedrals as ships. The superstructure of Ely Cathedral seen across a green sea of wheat, a tanker treading down wind-rippled waves. Lincoln Cathedral sailing its hill in massive pride. The futuristic super-yacht of Coventry, chained forever to the blackened wreck of its own shadow. St Davids in dry dock, hidden in its sunken hollow. Ships, all of them – ships of stone, some moored in tightly provisioned ports, others out in the open in full sail, with ribbed interiors as tall as upturned battleships, with turrets and crows' nests, orlops and bilges, galleys and engine rooms, shanties and slang and superstitions, and a jovial (and sometimes not so jovial) crew with all its complicated hierarchy of skills and duties, gripes and satisfactions.

There are over one hundred cathedrals in England, Scotland and Wales – not just Anglican and Roman Catholic, but Greek Orthodox, Ukrainian Catholic, the Belarusian Autocephalous Orthodox Church, the Ancient and Old Catholic Church, and other even more more unorthodox denominations. As a travel writer I've visited most of them. What striking buildings they are, and what a story lies behind their huge, apparently solid façades – a narrative of bloody deeds, miracles, fanaticism, intrigue, ruin and rebirth.

It's a thrilling, ongoing soap opera of characters, from the monarchs who agreed their building and the grand lords and bishops who envisaged and ordered them, down to the peasant labourers who erected (and died on) the scaffolding, and the innkeepers and prostitutes, holy people and rogues who served and cheated the workers. The finagling and manoeuvring over where they'd be built, the towns that grew up in their shadows, the prosperity and pomp that followed them. The effects of the pilgrimages and the Black Death, the Reformation and the Civil War with its icon-smashing and desecration. The revival brought about by the Industrial Revolution, the hope and disillusion of two World Wars, and the uncertain future of these giant, fragile, irreplaceable national treasures.

Ships of Heaven is not an architectural or historical guidebook, or a gazetteer of Britain's cathedrals. There are more than enough of those. Rather, it's a voyage of discovery round a personal selection of cathedrals, some old favourites that I've visited many times, others that I'd never before set foot in.

Cathedrals are not just assemblages of dead stone shapes; they are lively organisms, in the same way that a ship is. There's not much about ogee arches or liturgical niceties in these pages. It's those kinds of technicalities that have put me off cathedrals in the past. Little details attract me: Green Men peeping from the pillars, slabs of fossil stone in the mason's yard, a cathedral cat snoring by a radiator.

Cathedrals are packed with stories ancient and modern: statues to the dead of forgotten battles, monuments to tiny children snatched away, windows that honour women who fought for their rights. The holy bones of saints, come to light during renovations. Beautiful treasures of glass and stonework, smashed by the pikestaves of religious bigots. The arrogance of puffed-up prelates. Murder and arson, slander and theft. In modern times, the bravery of the two Bishops of Liverpool who pushed back together against sectarian bigotry. The struggles of women to attain holy orders. Guilt and atonement in Coventry, then and now, for the horrors of war. The humility everywhere of simple souls.

In the final analysis, the Ships of Heaven stand or fall by their crew. Believers and non-believers. Architects, archaeologists, the woman who dusts the monuments, the man who winds the clock. I talked to stonemasons at their workbenches and embroiderers at their needlework, bishops and treasurers in their offices, worshippers in candlelit quires and lost souls in back pews. Here is the account of a year's passage with this grand flotilla.

Cathedrals

A Short Inspection

Anglo-Saxon: Early Days

Cathedrals – the regional seats of bishops – were centres of power and prestige from the outset, and the tale of our Ships of Heaven begins with Canterbury Cathedral, founded as a small, stone-built church by St Augustine in the last years of the sixth century, fewer than two hundred years after the Romans left Britain. Augustine's brief from Pope Gregory was to convert the pagan British, and his cathedral at Canterbury was the focal point for that. From this centre, a religious order and discipline spread outwards slowly through a part pagan, part native British Christian country.

Other cathedrals soon followed – Rochester and St Paul's in London (604), York (625) and Winchester (660). Seven had been founded throughout the land within a hundred years of Augustine's arrival, by newly converted kings fearful for their souls, by bishops and abbots, missionaries and possessors of saintly relics. By the time the Normans invaded in 1066 there were eleven cathedrals – none of any magnificence architecturally, but all powerful and influential places.

Norman: Stern Solidity

It was the Normans, exponents of Romanesque architecture, who got the great phase of cathedral-building under way, and Durham, started in 1093, was their first masterpiece. They began building it less than thirty years after their invasion, in a region still turbulent and rebellious. The Norman ethic in this first phase of their rule was practical and military rather than aesthetic, and Durham Cathedral was a powerful example. It had to be impressive; the new rulers were making a plain statement of dominance to the angry and disaffected locals in raising a building that was, in Sir Walter Scott's economical phrase, 'half church of God, half castle 'gainst the Scot'.

Other strong, foursquare cathedrals soon followed, covering north, south, east and west of the kingdom – Exeter, Lincoln, Chichester, Salisbury, Norwich, Ely and Carlisle, all started within forty years, all with the protection of a nearby castle. The new cathedrals were as much a statement as the castles: the Normans had the temporal and spiritual upper hand. The same 'We're here to stay' message marks them out – sturdy fat pillars, heavy stonework, zigzag chevron decorations. But looking at these Ships of Heaven today, one sees the marks of other, later makers all over them, as the blunt old battleships of the Norman cathedrals were slowly transformed into grand and beautiful yachts in which everyone could sail away to Heaven.

Gothic: Light and Elaborate

The Normans got their feet under the table and settled in for a hundred years of rule. They were succeeded in their turn by three centuries of Plantagenet rule, and a brief hundred-year flurry from the Houses of Lancaster and York. During these turbulent times at home and abroad, the Catholic Church in England became ever richer, its land-owning monasteries more powerful and wealthy on the donations of pilgrims and the tithes of tenants. The upper echelons of secular society were getting richer and more luxury-minded, too, as a merchant class arose, wealthy from sheep and shipping. Crusaders and foreign travellers brought back new styles of art and architecture which infiltrated the cathedrals, and the challenge was to incorporate them in the most sympathetic – or least clumsy – way.

Architectural fashion and engineering improvements went hand in hand with gradually increasing confidence on the part of the ruling dynasties, both secular and religious. The aim became to lighten the impression the great buildings gave, to raise the focus from solid ground towards Heaven by means of spires and pinnacles, to insert beautiful glass into enormous windows, to embellish the cathedrals and their shrines with the very best of stonework, wood carving and ironwork. This might have been for the glory of God, but it was also for the glorification of men, specifically monarchs, prelates and rich men who endowed the monasteries and spent their money on securing their entrance into Heaven. They reminded God and their fellow men who was footing the bill by building towers, spires and porches with their initials in flintwork, putting in fabulously coloured and expensive stained-glass windows with their images included, elaborate marble tombs for themselves, and beautiful chantry chapels whence prepaid prayers for their salvation could reach the ears of the Almighty after their deaths.

The cathedrals reflected all this in the three stages of Gothic architecture that superseded, swallowed up or incorporated the Norman originals: Early English (late twelfth to early fourteenth centuries) with its tall, pointed lancet windows and rather severe lack of embellishment, and then Decorated (late thirteenth to late fourteenth) with more stonework elaboration and bigger windows with lots of tracery. There was a very noticeable hiccup immediately following the death of nearly half the population of England in the 1348–9 Black Death pandemic. This new era ushered in the less costly and soberly plain Perpendicular, a style more suited to the sombre mood of the times, but soon it had burst out in the exuberantly intricate trelliswork of fan vaulting and lace-like flying buttresses which owed their existence as much to sophisticated structural engineering as to artistic expression.

Not that medieval architecture was always successful. Most of the medieval cathedrals lean well out of true, thanks to the weight of their roofs, spires and towers. Some of the most impressive towers and spires were wobbly, and several collapsed altogether.

There is one 'pure' English cathedral, built all of a piece in one style, and that is Salisbury. The original version was one of the Normans' earliest, but they built it high on a hill without a proper water supply. The town that grew up around it was thirsty, dirty, disease-ridden and untenable. The Bishop of Salisbury refounded church and town down in the meadows by the River Avon in 1220, and the whole cathedral was completed in less than forty years, a unified Early English vision in pale dove-grey Chilmark limestone.

Salisbury was one example of the soft beauty of southern English limestone. Exeter is built of rich golden limestone known as hamstone. Norwich and Lincoln in the east had a sharper tinge to their silvery stone, while out in the west and north cathedrals such as Carlisle, Durham and Hereford, fortress-like guardians of remote and debatable lands, were made of solid red/pink sandstone. Such regional differences are part of the fascination of these wonderful buildings.

Trickle-down

Where each cathedral finally came to anchor with its crews of monks and priests might be a matter of royal will or military imperative, of aristocratic decision-making, or of episcopal or monastic influence. Enormous and lasting power, wealth, and spiritual and worldly consequence hung on the decision. And the cathedral had to be paid for, with donations by the founder, with endowments, with taxes or tithes, with contributions from flocks of pilgrims if the cathedral was lucky enough to house the relics of a popular or healing saint.

The building of the cathedral itself took place on a timescale unbelievably long to modern minds. Salisbury might have been built in thirty-eight years, but the norm was nearer two hundred years or more – York Minster, for example, developed gradually over four centuries between 1080 and 1472. There was work for masons, architects, woodworkers, ironworkers, quarrymen, scaffolders, ladder makers, tool repairers, glass painters. And to service them: blacksmiths, ropemakers, clothiers, innkeepers; prostitutes for their bodily needs, priests for their souls; butchers, bakers and candlestick makers. To accommodate them, a large 'footprint' all round the nascent cathedral, to be filled with housing, hostels, taverns, shops, mortuaries. And once the cathedral was up and running, even if incomplete, there were pilgrims visiting the shrines of saints, sick folk looking for help, crowds in town for the ceremonies, crowds for the high days and holidays and fair days. Not to mention the above-listed craftsmen, and the generations who succeeded them, who had to remain on hand to maintain the huge and complex structure.

So bustling, prosperous, money-making, lively towns, parts of them beautifully built of stone or brick, most ramshackle and more or less haphazard, developed and grew in the shadow of the cathedrals; also harbourside facilities to build and service the Ships of Heaven, with much the same purpose and atmosphere as a seaport. Monasteries were built or hugely developed alongside. The countryside for miles around, too, had to adapt its production in order to feed and clothe the newcomers. It was an effect mirrored later in the millennium by the influence of the Industrial Revolution and the advent of the railways.

But it wasn't just about worldly preferment or gain. Planning, building and maintaining a cathedral united people in pride and excitement. To play your part unstintingly – to carve the reverse side of a stone leaf as assiduously as the front, because God would see it even if no one else did – was to go some way towards saving your soul. It was a way of thinking outside personal gain, because you yourself wouldn't live to see it completed.

Chapter and Worse

The bishop headed the cathedral staff; his Chapter (senior clergy) ran things; the monks or other clergy prayed and sang and shepherded the visitors. The power the bishop wielded could be enormous – if handled the right way, he could prove a fount of patronage with regard to land ownership and rent, contracts, rights to hold markets and many other preferments. He and the cathedral Chapter could settle disputes in your favour, if so minded. If mishandled, though, you could find yourself beyond the pale, economically, socially – and spiritually, even as far as excommunication or facing a charge of heresy, the most dangerous form of ostracism.

Some bishops, such as the so-called prince-bishops of Durham, enjoyed wealth and exercised power and influence not far short of that of a king. When cathedrals clashed, like the row just after the Norman Conquest between Canterbury and York as to which was supreme over the other, the argument could go on for nearly three hundred years. Bishops received their lands and wealth from their temporal master, the king. Yet spiritually the king could be in need of admonishment – always a tricky thing for a bishop to handle. Kings and bishops could cut across each other in pride and anger – King Henry II and Archbishop Thomas Becket are the best-known examples, and that ended with the archbishop murdered on his own altar steps. Further down the scale, internal disputes, squabbles, petty meanness and ignoble dealing are all recorded – sometimes in stone and wood, as the masons working on the Gothic embellishments slyly added likenesses of thieving priests, greedy nuns, lascivious monks, over-proud bishops and puffed-up kings.

The Hidden World

It's these funny, quirky and often coded features that offer a window into the medieval mind. Parables, symbols, messages about pride and its falls, power and its misuses, are rife. Mappa Mundi, the chart in Hereford Cathedral of the 'known' world at the dawn of the fourteenth century, shows centaurs and salamanders, unicorns and mandrakes, men with eyes in their chests, and men sheltering from the sun under their own enormous feet.

Then there are the symbols that fascinate modern minds because their meaning has been forgotten: the enigmatic Green Men, spewing or choking on tendrils and leaves, who peer out of hiding in Ely, Norwich, Bristol and most other cathedrals with equivocal frowns or leers. They bring a smack of the wild into the geometric order of the cathedrals' architecture.

The cathedrals were not solely used for religious purposes; by far the largest buildings in the area, their naves were utilized much more commonly than nowadays for speeches, proclamations and public meetings. They were resource points for people in need of healing, education and legal advice, for example. And of course they were centres of architectural innovation, creative art and excellence.

Reformation and Upheaval

With the Reformation came a shattering upheaval. The monasteries, so closely associated with the cathedrals, had become thoroughly rotten and corrupt. They were closed and unroofed. The jewelled shrines of the now discredited saints were broken open, their old bones thrown out or burned. But the cathedrals themselves survived – the ones with secular clergy just carried on with a switch of liturgy, and those with monastic foundations were reformed and continued as Church of England. A hundred years later, as Civil War and Puritan zeal swept the land, iconoclasts came to smash the glorious painted glass and scratch out the eyes of angels and saints on painted screens.

It took two centuries of neglect and decay for the Anglican Church to recover from the slump it entered after the Civil War. Many cathedrals were strapped for cash and couldn't maintain their fabric. But the nineteenth century saw a tremendous revival in the country's fortunes on the back of the expanding Empire and the Industrial Revolution. Anglicanism got a revitalizing shot in the arm, Roman Catholicism came out of the shadows after centuries of penal discrimination, and the cathedrals entered a Golden Age. New stone and marble monuments were peppered round their interiors, the Arts and Crafts Movement was deemed suitable for new decorations, carving and windows. Bishops became 'grand' once more, and cathedral towns 'precious' in high Victorian manner, as lampooned by Anthony Trollope in his 1850–60s Barchester novels (widely said to be based on Salisbury). And after a hiatus of three hundred years, new cathedrals were built, many in response to the huge increases in population of northern cities during the Industrial Revolution. Once more cathedrals were rising as centres of art, craft and teaching, but within vast communities already fully formed. The social history – industrial, working-class and reformist – of these cathedrals was very different from their medieval predecessors, but as lights in often dark places they performed the same functions.

Modern Times

The twentieth century saw new cathedrals built in Britain, some of traditional neo-Gothic form (Liverpool's Anglican cathedral), others of bold modern style (Liverpool's Roman Catholic cathedral). Brick-built Guildford Cathedral, begun in 1936, was completed in 1961 after a pleasing exercise in democracy in which the public sponsored the work, brick by brick. And the new Coventry Cathedral, rising in the 1950s from the bombed-out ruin of the old one alongside, was all about atonement and reconciliation, a struggle through a dark place towards the light – a remarkable effect of the Second World War.

1

Wells

A Ship of My Own

I AM BACK ON CATHEDRAL GREEN in the city of Wells. A west wind is blowing. Clouds are rushing east. And the west front of Wells Cathedral still sails towards me, high overhead, as it did sixty years ago. I don't fall flat on my back this time, but there's the same whirlpool feeling inside my head. I squint up at the ranks of the great and the good and the not so good, all prim and admonitory in their limestone immobility. And I see myself in a schoolboy's shorts and sandals, walking into the cathedral under their disapproving gaze for my midday appointment with Jack Blandiver and his remarkable clock.

Wells Cathedral was 'our' cathedral. We lived near Gloucester, seventy miles away from Wells, and Gloucester had a perfectly serviceable cathedral of its own. Quite a famous one to us as children, too – Beatrix Potter had put it in her picture of the Tailor of Gloucester and his cat Simpkin in the snow on Christmas Day. But our family came from a village just outside Wells, that was where we often visited and felt we belonged, and Wells was the cathedral that I knew best. The stone figures on the west front with their little short thighs and elbows bent the wrong way had become familiars. So had the scissor arch across the middle of the cathedral, like a cross old owl staring at you with his beak and eyes wide open.

On mornings when my parents had boring grown-up things to do in Wells, it was a thrill to be left in the cathedral to wait for midday. Sitting in shorts on the stone bench in the north transept was a cold hard business, but that didn't matter. When midday struck, all sorts of magical things would happen at once. Outside, two grey effigies of men in armour swivelled smartly on their turrets, halberds in hand, to strike a pair of bells that hung over the big clock on the wall. I couldn't see them from where I sat within the cathedral, but I knew these gallants kept time more or less in step with Jack Blandiver. Jack was another model figure, a sprightly little man in a red coat and white stockings who perched in his own high niche inside the north transept. He sat on a wooden settle that stuck a little way out from the wall, so far up and with so far to fall it gave me a funny feeling inside. He wore a smudge of moustache and a pair of triangular sideburns. His eyes were circled with thick black liner. As the men-at-arms rang the noon chimes outside, Jack Blandiver would kick back abruptly with his heels at a pair of bells hidden under his seat – *bing, bong! bing, bong!* – and strike forward with the two beaters in his hands at another bell hanging in front of him.

Something about the jerky, tic-like movements and the intensity of his thousand-yard mascara stare lent Jack Blandiver a sinister air. One couldn't spare any more attention for him, however, because on the wall opposite me, with a dusty whirr and a bang, the oldest clock in the world was creaking into its midday display. Above the enormous wooden clock face with its painted likenesses of sun, moon and stars, four tiny mounted figures of jousting knights began to orbit round one another. Two would pass each other by without incident, but the crux came when the other pair met in their circling. One, a sturdy, beefy-faced fellow with a handlebar moustache, dressed in a red jerkin and cap of green, lowered his lance on each revolution and neatly struck his opponent in the chest. This unfortunate, a sallow-faced wight in faded gold armour and a helmet, would be hurled backwards, his back bending at a spine-snapping right angle with a loud crack as he was laid flat out on the back of his horse – as flat as myself on the grass of Cathedral Green when the Ship of Heaven ran me down. Red Jerkin the upright victor and Gold Armour the supine loser would then continue their opposing circles, round into the darkness behind the mechanism, out again into the light with Gold Armour upright in the saddle once more as he bore round inexorably for yet another flattening at the hands of Red Jerkin.

If Mum or Dad deposited me after the witching hour of noon, it was scarcely worth waiting till the next hour struck. The jousting knights were programmed to make twelve full circuits at noon, but at one o'clock they made only one. The man in the red jacket had time to land no more than a single lance blow; his golden opponent was snapped back in his saddle just the once. I can still recall the sense of indignation at having been dealt short measure.

Knights and dragons went together, and if you were fed up with waiting for the combatants of the clock, there were plenty of dragons to find in the cathedral. Spotting them entailed squinting up the long pale columns of the nave, where among the carved leaves you could spy dragons fighting, twin dragons sharing one tail, little friendly dragons peaceably eating the foliage. Better than those, though, were dragons one could actually handle, those carved in wood that were hidden away in the choir stalls. I liked the name of the solid old seats, 'misericords', with its intimations of misery and mystery. Those seats were heavy, the hinges stiff, and the verger would tick you off if he found you crawling about in the sacred (if dusty) space between the stalls. But under there I found more magic. Dragons eating their own tails, chewing their own backbones. A dozy dragon with a great fat head. Violent images, too: a dragon being speared down its throat, another being stabbed through the head. You could run your fingers across their ears and bellies, feeling the tiny cuts that the wood carver had made long ago. It brought them alive, in a way.

I didn't really take any interest in the cathedral's music. I liked to hear the sonorous tides of the *Messiah* in Advent, the familiar carols at Christmas and the *St Matthew Passion* coming up to Easter. But it was all a bit like lying back in the bath before bedtime. The singing, as soothing as warm water, would wash me clean away into slumber. I preferred to wander up the wide crooked steps to the chapter house, into the aisles where funny little stone people capered at the tops of the columns: a man with toothache stretching his mouth out sideways, a man picking splinters out of his feet, and a naughty varlet stealing grapes and getting well thumped for his sins.

Outside the west front of the cathedral you went down through a little chink of archway called Penniless Porch into Wells's marketplace. A much bigger archway opened off this space, and through it you got your first glimpse of the Bishop's Palace. The Bishop of Bath & Wells was a figure you saw rarely, but everyone spoke about him with a sort of reverence. If he came into the cathedral, or into a room where you were, there was a pop-star frisson about him, even though he was an old man. Wells people were proud of the fact that their bishop lived among them, in the house that had been lived in by their bishops for the best part of eight hundred years. He lived in fine style, or at least in fine quarters – a palace, no less, surrounded by a walled moat where swans would come to ring for their food by tugging a bell rope beside the drawbridge. That was a fabulous, fairytale touch for a child.

Wells was my cathedral, its frolics and personalities, its carvings and clock. It dominated the life of the little city. Its flat-topped towers, too bluntly finished for beauty, were a personal landmark in a country-side I knew and loved. When I had little children of my own, it became an immutable weekend ritual to walk from our village to Wells across the muddy cattle pastures, over the Palace Fields towards the towers, along the moat with its hybrid ducks and quarrelsome black-headed gulls, stopping to feed redundant breakfast toast to the swans, pausing to drop a penny to the tangle-haired melodeon player in Penniless Porch, before arriving at the cathedral for a quick scoot round and tea in the Cloisters Café.

New buildings have arisen on the city outskirts. Old certainties fall fast. But the towers of the cathedral still sail ship-like against the blue sky, as they did for me all those years before. Surely the permanence of that great, solid, dependable block of architecture and history must be set in stone for another thousand years.

'Oh, a cathedral isn't a fixed entity,' says Bishop Peter Hancock. He leans forward and pours me a cup of tea. 'A cathedral isn't a monolith. If it's a ship, then it's a huge cargo carrier, but it doesn't maintain one unchanging shape and nature. It bends with the waves of history, of public feeling and the times. At one time, say in Cromwell's era, it's plain, unmusical and stern; at another, during the last century for example, it becomes colourful and daring and full of joyful songs.'

We are talking in 'Bishop Peter's room' in the palace, a calm, book-lined study through which secretaries and helpers flit from time to time. There are no lawn sleeves or gaiters about Bishop Peter, although he has his purple shirt front and white tab collar on, and a gold crucifix on a chain.

It's rather remarkable, in fact, that we are sitting here at all. Before coming to meet the bishop I searched the Internet for 'Wells Bishop's Palace', and unearthed a storm of remarkably vehement online outrage. 'OK, parishioners, on your knees,' posted BrazilPat. 'The C of E machine needs loads more money to pay for their excesses. Pray up & cough up.' 'So he is "slumming it" in a grade 2 Georgian rectory,' spluttered David from Northwich. 'Howbeit the most High dwelleth not in temples made with hands, you have got to laugh lol.'

When Peter Hancock was appointed Bishop of Bath & Wells in December 2013, he walked straight into a row not of his own making. 'I'd been appointed,' he says, 'but hadn't yet taken up the role, when the Church Commissioners decided to move the residence of the bishop. There were a number of reasons why they came to that decision. The upkeep of an historic palace is very expensive, and they felt it was inappropriate in these times of financial hardship to house a bishop here. I didn't have any say in it – and there wasn't much I *could* say, anyway, as I had not yet come into post. Since then I've learned just what an attraction the palace is. We get four hundred thousand people over the drawbridge every year. The Trust now employ over forty staff, some of whom live within the palace precincts. It means I am actually something of an abbot here with a community to care for!'

The Commissioners bought a former rectory in the nearby village of Croscombe as the bishop's residence, for close to £1 million. It was only supposed to be a temporary stopgap until a more suitable house could be found in Bath or Wells. But that wasn't explained properly, and a rumpus ensued. Local grumblings quickly fanned themselves into a Twitterstorm. A more measured statement of opposition was issued by senior staff of the Diocese of Bath & Wells, taking the Commissioners to task for failing to ask what ordinary people thought. 'Despite ample time and opportunity, the Church Commissioners have failed to undertake effective consultation at a local level. Instead they have taken a unilateral decision which has, sadly, cast a shadow over the announcement of our next Bishop.'

The Commissioners' high-handedness not only attracted this rap over the knuckles from the senior clergy, it also aroused the sleeping dragon of local opinion. A petition was got up, attracting over two thousand signatures. The Commissioners' actions smacked of a Barchester sense of entitlement in the era of Internet democracy, and the whole affair pointed up a very significant attitude among the local public – that twenty-first-century men and women still valued the connection between bishop and palace, cathedral and city, and were prepared to fight to preserve 'their' bishop in what they saw as his rightful place among them. Sentimental, romantic, a soft-focus *Vicar of Dibley* view of bishops, palaces and cathedrals? Perhaps. But the strength of feeling couldn't be shrugged aside by the Church authorities. The Archbishops' Council of the Church of England deliberated, and decided to revoke the move. 'The people of Wells felt they were losing "their" bishop,' Peter Hancock summarizes, 'and they rose up. The decision had to be reversed.'

What was the Diocese of Bath & Wells looking for when the post of bishop became vacant in 2013? 'Well,' says Bishop Hancock, 'a bishop's appointment used to be a lot more political, but the Church takes more responsibility for it nowadays. The process is much like any other job. There's a longlist drawn up; perhaps three or four people are then invited to interview, and then someone's asked if they would like to fill the role – in this case, me. The diocese has a big say in what direction they want their new bishop to lead them. Bath & Wells is primarily a rural diocese and they were looking for ways in which the Church could engage more effectively with the whole diocese, but especially with rural communities, with agriculture and the environment.'

I've got a lot of learning to do when it comes to the Ships of Heaven, that's becoming clear. I've always assumed that a cathedral is just the biggest, finest, most handsome church in its diocese, and everyone from the bishop and dean downwards is based there and has it as their main concern. To be frank, I'm not really sure what a bishop does, or a dean for that matter.

'Well,' says Hancock, 'the two roles are quite different. The bishop is concerned with the wider church and with all the communities which make up their diocese. The dean has a particular responsibility for the cathedral. The Dean and Chapter, the group who run the cathedral, have a significant amount of independence. But it's essential for them to work together. It is very important that bishop and dean have a good working relationship, that diocese and cathedral support each other, especially if there are any problems or concerns.

'As bishop I have a role as Visitor, primarily an advisory role, as far as Wells Cathedral is concerned. A bishop has to play that role very carefully and tactfully, so as not to step on the dean's toes, or those of the Chapter, the group who look after the running of the cathedral and its worship. The position of Wells is unusual in that bishop, dean and clergy all live very close to one another within the curtilage of the Liberty, the historic enclave round the cathedral and palace. So it's vital that bishop and dean get on, and I'm very pleased to say that the dean here, John Davies, is delightful, an excellent colleague and a good friend. He doesn't confine himself entirely to the cathedral however; he makes a point of getting out and about. He and other members of the Chapter regularly preach and minister all round the diocese.'

The challenge and the problem for any bishop with a strong sense of mission is how to spread and resource the message in an era of declining church attendance and unwillingness to accept anything that smacks of authoritarianism. The fact is that all across Britain, church attendance has been steadily declining. Only one in twenty people goes to a parish church service on a Sunday; that's fewer than one million churchgoers, for the first time since records began.

'We've got to be more flexible and responsive,' says Bishop Hancock. 'There's been a significant drop in children and young people attending church services on a Sunday. So maybe we need to find other times when young people can meet together – and maybe not in a church. When I first served as a curate in a parish, baptisms were held at three p.m., when the church was cold and empty. So we moved them to the morning, when the family coming in would mingle with the congregation going out, and the church would seem warmer and less intimidating. In baptism we say that we are welcoming someone into the family of God, so wouldn't it be better if they could actually see the church operating as a family home?'

There are nineteen deaneries or groups of parishes in the Diocese of Bath & Wells, and Peter Hancock wants them to be 'engines of change'. He has asked each rural dean to draw up plans and objectives. How to engage with children and young people, with homeless people, with the elderly, with schools and nurseries, with the lonely and bereaved. How to include those with particular needs in everyday worship – those who may be deaf or who live with illness or disability. 'If we're not doing that, we're falling short.'

But what about resources, in an age that's strapped for cash? Who's going to get these admirable aims carried out across a diocese of some 560 parish churches, nearly two thousand square miles and almost a million people? 'We have our paid clergy, but we also have a huge resource of self-supporting ministers, retired clergy, lay readers, lay pastoral carers and lay worship leaders. They aren't just enthusiastic amateurs. These are people who are responding to God's call and who put their gifts and faith to work. They have all taken courses to qualify them: learning how to lead worship and prayers; how to preach and teach; how to listen and care for others. There is an incredible amount of expertise and energy, right across the whole diocese, and it is humbling to see people using their gifts to serve their communities.

'As far as the cathedral is concerned, it's a question of a feeling of belonging. Wells Cathedral, for example, might seem pretty remote if you live in the west of the diocese on Exmoor – Simonsbath, say, or Exford. But Taunton's only an hour over the hills. If you let us know you're coming, we'll welcome you with warmth and friendship, you'll get a cup of tea and a seat at the front, we'll pray the prayers you ask. So you can feel that the cathedral is for you, is *yours*.

'Wells Cathedral,' says the bishop, as our allotted hour runs out, 'it isn't a pilgrimage cathedral, like Canterbury with Thomas Becket or Winchester with the bones of St Swithun. Wells never managed to acquire its own saint, so it never had that wealth from formal pilgrimage. But people still come here as pilgrims. They want a finish, a prayerful end to a journey, or just a place to tell stories of what they've been through in life. A space to express big hopes, dreams and fears. In our busy, noisy world many people seem to suffer from a lack of connection with anything or anyone. But in a cathedral people often discover what they have never experienced before, a connection with God. These are presences that hover in the air of a cathedral, like angels.'

In a corner of Penniless Porch a bearded man still tinkles out a tune on a clarsach. The cathedral cloisters look much as they did when I used to munch chocolate cake with the children here. But now the café has gone elsewhere, and the cloisters on this cold afternoon are clean and uncluttered. I don't think I've ever really looked properly at the fifteenth-century carvings in warm, honey-coloured hamstone that embellish the vaulting of the ceiling. Their details are quite markedly blurred, perhaps because the weather has blown in on them from the cloister garth, the garden at the centre of the hollow square. The bosses, great and small, show flowers, leaves, bunches of grapes, coats of arms. A pelican pecks nourishment from her own breast for her young. Dragons shrug free of their patchy coats of whitewash. Four faces meet at the intersection of two ribs, their features indistinct, only distinguishable one from another by their hats and hairstyles. A Green Man stares down with a skull's grimace, overwhelmed by great curly kale-like leaves sprouting from mouth, eyes and brow.

I'm always drawn to carved folk musicians in the odd corners of cathedrals with their burlesque looks, foreshortened limbs and cramped positions – quite different from the beautiful musical angels shown in stained glass or painted panels playing harps, shawms or psalteries with languid grace. The peasant music maker with his bagpipes or bumbulum is clumsy, almost furtive of attitude, distorted by being obliged to fill an awkward angle or obscure cranny. It's as though the stone carvers knew that folk musicians were socially significant people with an advanced skill, but felt obliged to tuck them away for the Bruegelian characters they were. Overhead in the cloisters I spy a pair of pipers, their legs painfully hunched up, posed on either side of a stone rib. One musician is playing a straightforward-looking oboe or shawm, but his colleague's instrument is more mysterious. He's blowing a single pipe that leads into a double chanter, like Cornish bagpipes. Both hands are busy on the holes of these paired chanters. But the piper also has a windbag under his arm and a drone resting on his left shoulder. Is it an accurate representation of an exotic instrument powered by breath and also by bag? More likely the carver didn't know or care about accuracy, but just did his best to depict a complicated instrument he didn't really understand.

An epitaph for the Revd Robert Foster, 'Prebendary and Priest Vicar of this Cathedral' (died 20 September 1836), catches my eye:

His eye sight, weak from his birth, waxed more and more dim
with advancing years, till at length those that look out of the windows were darkened. But a light sprang up in the darkness. While
those around him shed the silent tear, contemplating his painful
loss, a holy joy would brighten up his countenance, so that of him
it might be truly said, He kissed the rod that smote him.

I remember spelling this out as a child – one rather too frequently smit-
ten with the rod for one or another malfeasance. I had a kind of fellow
feeling for poor Mr Foster, although unable to imagine kissing my
headmaster's cane under any circumstance whatsoever. I read his title
again – Prebendary – and it reminds me once more that I don't have
much of a clue about these cathedral officials, precentors, archdeacons,
prebendaries and deans, commemorated so kindly in carved epitaphs
and drooping cherubim. The dean, for example. I remember the fact of
the Dean of Wells from childhood, that such a personage existed, and
that he, or his office, was somehow very grand. Now I need to get a
rather more grown-up handle on the realities of cathedrals, and those
who move in the shadows behind the slate and marble.

'He's best addressed as "Mr Dean",' I'm told as I am shown into the
cathedral office. 'Oh, John is fine,' says the Very Revd Dr John Davies,
Dean of Wells, as he leads the way into the chapter room. He has been
in post for fifteen months – long enough to win the trust and admiration of Bishop Peter Hancock, who appointed him from his previous
post as Dean of Derby.

'What does a dean do? Well, my job is to preside over the governance of the cathedral in spiritual matters, in mission, in finances, in
matters concerning the diocese and the bishop, relations with the city
of Wells and its environs, in outreach and education. To make sure,
first and foremost, that the cathedral runs as well as it can, that it's not
one more problem the bishop has to solve. A broad brief? Yes, you could

say so! Insofar as there is a buck, it stops with me. However, I have a Chapter or governing group of five to help me – the chancellor, the treasurer, the precentor, the archdeacon, and . . . who's the fifth? Oh dear, let me think . . . ah yes, me, of course!

'The 1999 Cathedrals Measure changed the way that cathedrals are run. That was in response to the Howe Report in 1994, which criticized cathedrals for the insular way they were run by exclusive, unaccountable governing bodies. Since then Chapters have been under greater scrutiny. They are no longer composed of clergy alone; now they include lay people to broaden their scope. At Wells we have three lay people – one has great experience of how worship is conducted in other cathedrals, another is expert in fundraising, and the third in project management. They bring these skills to the meetings; it's a very welcome step forward. And in fact there's now a proposal to bring in more lay members, to enlarge Chapters further – maybe to a dozen people in the case of Wells. I'd really welcome that. The scope of what the dean deals with changes all the time. Last week the city's LBGT group were at this table, for example; this week, the Knights Templar.'

Some Chapters, led awry by too much unaccountable power, have badly needed sorting out. The most notorious recent case was a poisonous row between dean and sub-dean at Lincoln in the 1990s. I'm due to visit Lincoln Cathedral in a week or so, where I'll find the details of that sorry mess still raw in people's memories. John Davies mentions a couple of current examples, one cathedral whose dean has fallen out with everyone, another where the dean and the administrator have formed a duopoly and shut the rest of Chapter out.

'If there's a mess, a problem with a dean and/or Chapter, it's up to the bishop to sort it out, not the state. But Dean and Chapter are independent of the bishop, and that's a vital element to maintain. The whole history of the governance of the Anglican Church is about power and its exercise, about individual priests being free to use their independent judgements. However, that's under the general rules and mission of the diocese, which is guided by the bishop.

'It's true that we do leave the bishop in the body of the cathedral at the making of prebendaries; I install them in the chapter house without the bishop present. It symbolizes the balance and separation of powers – a way of resisting absolutism, if you like, of emphasizing Chapter's independence from the bishop. Practically, of course, it's far better if the two sides work closely together. How closely depends quite heavily on the personal relationship between dean and bishop.

'The cathedral as it relates to the wider diocese – that's another delicate relationship. Parish clergy, especially, can get a case of "cathedral envy". They see the money that pours into cathedrals, the support we have here, the excellence in music and worship, the respect – "Good morning, Mr Dean" – and so on. Everything zeroing in on the cathedral, the big ego. It can look very self-satisfied, like cathedrals are up themselves.'

The bland leading the bland, the Tory party at prayer, all those hoary old jibes? 'Yes, exactly. And the bishop and I both want to change that perception. I preach out at other churches all over the diocese every month or six weeks – I offer myself, and also I invite them back. Come to the cathedral, bring your parishioners, come and preach here, have tea and a tour. I don't like this "Welcome to *our* cathedral, have a cup of tea with *us*, join in *our* worship." It is *your* cathedral, or should be.'

Cathedrals as bright stars, radiating light and energy outwards, rather than black holes sucking everything into their powerful embrace – it's a dynamic aspiration. 'This is fundamental,' says the dean. 'We start every day in the cathedral with a celebration of the Eucharist, a sharing of the body and blood of Christ – and what more outward-going, non-possessive act of sacrifice could there be than Christ giving his life away? Cathedrals are not for their clergy or congregations to possess; they are for giving away.'

Back in the cathedral, touring with one of the guides, I learn all sorts of things. The monks that have always paced the cloisters in my imagination never existed. There never was a monastery here – the cloisters were built for priestly processions. Wells Cathedral, constructed from east to west between 1175 and 1240, was the first English cathedral to be built completely in the Gothic style, an architectural mode borrowed from France but marked as peculiarly English by the great length and sideways sprawl of cathedrals in these islands. Now that's been pointed out, I can see it clearly as I look down the length of a nave uncluttered by any furniture (the cathedral is having a chair-free month). 'A ship's hull,' says the guide, and I smile to myself. 'All brightly painted in medieval times, of course, a wonderful riot of colour. That all vanished under whitewash at the Reformation – not a hint of colour anywhere in the new austerity. Then the whitewash was peeled right back to the bare stone by the Victorians – the "Great Scrape", we call that period. They removed all the monuments from the walls and the aisles and collected them in the cloisters. So today we enjoy the integrity of the stone itself, with nothing to detract from it.' Yes, now I can appreciate that, too – the cloisters lined with epitaphs and funerary slabs intended for the nave, leaving the pale gold of the limestone, quarried at Doulting just down the road, to dominate all other visual impressions in the main body of the building.

What about the 'angry owl', the scissor arch, that great construct swirling in perfect symmetry across the end of the nave? I've always thought of it as timeless, two gentle sigmoid curves crossing each other and pierced by a pair of bevelled portholes, something so perfect, so absolutely right-looking, that it could have been designed yesterday or a thousand years ago. There are three of them, says the guide. Good Lord, so there are, forming a three-sided box. I have literally never, in nearly seventy years, noticed the other two that stand at right angles across the transepts. Familiarity breeds blindness, I suppose. All were inserted in a bit of a panic between 1338 and 1348, when a recently built upper storey and lead-coated spire had wobbled the central tower. The water table was very close to the surface directly below, and the additional weight was too much for the soft ground. The whole tower had begun to subside, and it was only the insertion of the scissor arches that stabilized things. Existing arches were fortified with blocking stones, flying buttresses added to give a bit of counter-thrust, but it was the scissor arches that saved the day. On those three supports, as beautiful as they are effective, the tower has stood for another seven hundred years. We know the name of the man who dreamed them up and saved the tower – master mason William Joy.

I drift about the cathedral in the wake of the guide. Imperfections, quirks, quiddities give a human, manageable feel to the giant essay in stonework. The text round the lip of the pulpit, squashed up and abbreviated because the carver miscalculated his distances. Empty recesses in tomb slabs on the floor where the memorial brasses were wrenched up after the Reformation and used to patch up the leaky roof. The chapter house of 1306, octagonal, splendid, its central stem branching up and out into intricate rib vaulting. The Lady chapel, flooded with coloured shafts of sunlight through windows spattered with tiny fragments of glass. 'Jumble windows, we call them,' says the guide. I look more closely, and see a maze of heads, animals, grinning lions, foliage, limbs. 'All this glass comes from windows smashed when Puritan soldiers were billeted in the cathedral around the time of the Civil War. Didn't agree with anything living being depicted. They broke all the bottom windows – that was as far up as they could reach.' In the tracery lights above the south windows, medieval faces with weirdly staring eyes look down. The pikes of the unlicentious soldiery couldn't reach that far.

It is a compendium of human outreach and folly, this cathedral I thought I knew. Grand and mad beyond belief.

A little homely tableau, albeit not exactly human, forms a finale. By a radiator grille near the north door luxuriates the cathedral cat, a plump tabby tom nearly two feet long, head pressed against the wall, in glorious centrally heated sleep. What's his name? 'Pangur,' says the guide. Oh, Pangur, namesake of the most famous cat in poetry, hymned in simple stanzas of affection by an Irish monastic scribe some four hundred years before Wells Cathedral was built! Whoever came up with that name, you handsome radiator hugger, deserves a place in Heaven.

Pangur Bán

I and Pangur Bán my cat,
'Tis a like task we are at:
Hunting mice is his delight,
Hunting words I sit all night.

'Gainst the wall he sets his eye
Full and fierce and sharp and sly;
'Gainst the wall of knowledge I
All my little wisdom try.

Better far than praise of men
'Tis to sit with book and pen;
Pangur bears me no ill-will,
He too plies his simple skill.

When a mouse darts from its den,
O how glad is Pangur then!
O what gladness do I prove
When I solve the doubts I love!

'Tis a merry task to see
At our tasks how glad are we,
When at home we sit and find
Entertainment to our mind.

So in peace our tasks we ply,
Pangur Bán, my cat, and I;
In our arts we find our bliss,
I have mine and he has his.

Oftentimes a mouse will stray
In the hero Pangur's way;
Oftentimes my keen thought set
Takes a meaning in its net.

Practice every day has made
Pangur perfect in his trade;
I get wisdom day and night
Turning darkness into light.

Translated from the Irish by Robin Flower

Lincoln

Everyman's Barque

Lincoln opens to view at Least 6 miles off; it Stands on a very high hill and Looks very ffine; at the Entrance the houses Stand Compact together. The Streetes are but Little but its a vast hill to ascend into the town where the Minster stands, by that Means its very perspicious and Eminently in view a great Many Miles off.

The Journals of Celia Fiennes, 1697

A THICK BELT OF OOLITIC LIMESTONE snakes beneath England from southwest to northeast. In the flat lands of Lincolnshire it forms a ridge of hilly ground, and Lincoln Cathedral sails high at the centre. This is a cathedral you can see from twenty miles away in all directions, its three towers printed on the skyline. Celia Fiennes, intrepid horseback traveller through England in the 1690s, was mightily stirred by the spectacle. What an impression it must have made, when it first arose, on locals and travellers alike. Beckoning and threatening, carrot and stick. Come to me, you sinners, or go to Hell. Come up to where God is; rise into the presence of goodness and glory, and of material advantages, too – health, wealth and excitement, the stimulation of the big city and the bright lights. And if you don't – God is watching you, and the bishop is watching you, and the king, too, all embodied in the cathedral, looking down on you like Sauron's Eye.

I climb the steep hill and make for the west front. Lincoln Cathedral, like most of Britain's Ships of Heaven, gives the impression of sinking among its satellite buildings as you draw alongside. The body of the cathedral hides itself modestly behind the ornate barrier of fourteenth-century Exchequergate, though the west towers peep over the top – you can't escape those towers. As I pass through the narrow arches and come out into the cathedral close, the revelation of the building hits me like a blow in the eye. It is as immense as Wells's west front. No, more immense – a Gothic cliff of narrow lance-headed arcades streaking away skywards towards the twin lighthouses of the west towers, leading the eye straight up past ranks of seated bishops, saints and angels, up through pinnacles, crockets and spires to Heaven.

And if a wilful sinner rejects the upward and obvious trajectory of the straight and narrow, he can't say he hasn't been warned. The lower courses of the cathedral's west façade writhe with unambiguous carvings depicting the malefactor's fate, be he baron, bishop or bumpkin. Down here where it's all muck and misery, naked souls writhe in the clutches of demons. A couple guilty of the sin of luxury brandish gold rings as their innards are scratched out by a tongue-waggling devil, their sexual parts devoured by a pair of dragons. A bull-headed monster pulls the hair of a gay couple, a youth and a bearded older man, while snakes bite into their limbs. But there is consolation and hope of salvation for sinners, even in the toils of sin. At the end of the row Jesus, crowned as a king and sublimely calm, treads Satan into the ground while helping a clutch of entreating souls to climb from the very maw of Hell.

This is a stunning introduction.

Inside the cathedral, the light is subdued. The nave windows are all of coloured glass – a sumptuous effect, but one that mutes the atmosphere. Were it not for the pearlescent light admitted by the row of clerestory windows high up in the nave walls, there would be perpetual twilight in the building. It's an ambience that can strike as sombre or calm, depending on your mood as you enter.

The image of medieval cathedrals as monolithic and immutable slabs of stone, set foursquare on unshakeable foundations at their creation and hardly altered since, is a tempting one. I've always rather lazily imagined them like that. A massively large and heavy object like a cathedral, pressed to earth and consolidated by its own sheer weight, must surely have stood, and be going to stand, for ever and ever amen. But, I soon come to realize, cathedrals are as unstable as any other buildings – more so, considering their age, weight and condition. They were built with amazing skill and daring, but on imperfectly plumbed foundations. Designed not by modern technology but by the pricking of a master mason's thumb, they have been embellished on the hoof over many hundred years as styles and fashions dictated, whether the structure can really bear it or not. Like ageing boxers going to seed, their increasingly shaky legs can hardly support the weight they have gained, tens of thousands of tons of it, towers and spires, gargoyles, parapets and acres of lead sheeting, piled on their upper works through the years.

Bits fall off. Ancient stones crumble and drop into space. Walls lean and crack, turrets slump. Internal timbers groan and shift. The fabric is a constant threat, an unceasing worry. Planned reparations alternate with periods of emergency firefighting. The tottering tower of Wells Cathedral, saved from destruction by the insertion of master mason William Joy's ingenious scissor arches, is not an aberration in the story of the Ships of Heaven, but a commonplace.

Neville Birch is our guide today. What he has to say about the origins of Lincoln Cathedral casts the building in the light of a much mended, much patched old barque, only the stern gallery remaining of the original structure, the rest of it wrecked and salvaged, burned and reconfigured over the centuries – a template for the story of all the other cathedrals, as I'm beginning to appreciate. Maybe it was this everyman quality of Lincoln's, its dogged 'been-through-the-mill' status, that saw it win the 'Twitter Cathedral World Cup' by popular acclaim in 2017.

'After the Norman Conquest in 1066,' Neville tells his charges, 'things weren't like you might imagine. King Harold and his army had dashed up to Stamford Bridge to defeat a Danish army on 25 September, then dashed back down to Hastings to be slaughtered and beaten only three weeks later. It wasn't a smooth transition of power to William at all. The country was in chaos. Most of the northwest was under Scottish rule. There were rebellions in Wales, in Northumberland, more Danish invasions up north. Basically, after a few years the Normans panicked and decided that cathedrals must be moved to the safety of walled towns.'

The diocese that contained the city of Lincoln was known as the Diocese of Dorchester. It was vast, stretching from the River Thames to the Humber, but its bishop's seat of Dorchester was a tiny little town on the Thames in the far south of the diocese. The city of Lincoln was the only properly fortified place in the whole diocese; the Romans had walled it a thousand years before. So the Bishop of Dorchester, Remigius de Fécamp, a strong supporter of King William, was appointed Bishop of Lincoln, came north some ten years after the Conquest, and eventually built a new cathedral inside the Roman walls. 'Remigius,' says Neville, as though ruminating on a close acquaintance. 'Built like a Sumo wrestler, he was, four by four. Everyone knew Remigius. You'd keep out of his way in a scrap!'

Remigius's cathedral had no undercroft, and no foundations to speak of. 'Three feet beneath this floor' – Neville taps his shoe on the flagstones – 'it's solid rock.' The cathedral suffered a fire in 1124 that destroyed the tower and roof, but it remained upright for about a hundred years. Then in 1185 came an earthquake, a fearsome event that caused the entire building to collapse, all except the lower part of the west front. Stained-glass windows in the chapter house vividly depict these catastrophes – the great fire of 1124 with red dragons of flame consuming the church ('Ardet Ecclesia Cathedralis'), the earthquake of 1185 sending tower arches toppling among the terrified clergy ('Ecc. Cath. Ruit. Turris. Principilis').

I lag behind the tour to admire the boat shape of the Gothic cathedral that rose from the Norman rubble. Each pillar of the nave has a core of creamy limestone, clamped in half a dozen slim columns of dark, shiny Purbeck marble. The effect is of rigidity, the pillars stiffened as though with iron rods. But this is an optical and an actual illusion. The 'marble', quarried on the Purbeck peninsula of south Dorset, is not a tough metamorphic rock at all, but just another form of limestone, basically marine snail shells crushed up fine in a mortar of mud. It does take a beautiful polish, and that's why the architects of the resurgent Lincoln Cathedral chose it more than eight hundred years ago.

The new cathedral lost its main tower after forty years to another collapse, a structural failing this time. Early in the fourteenth century they raised the height of the central tower and topped it with an enormous spire, made of wood but sheathed in lead. That amazing projection reached a height of 525 feet, three feet taller than the Great Pyramid, and made Lincoln Cathedral the tallest building in the world. So it remained, till a great storm of wind in 1549 blew down the spire, already shaky through the rotting of its timber frame. A pair of lesser spires graced the west towers, but they had to be removed early in the nineteenth century when their weight, added to the vibrations of the bells, threatened to bring down the west front once more.

What a farrago of change, of shape-shifting, of pride going before a catalogue of falls.

I catch up with Neville the guide as he lays his hand on one of the columns of dark Purbeck marble that enwrap the limestone pillars of the nave. It's thirsty stone, Purbeck marble, he says. From the rock underlying the cathedral it sucks up water whose chemicals attack the foreign stone. In spite of appearances the columns are rotten with decay, their convex surfaces crumbling here and there. A palm passed across one of these scabby patches dislodges a dandruff of powdery flakes. 'Doesn't happen with *our* stone,' says the guide with quiet chauvinistic pride, contemplating the pale oolitic limestone of the pillar at the centre of the ring of dark columns. 'Lincoln stone, strong as steel.' He slaps it affectionately, as a farmer might slap a favourite cow. 'It's supporting the marble, not the other way round. Take that good Lincoln stone away and the whole thing'd go.' I imagine a Samson-like figure prising open the nave roof to draw the pale limestone core up and out of its dark ring of columns, as a mended arm is withdrawn from a plaster cast, then the Purbeck marble crumbling into dust like an empty promise.

Two magnificent medieval rose windows sail at either end of the transept, the Bishop's Eye looking south, the sunny side traditionally associated with goodness and the Holy Spirit, the Dean's Eye facing north, the dark side in both meteorology and religious iconography. Certainly something dark got between the Dean of Lincoln and his sub-dean, round about the time of Prime Minister Margaret Thatcher's political apotheosis. When Mrs Thatcher appointed Brandon Jackson, the abrasive and energetic Provost of Bradford, to the post of Dean of Lincoln in 1989, the intention was to shake things up in the very conservative world of cathedral administration. Back then cathedrals, Lincoln included, were run as autonomous bodies by Chapters of clerics appointed for life. Mrs Thatcher and her supporters wanted to see a lot more anti-elitism, a lot more free market, individual responsibility and accountability across the board – and that included the cosy world behind the scenes at the cathedrals.

New broom Dean Jackson, in the words of Andrew Brown of the *Independent*, 'burst into the feline world of the cathedral close like an angry if bewildered terrier'. His opponent was Rex Davis, sub-dean and treasurer since 1977, leader of the Chapter, an Australian, fully as bloody-minded as Jackson. The two men conceived a dislike and contempt for each other from the outset. A row erupted almost at once, and blazed very publicly for the next seven years.

The main spark for the controversy was a trip to his native Australia by Rex Davis in 1988, before the appointment of Brandon Jackson, to display Lincoln's copy of Magna Carta (one of only four originals in existence) at Expo 88 in Brisbane. With Davis went his wife, two daughters and two family friends. The jaunt lasted six months and cost Lincoln Cathedral £80,000; public donations to defray these expenses amounted to just £963. Davis said the game had been worth the candle in terms of raising public awareness of Lincoln Cathedral; Jackson was outraged at this evidence of unaccountability over what he saw as a fundraising trip that had disastrously failed – not to mention its aspect as a 'jolly'. The new dean leaked the story to the press. Rex Davis and the three canons who made up the Chapter were counter-outraged, and reported Jackson to the bishop, Robert Hardy. The bishop was outraged and launched a Visitation. In his September report he came down on the side of the dean. But he expressed his annoyance with all parties very forcefully:

> The plain fact is that the Dean and Residentiary Canons have been at odds with each other, and the intemperate language and indiscretions on both sides have simply added to the sense of conflict. There does not seem the will to change. I consider the attitude of the Residentiary Canons to me to have been on occasion reprehensible and that they and the Dean have conducted themselves shamefully in the media. As far as I am concerned, the past eight months have been the saddest period of my ministry. The whole Chapter seems to have little perception as to how all this comes across to the general public. It all seems a very long way from Jesus of Nazareth.

The sub-dean and Chapter refused to resign. They leaked disobliging letters from Dean Jackson to *Private Eye*. Jackson called in the Fraud Squad; the bishop called in professional counsellors. Davis and Co. stuck to their guns. The Archbishop of Canterbury called for both sides to 'consider their positions'. No one budged. It would have cost over half a million pounds to sack the sub-dean and Chapter, so attempts on that front were abandoned. Sniping continued unabated. Briefings were issued. The dean called the sub-dean 'wicked' and asked for the cathedral to be exorcized. The sub-dean called the dean 'repulsive and wrong'. In 1992 two of the canons retired, but Rex Davis was still there, immovable, convinced of his rightness, refusing to go.

In 1995 Brandon Jackson was accused of sexual misconduct by a female verger, but a consistory court acquitted him. Two years later, he resigned. Rex Davis stayed right where he was until his compulsory retirement at the age of seventy in 2003. The retelling of the whole sad and grubby saga still upsets those who served at Lincoln in that miserable era.

*

Medieval cathedrals were one and all desperate to claim a credible, miracle-working saint. No saint, no shrine. No shrine, no pilgrim revenues. And those could be vast, in an age when healing of body or mind had as much to do with hope and faith as it had with verifiable medical skill. Wells Cathedral never was able to muster a saint, but Lincoln did better with St Hugh, Bishop of Lincoln from 1186 to 1200. A great educator and by all accounts a witty and relaxed man, Hugh had a pet swan, always a popular figure for iconographers. When the bishop died, King John helped carry his body through ankle-deep mud to its resting place, a marble tomb in the cathedral choir. Unusually for a man of his time, Bishop Hugh had always questioned the validity of miracles attributed to others, and had wanted none attributed to him. Nevertheless, by the time of the Reformation, he was second only to Thomas Becket of Canterbury in popularity as a pilgrimage saint.

In his lifetime Hugh was a champion of the much-persecuted Jewish community. Half a century after his death, in a bizarre footnote, ninety Jews were arrested in Lincoln in 1255 and accused of the ritual murder of a little boy, also named Hugh, whose body was discovered in a well in the city a month after he had gone missing. Paranoia fed the 'blood libel', and eighteen of the accused were hanged. 'Little St Hugh', although never formally canonized as a saint, became an object of veneration almost as passionate as that of his namesake. Bathing one's eyes at the fatal well was known to ease all manner of eye trouble, though it signally failed to cure the centuries of blind prejudice against the Jews. Pilgrimages to sites around town associated with Little St Hugh persisted until about a hundred years ago, and his tomb chest still stands in the cathedral, although the truth of the matter – anti-Semitic hysteria – is admitted and decently lamented in a notice nearby.

'Let's go up behind the scenes,' says Neville Birch. We pass through a modest door, out of the visible world and into the bowels of the machine. Up a spiral stair we file, to reach a narrow passageway in the

41

wall. The pale gold stonework is pitted with medieval chisel gouges, cuts and scrapes. Up again to emerge among the dust and sunbeam motes of long galleries like the tween-decks of a ship, stretching away under slanting ceilings of pine boards. 'They couldn't nail the lead roof sheets straight on to the oak timbers,' says Neville, 'because the natural tannic acid in the hardwood would rot any iron nail. So they had to insert a layer of softwood between the lead and the oak, and nail down into that to preserve the nails.'

All manner of paraphernalia lies about, the wherewithal and jetsam of keeping the massive organism going through the ages. A clutch of venerable heating pipes, warm to the touch. A big cast-iron winch left behind after some repair operation – it was superseded by naval compressed-air technology, says our guide, and was too big and awk-ward to retrieve. A water tank. Copper piping. A spaghetti tangle of colour-coded electric cables and fuse boxes. Two archaic fire hoses in scarlet coils, with a brightly polished brass nozzle alongside.

A gallery high in the west end gives a breathtaking glimpse down the full length of the nave. Then we are in the bell-ringing chamber. The ropes hang from the wooden ceiling in spirally wound loops of red, white and blue. There are twenty bells, including Great Tom, five and a half tons of cast iron. Celia Fiennes says:

> 8 persons may very well Stand up in the hollow of the bell together . . . its as much as a man Can Reach to the top of the bell with his hand when he is in the inside; its rarely Ever rung but only by Ringing the Clapper to Each Side wch we did and that sounds all over the town.

Great Tom's vibrations shudder the stonework. No wonder they silenced the bells and whipped the spires off these shaky western towers in 1807. 'It's been hard to find ringers,' Neville laments, 'although it's better now than it was. They are complicated patterns you've to learn – you need a damn good memory, or else a big crib sheet. However, there are compensations. If another ringer makes a mistake in practice, he has to buy the beer in the pub afterwards.'

Up to the next level of the west end, where we traverse the roof space among oaken spars and bracing beams. Neville indicates a square of lead made for the original roof. It was about to be melted down for recycling when someone noticed a set of spidery outlines scratched in the rough surface. Three medieval roofers had signed their work by incising the outlines of their shoes in the lead – one with a round toe, one pointed, one square. It is curiously moving to find this link with these all-too-anonymous men of the long past.

We climb another spiral stair, duck through a low doorway and are out on a narrow strip of parapet looking south over the neatly squared-off ruins of the former Bishop's Palace to a sprawl of the modern city and miles of low green country beyond. A wire is stapled to the wall. 'For abseilers,' notes our guide. 'Later in the spring they'll nip over the side with a sketchpad and make notes on what needs to be repaired.' I peer over the edge. It's not just the wind that has me shivering. I run my hand along an edge of lead, thinking of the medieval roofers and their shoe jape, the lack of any safety equipment when they were hammering lead panels into the softwood layers above the roof beams, their larking about up here. The lead feels cold and floury under my fingertips. 'That'll be as soft as putty and too hot to touch on a nice summer's day,' remarks Neville.

Another dark passage to shuffle through, and we find ourselves at the crest of the west front, with a waist-high parapet between us and a two-hundred-foot drop to the ground. It's a reeling view, looking west to the great dip of Lincoln Castle's curtain wall. The medieval town is laid out below in black-and-white houses, cobbled streets and crowded alleys squeezing inwards and upwards towards the castle and cathedral in their dominant position, the massed roofs spreading out and away in red pantiles and grey slates.

On a clear day from this eyrie you can see the hills of the Peak District nearly forty miles off. Today's sky is leaden and steamy, though.

The westerly wind batters and grunts around the cathedral. Now for the central tower, where a pair of peregrines is nesting, with four chicks just hatched. Cathedral towers look so solid, so tall and strong. But they are subject to continuous if hardly measurable movement, to cracking and potential crumbling. As we traverse the clock room the quarter-to strikes with a dusty, creaking thump that shakes the structure.

In 1932 the citizens of the USA, many with Lincoln roots, subscribed £40,000 to save the central tower from yet another collapse. This is the fourth such tower to rise over Lincoln Cathedral. Tower No. 1 burned in the fire of 1124. Tower No. 2 fell in the earthquake of 1185. Tower No. 3 collapsed in the storm of 1549. Tower No. 4 is still here. But as we emerge on to the leads of the central tower I notice a scurf of stone fragments all along the foot of the wall, tumbled from the fabric overhead. These hundreds of pieces have fallen since the cleaner was last along here with a broom.

We look down across a kink in the nave roof, like a broken nose not properly mended, where the architects didn't quite get the join right during the post-earthquake building. Beyond the roofs of Lincoln the flat countryside spreads massively out on all sides. To the south lies industrial Lincoln, where the manufacture of steam pumps and thrashing machines and traction engines secured the city's nineteenth-century prosperity.

Beyond the sprawl, the slender hundred-foot Bomber Command Memorial Spire rises on Canwick Hill. During the Second World War the flat fields of Lincolnshire were studded with the airfields of Bomber Command. High-perched Lincoln Cathedral with its landmark towers became a rallying point for bomber streams before they headed out over the North Sea on their incredibly dangerous missions. Rumour says that the cathedral remained unbombed by the Luftwaffe because they, too, found the familiar silhouette too important as a navigation point to think of destroying it.

I can make out two Roman roads: the straight course of Ermine Street, arrowing north towards the city all the way from Colchester, and in the southwest the Fosse Way approaching from Exeter. Twenty-five miles away to the southeast Boston Stump, the great tower of St Botolph's Church at Boston, raises its ghostly white finger. Now I can appreciate how powerful a magnet the raised rock of Lincoln has always been for travellers in the flat fenlands all around. This prospect from the tower was the most extensive view anyone in the region could command for the best part of eight hundred years, until aircraft stole the magic.

A great shout arises, a throaty male roaring of the kind the citizens of Lincoln must have quaked to hear as Viking armies approached their refuge. Today it comes from the mouths of 9,934 Lincoln City supporters, packed into their Sincil Bank football ground in the south of the city. Winger Terry Hawkridge has just sealed promotion to the Football League for the Imps with the second of a brace of goals against Macclesfield Town. The greatest moment in the club's history, and from 270 feet in the air we hear its reverberations. Later today I'll encounter Imps supporters wandering through the medieval laneways of their city, dazed and grinning, yelling at one another and the world at large. They are good-natured and unthreatening, but there's a tang of Bernard Cornwell's descriptions of drunken soldiery abroad in a sacked city.

We cross the dusty catwalks and descend the spiral stairways to ground level and the everyday. Leaving the cathedral by the west end, I pause to run my hand across the rough stones of the tower base that survived the earthquake of 1185. Lincoln is one of very few cathedrals to be built of the stone it is founded on, one of even fewer to have its own dedicated quarry close at hand, in Riseholme Road. The cathedral has owned the quarry since 1876, but it is almost worked out now. I walk away into the misty afternoon, thinking how little I know of the masons and cutters who have 'worked their hands in stone' here over the past eight hundred years, the people who have sawn and hauled, chipped and smoothed, coaxed and bullied these stones into shape and into place.

*

Next morning, as I walk along Eastgate, I spy a half-open door in the wall. I poke my head through the gap. A builder's yard, and on the far side a long, low building. By chance I've stumbled on the workshop of Lincoln Cathedral's stonemasons. Inside the shop the air is blurred and greasy with stone particles, but everything's neat and tidy. A place for everything, and everything in its place. Sixty cold chisels hang in a long row. Extractor fans housed in long trunkings are poised over the workbenches to suck away the stone dust. 'My lungs are half full of stone dust,' Paul Ellis says, 'and the other half's iron dust. You wouldn't want a stonemason's chest, believe me!'

Paul is a stone carver, a master of his trade. He's a stocky, tattooed Nottinghamshire man in his fifties, softly spoken and quietly humorous. He heard the call of the one he calls the 'Big Feller' fairly late in life, and his faith is ardent and sincere. Paul wasn't very interested in school. His family has a long tradition of military service, but he started his working life as an engineer. At one point he very nearly did join the army, but he went into stonemasonry when his soldier brother suggested he'd do better working with his hands. He's been thirty years a mason now, fifteen of them at Lincoln. Today he's working on a stiff-leaf capital, but he downs tools, once he sees my interest, to give the rest of his day over to me.

'I'm not so much a stonemason as a stone *carver*. You graduate from being a basic stonemason to being a stone carver, and that's what I call myself. Every stone carver has their own style. Mine's a rough one.' Paul indicates the stiff-leaf carving he's making to replace a crumbling thirteenth-century capital. I bend close to the carving and see that the worked surface is a maze of little ridges and cross-cuttings. 'I don't leave the stone as smooth as some. A mason who knows how I work would recognize that piece as mine.'

The concept of anonymity, of letting the work speak for itself, is important to many craftsmen who work on the cathedrals. And yet their work is as much about art as it is about craft – work in which the creative ego can't help but express itself. Paul is well aware of the contradiction.

'Lincoln Cathedral has great similarities with Trondheim in Norway, and the masons over there, working in soapstone on that lovely cathedral, they are wonderful craftsmen. When they have achieved a certain number of years at the job they're presented with a pewter plate, and round the rim it says: "God in Heaven sees your work". I like that, the feeling of anonymity, of an agreement just between the two of us, me and the Big Feller upstairs. He sees what I do. I don't need any other recognition. The medieval masons were almost all anonymous, too, and I'm just following in their footsteps. But that doesn't mean my work lacks personality. Like every other stone carver, I leave my mark, my signature. I can't help that.'

I comment on the beauty of the stone, a dense silver-grey shot with darker threads of fossilized shells. 'Lincoln limestone silverbed, we call it. Dug in the cathedral's own quarry down on Riseholme Road, near Ermine Street. In medieval times they would have dug the stone for building the cathedral all over the hill. Nowadays Lincoln's the only cathedral that still operates its own quarry. That's special, that.

'The cathedral's full of stiff-leaf – Gothic-style foliage. It's eight hundred years old, and it's coming to pieces, especially on the outside of the building where the weather degrades it. We spend a lot of our time restoring it. Gothic, though . . . that to me is an anal style, very geometric and tight. It's the Romanesque that came before that I love; it's freer, sometimes a bit wonky, but more natural, more human. Gislebertus, he was the man – do you know his work in France?'

Paul stoops to a locker stacked with dusty folders, and extracts a large book about the maestro of Romanesque stone carving. Across the nine-hundred-year divide, Gislebertus beckons our attention towards a gang of ghastly devils meting out torments to unrepentant sinners, a sinuous Eve as languorous and seductive as a houri, the Three Wise Men asleep under a ribbed blanket while an angel attempts the gentlest of awakenings.

'Here at Lincoln we restore the work that's there, if we can. But if a stone is actually failing and in danger of falling out of its hold, then we have to replace it with something we've carved from new. I don't make maquettes, I work from photos. That's one luxury the medieval masons never had. I try to be as naturalistic as I can. I like to add stuff in, topical things or personal things, like the fox hunt I did along the west front. I carved it at the time there was a row about fox hunting, so it's my little commentary on that.'

A plaster cast of a bishop's head in a mitre hangs on the workroom wall. 'That's Archbishop Stephen Langton, and I did it for the eight-hundredth anniversary of Magna Carta in 2015. But look a bit closer – can you see Brian Clough? I wanted to show a man in his sixties with a face that's been through a lot, a bit jowly and saggy, and being a Nottinghamshire man and a Forest fan I naturally thought of Cloughie.

'You might think, looking at our work here, that this country is full of fantastic masons. It's not, though. The Germans and the French, they are so far ahead of us. If you're training as a stonemason in Germany, you have to put in three years' apprenticeship as what they call a journeyman after you finish. You wear a special costume so you can be recognized and looked after on your travels, and you have to spend at least three years away from the place you trained in, travelling and working, getting your breadth of different experience.'

Photographs show German journeymen, young men and women, extravagantly curly sticks in hand, soft bags with their few belongings and the tools of their trade over their shoulders, wearing their traditional *Kluft* or costume of soft black hat, waistcoat (the number of buttons corresponds to the number of hours they will expect to work on any day) and outrageously flared trousers. They must be single, childless and clear of debt, and they are obliged to wander the world for at least a year and a day *auf der Walz*, on the road, getting work wherever they can. When they return home at the end of their travels they must be in possession of no more money than they had when they set out. What they gain is a wealth of practical and worldly experience that money never could buy. These young itinerant workers with the

carnival aspect of pearly kings and queens pitch up at Lincoln, Gloucester, Canterbury and other cathedral workshops to learn their trade,
and Paul Ellis sees a painful contrast between their eager attitude and
that of young Britons in the stonemasonry business.

'In France they call them the "Compagnons", and it's a similar
story. There's so much greater width of experience, much deeper understanding required before you can consider yourself a stonemason. But
here they chuck diplomas and NVQs [National Vocational Qualifica-
tions] around like sweets. End of your three years, no matter how
incompetent your work might be – here y'are, you've got your diploma,
well done!

'I'd like – d'you know what my dream is? – I'd like to see an old
abbey restored, and became a national centre for training stonemasons. Even better, a network of regional centres. That's my dream,
because at present there just aren't enough good, experienced young
British men or women coming through. Anyhow . . . like to see some of
my work in place? Come on, then, and bring them binoculars.'

Round at the west front, among the capitals to the left of the door
into the Morning Chapel, Paul's fox hunt wriggles in and out of the
stiff-leaf. You could very easily miss it if you didn't have your eyes
peeled. A horse comes charging out of the foliage towards the onlooker,
the huntsman aboard, tooting his horn. Hounds quest at the feet of the
stone fronds, one giving tongue, while above them the fox peeps out
between the leaves. 'See that one?' Paul indicates one of the hounds.
'That's what I call the dog's bollocks, that one. I carved him complete
with his two little nuts. But I've hidden them away out of sight, where
only the pigeons and the Big Feller will ever see them.'

We stroll round the building, inside and out, unlocking doors with
Paul's private bunch of keys. In the Angel Choir he points out some of
his favourite examples of the carver's art: angels soaring to the roof;
dragons with writhing tails sinuating in the spandrels. In the chapter
house it's a tiny face behind the dean's chair with a curly moustache
spreading across the cheeks rather than the upper lip – what naval slang

calls 'bugger's grips'. Like all the cathedrals, Lincoln is full of such oddities – most famous of which is the Lincoln Imp, who sits in a spandrel high above the choir, right leg cocked over left knee, a gap-toothed grin across his pudgy little face.

Outside, I stare upwards. The perspective is so odd. I concentrate through binoculars on the fine details of carvings a hundred feet over my head – bags under the eyes of a bishop, the snaggle teeth of the demon who leers at him. Then a step back and a lowering of the lenses, and the grotesques shoot up and away, and are nothing more than featureless blobs against the sky. I haven't a chance of finding out anything biographical about the individual men and women whose facial twists and character flaws were set in stone for evermore in these caricatures, nor about the medieval carvers who gave expression to such little jolts of humour all those centuries ago. But here at my elbow is Paul Ellis, their present-day counterpart, talking with quiet amusement of the contemporary characters – albeit in medieval garb – that he has infiltrated into the fabric of the great church: groundsmen and craftsmen immortalized in silverbed stonework.

Near the Dean's Eye, crouching at the base of a pinnacle on the northwest transept, is Norman Bonner, recently retired leader of the joinery team, his curly hair protruding from a close-fitting cap. In one hand he holds an old-fashioned box plane, and in the other the chain of a beautifully carved thurible. Nearby looms Acker the mason, grasping a cylindrical mallet with a dent in it, and a bottle of Imp Ale. Perched in another cranny high on the cathedral wall is lead dresser Tony, wrapped appropriately round a section of lead pipe. 'A right Tory, Tony. So I put a Lincoln Imp on his back, peeping over his shoulder, and I told him, that's Maggie Thatcher, Tony – you'll never get her off your back now!'

On a buttress top sits Stuart Boyfield, bearer of the title 'domus supervisor', guardian of keys, whose job includes unlocking and locking around the cathedral and the works yard first and last thing. His laughter lines and heroic chin are carved to the life. He wears a cape with a big baggy hood, and dangles a bunch of keys and a watchman's lantern. On his back rides a wicker basket, its lid slightly ajar, revealing the sly hand of an imp clutching a key. 'We all know where Stuart keeps his spare key,' says Paul, 'so I assume the imps do, too.'

Paul takes off his cap and scratches his smooth-shaven head. 'What makes this cathedral a living building? It's alive with people's work, ongoing. In a purely commercial business, there'd be no sense in putting so much time and detail, so much of yourself into it. But here you're given the time and the leeway, the freedom, to carve the way you think best. Stuart up there, for example – he's given thirty years of his life to this building, that makes him part of it, and now I've made him permanently part of it. He'll be up there for a hundred years, probably, and he deserves to be. After him as a carving, and me as carver, there'll be another two blokes, and two more after them. Continuity, you see – that's what makes it a living building.'

Humorous caricatures of cathedral craftsmen are one thing, but Paul's carvings allude to contemporary goings-on, too. To commemorate the life of Nelson Mandela, he carved a smiling likeness of the great South African statesman on the south wall, next to a medieval carving of what appears to be another black countenance, a highly unusual feature on an English cathedral. And down at ground level outside the south transept there's a macabre carving that caused a lot of controversy when it was first installed: a grinning skull with pound signs for eyes, a gold coin stuck between its teeth, a money bag in its bony fist. 'That's all about greed. I carved it when the banking crisis was on and the economy down the toilet. Sometimes I find coins on the top of the money bag – people leave them there, a kind of offering, like. Talking of money . . .'

Paul leads the way back into the cathedral and makes for his Clough-alike bust of Archbishop Stephen Langton. 'When we were fixing old Stephen in place, I thought that the stonework around the window felt odd, a bit thin and skimpy. So we probed a bit deeper, and hidden behind where the old carving had been we found a piece of greaseproof paper. We very carefully unwrapped it and found a slip of cardboard inside, signed with the names of the four masons who'd last worked on the carving, and the date of 1965. So we wrote our names on the back of the card, dated it, and put it back behind the stonework along with two pound coins. I was moaning to my mate about how mean those old masons had been, not to leave any money for the next finders, when what should we see, fallen on the floor right under the window, but a ha'penny! So they had paid their dues after all, them four blokes.'

3

Salisbury
Ship Shape

He got down on his knees, hard, eyes shut, crossing himself and praying. I bring my essential wickedness even here into thy air. For the world is not like that. The earth is a huddle of noseless men grinning upward, there are gallows everywhere, the blood of child-birth never ceases to flow, nor sweat in the furrow, the brothels are down there and drunk men lie in the gutter. There is no good thing in all this circle but the great house, the ark, the refuge, a ship to contain all these people and now fitted with a mast. Forgive me.

He opened his eyes and stood up, looking for his happiness to see where it had gone . . .

William Golding, *The Spire*, 1964

DEAN JOCELIN HAS JUST CLIMBED a half-built cathedral tower that will support his grand design, the spire. The foundations for this medieval manifestation of hubris are non-existent, its supports already bending and cracking. We follow Jocelin, a good man in a naughty world, as he slowly loses his mind and will in a struggle with spiritual and sexual obsession. He morphs into a beaky gargoyle, clamped to his own folly. But does he lose his soul? William Golding holds back on that.

At the time he was writing *The Spire*, Golding was a schoolmaster at Bishop Wordsworth's School in Salisbury. Day in, day out, Salisbury Cathedral and its spire were in his vision. This particular Ship of Heaven, uniquely harmonious and ship shape in its architecture, may be anchored low in its hollow between the Wiltshire hills, but there's no escaping the magnetic pull of its cloud-scraping mast. At 404 feet the tallest in the British Isles, Salisbury spire beckons you from many miles outside the city.

On a drizzly summer morning I'm standing looking down at the city and the spire from a vantage point two miles north. The ramparts of Old Sarum, a great Iron Age hill fort, swing round in concentric circles from my stance at their rim. The Romans were up here; they called the place Sorviodunum. The Saxons knew it as Searoburgh, the 'dry town' – a fortified hilltop superbly sited from a defensive point of view, but drastically short of water. That drawback would contribute to the eventual abandonment of the whole settlement, but not before Old Sarum had seen the rise and antagonistic clash of a thriving town, a pioneering cathedral and a massively strong castle.

It's hard to believe that these brambly slopes were once cut through with busy streets. And incredible to think that a large Norman cathedral once rose above the packed roofs of a large, prosperous settlement on what is now an empty green disc of meadow inside the ramparts. In fact the hilltop is shaped not so much like a disc as a wheel, its hub formed by a motte of very early Norman design. This flat-topped conical mound rises from a deep circular ditch at the centre of the fort. The castle sited up there shortly after the Norman Conquest on the orders of King William I commanded a masterful position. Now castle and garrison, cathedral, town and people are all gone from Old Sarum. No one has lived here since Tudor times. The only movement on the hilltop today is that of the flower heads of scabious and harebells in the spitting wind, the only sound the calling of some children down among the trees.

Old Sarum's first cathedral, built some twenty years after the Norman invasion, was comparatively small and narrow. It was during the following century that a large and very beautiful cathedral with long side chapels and towering transepts came into being, along with living quarters for the canons who served the cathedral and an elaborate stone palace for the bishop. I pace out its cross-shaped foundations. Such stonework as survives points to very fine workmanship. At the same time the original wooden castle was rebuilt in stone, later extended and fortified anew.

It's not surprising that rivalry and antagonism should breed between the two contrasting organisms, castle and cathedral, forced cheek by jowl into such close confinement inside their belt of walls on the isolated hilltop. Cleric and diplomat Canon Peter of Blois was paid a stipend as a canon of Old Sarum. Writing to his friend the Prior of Fountains Abbey, Peter described the hilltop of Old Sarum as 'barren, dry, and solitary, exposed to the rage of the wind', and the cathedral as a captive, 'like the ark of God shut up in the profane house of Baal'. The wind was sometimes so strong that it blew holes in the cathedral roof and made it impossible to hear preaching or prayers. Such water as there was had to be dredged from deep, unreliable wells or brought up-hill with great labour from springs below. This water was extortionately expensive to buy. The castle garrison controlled most of the wells, and cut off the supply when they felt like it. On holy days the soldiers took to obstructing the roadways by which the citizens could reach the cathedral. Soldiery and clerics were often at each other's throats; there were confrontations, acts of spite and occasional fights. In the end the Pope was petitioned, permission for a move was granted in 1218, and the clerics left Old Sarum to set up the new cathedral and town of New Sarum in a less awkward location altogether, down in the well-watered marshlands beside the River Avon.

Deprived of its civilian and ecclesiastical clout, the hilltop lost its significance. The fortress on the motte declined and decayed. Those folk who were left in the old town soon drifted away. By early Tudor times the castle was ruinous, and Oliver Cromwell finished the job by slighting it after the Civil War. No one at all inhabited Old Sarum. Yet it continued to elect two Members of Parliament, courtesy of a handful of landlord voters, none of whom lived anywhere near. It became the rottenest of rotten boroughs, a scandal that persisted for another three hundred years until the Reform Act of 1832 finally rang the curtain down on such scams.

Salisbury's main car park is a gloomy hole on a wet afternoon. A dozen shopping trolleys lie capsized in the murky Avon. Characterless super-market architecture gives way to the hideous grey bunker of Salisbury Playhouse. People hunch into their collars and hurry in the rain past chain shops cheek by jowl in the streets – Ecco, Costa, Wagamama, Caffè Nero.

The modest fourteenth-century arch of the North Gate is a space/time portal between this world and the next, the humdrum modern town and the quiet elegance of the Cathedral Close. The cathedral sails on a green sward, boxed neatly in by mellow old buildings, the trees and lawns of ordered and settled Olde England. The rain ceases to spit as though on command. My glance rises irresistibly to the tower top where, well over two hundred feet above ground, the octagonal spire begins a climb almost as high again, arrowing smoothly up to its peak against the leaden sky. It's a monumental achievement for any era of engineering.

The Jurassic limestone used to build the cathedral eight hundred years ago, easy to work and durable, came from quarries at Chilmark and Teffont Evias a few miles to the west. On a day as dour and dreich as this it's hard to appreciate its qualities fully, but the milky grey hue possesses a metallic glaze, an overall sheen. The whole cathedral, more than any other, has the appearance of having been lowered from the heavens all of a piece. I circumnavigate the building, ending up in front of the west end. None of the usual bulgy asymmetries of chapels and other outliers tacked on through successive centuries are visible, apart from a square cloister off the starboard quarter with the octagonal upper works of the chapter house peeping over its wall beyond.

Construction began in April 1220, as soon as the new site in the valley had been donated by Bishop Richard Poore. Release from the dire situation on Old Sarum hill generated shock waves of energy and generosity. Bishop, dean and canons contributed masses of their own money. The twelve-year-old King Henry III, or those controlling his purse strings, donated the necessary timber from his local estates and from far-off Ireland. One Alice Brewer, owner of quarries rich in Purbeck marble, granted the builders as much stone as they could extract over twelve years. The whole cathedral of New Sarum, including cloisters and chapter house and a separate bell tower, was built entire in just over forty years, all in the latest Gothic style now called Early English, bringing a unique unity of appearance and design. And the planned town newly laid out at the gates of the cathedral, having been granted the all-important royal charters for fairs and markets, grew and throve on the back of the enormous project. Only the spire was lacking, and by

1320, a hundred years after the first sod of New Sarum had been broken beside the River Avon, that too was up and sailing.

Surprisingly, considering the luminescence of the cathedral's building stone, the interior gives a dark impression when seen from the west end, getting darker, too, as the very tall and slender nave funnels towards the east. The upper arcade is light and silvery in colour, but the clerestory of tall slim Early English lancet windows is too high up to admit much helpful light, and the lower columns are of smoke-brown unpolished stone, cut on the cross in drum sections for strength. They are ribbed, as at Lincoln, with pillars of dark polished Purbeck marble. These nests of pillars emit a faint, mysterious shimmer of silver. From close up I see that this metallic gleam emanates from the close-packed fossilized shells of millions of snails – *Viviparus*, a freshwater gastropod of the Jurassic era, according to the guide who hurries over to find out why I am pressing my nose to the stonework.

The lower nave is lit by large slim windows, some glazed with pink and green lozenge panes, others with stained glass, casting a sombre light. At the east end a screen of pointed arches behind the high altar shuts out whatever daylight can make its way past external scaffolding and in through the east window, a 1980s design of very dark stained glass. Having walked the length of the cathedral from brightness into gloom, I turn to look back from east to west and am confounded to find the high inverted ark of the nave roof washed with waves of bright silver and gold, a breathtaking trick of light and architecture.

Halfway along the south aisle stands a tall brown alabaster monument to Edward Seymour, Earl of Hertford (1539–1621), and his family. 'They call us the Holy Dusters,' says a woman who bends over it with solicitous care. With a home-made implement, a hoover brush nailed to a stick, she's cleaning the pointed beard and neat little ears of Thomas, the earl's younger son. 'I come every week to give the monuments a good clean. My favourite? Probably this one to the Seymours, although the painted one in the south aisle down there to Richard and Katherine Mompesson is the strangest. I don't do more to that one than just' – she purses her lips and mimes blowing the dust away – 'in case I damage the enamel. They both have their hands pressed together in prayer, you'll see. Quite often I find a sweet or a chocolate biscuit lodged between their fingers.'

Near the southwest door lies the effigy of the energetic prelate Bishop Roger le Poer, Bishop of Salisbury from 1107 to 1139, who oversaw the rebuilding of the original cathedral on the hilltop of Old Sarum. His head is carved in bold relief, while the rest of Roger's body is incised in flat-pack style on his tomb slab, giving the impression of a bishop luxuriating in a bath of melted toffee. The great winged beast under his feet and the snaky tendrils of foliage that cradle him have a pagan smack about them.

Nearby stands a model of New Sarum's cathedral in the process of being built on the marshland site by the Avon. Its rough-cut, half-finished walls are stark white. Tiny workmen in blue caps and red aprons stand stock still, caught in the act of winching a cut stone block into place. Not for the first time, I'm struck by how little we really know of these diligent, ant-like figures, the shadowy personas of people sunk beyond recall in the marshy ground of the past.

Elias of Dereham (1167–1246), master mason and designer, was Salisbury Cathedral's project manager through most of the build. He also acted as steward to Bishop Jocelyn of Wells while that cathedral was under construction. Although he never gained an impressive title, Elias seems to have been a figure universally trusted, whether for his artist/craftsman talents, for legal advice or for his diplomatic skills. He was one of the key figures in getting King John to agree the terms of Magna Carta at Runnymede in 1215, and had a copy brought for safekeeping to Old Sarum cathedral. That document is on display today in the chapter house, a densely written, curlicued mass of script on parchment, an epoch-defining charter of freedoms that stipulated a curtailment of the king's hitherto unquestioned right to command, and a guarantee that justice should never be delayed, denied or for sale.

I stand and stare at what is one of only four original copies of this pioneering English 'Bill of Rights', and wonder, as so many visitors must do,
at its survival down these past eight centuries of damp rot and fire risk,
of pilfering fingers, of religious fanaticism and zealous destruction and
social upheaval.

In her tiny office, cathedral archivist Emily Naish burrows among
dusty folders full of blurred typeface. 'I inherited a 1950s catalogue for
the archive,' she says, 'all of it hand-typed and . . . let's say, idiosyncrati-
cally ordered.'

On her work-table we gingerly unroll and pore over medieval documents. They are written on fine sheepskin parchment, faintly greasy
and fibrous to the touch, in ink once matt black, now brown and
sparkly. 'Made from oak gall and iron salts,' Emily says, 'mixed with
gum Arabic, the sap of the acacia tree.' Most fascinating is a cartulary,
the back-up disk of its day, a compendium into which a wide variety of
important documents such as papal bulls or royal charters were copied.
The old parchment pages of 'Cartulary C' are closely lettered in dark
brown ink, with scarlet summaries in between. Peering closely I make
out a column of minuscule holes running down the page margin,
pricked out to indicate the spacing of the lines, and rows of stylus
scratches ruled across the page to underscore the lines themselves.
These details of preparation, meticulous, subordinate to the main purpose, designed to pass unnoticed once in place, somehow invoke the
individuality of the anonymous scribe.

This cartulary was probably compiled up at Old Sarum, and into it
the wording of Magna Carta was copied direct from Elias of Dereham's
Runnymede document, just before the old cathedral site was abandoned in 1220. There's a preamble in red lettering highlighting two
clauses in particular: freedom of the Church from royal command, and
a fixed scale of weights and measures. 'Plans for the new cathedral and
town at New Sarum were beginning to take shape,' Emily points out,
'and minds were obviously turning to establishing a market there. They
were working out the practicalities before they'd even begun to build

anything down there.' Also here is the papal bull of Pope Honorius III that ratified the removal of the cathedral from Old Sarum and granted privileges to the citizens of New Sarum. As long as the cartulary was preserved no one could deny what had been agreed, making it a tremendously valuable document.

We pick through other curios. Here is a nice little memento, a victualler's invoice presented to the cathedral authorities following a fire in 1672:

A Byll for Charge at the Fyer,

Making yow Pay noe More than I Pay to the Brewer	
1 Humerkin of Strong Beere	0 . 12 . 9
3 Barrells of Small Beere	0 . 10 . 1½
For some People that would drinke	
Brandy on Pint Cost	0 . 0 . 6
Some People that stayed above to see the	
fier out after all the Rest were gon	
being People that Lookes for	
noething for their Paines	0 . 2 . 0
For Pipes and Bread & Cheese	0 . 1 . 0
Paied on this bill	0 . 16 . 4½
Rec'd of Mr Read so:	1 . 6 . 4½

A footnote to the invoice claims some sort of moral high ground: 'They had the drinke, and tapt it their selves, and drew it out; I looke not for a Penny Proffitt.'

From the library I find my way over to the stonemasons' workshop. No one is expecting me, and none of the phlegmatic workers bats an eyelid. In the back regions a massive lump of stone lies in the masons' yard.

'Tisbury stone,' says Lee Andrews, the cathedral's head mason. 'Forty per cent silica, sixty per cent limestone, just been delivered from the quarry we use out at Chicksgrove, very near the original quarries.' It's hard 'B Bed' stone, Lee explains, to be used where it'll have to stand up to a lot of weathering. The other sort of stone from Chicksgrove is 'C Bed', which is softer, creamier, closer grained. It doesn't weather so well but it's good for carvings inside the cathedral. The block of B Bed stone in the yard is seven feet thick, and twice that length. It's the size of a small lorry, a roughly cut chunk full of fossil shells. It's seamed with small faults, too. 'Stone cracks heal themselves,' Lee says. 'See the calcite that's formed in this one, like scar tissue?'

The ragged rock will be cut into rectangular blocks with a giant suspended circular saw. The stone dust is damped down with water sprays; however, there's still a lot of it in the atmosphere. Protective hoods are available, but silicosis is still a big threat to masons. 'I wouldn't give you much for a medieval mason's lungs,' says Lee, in an echo of Paul Ellis up at Lincoln Cathedral.

Inside the workshop the masons are hard at it. Luke Kingston is working on a stiff-leaf label stop, David Vanstone on the base of a column for a gable end at the southeast corner of the cathedral. The round column base is beautifully smooth already. 'Not finished yet, though,' grunts David, workmanlike in his bandanna and scarlet industrial mitts. 'I'll be polishing it for the rest of the day.'

Lee unrolls a plan of the east end of the cathedral, the oldest and the least restored sector of the building. It's the part they're concentrating on now. The plan is colour-coded, red for stones that need replacing, green for mortar repair. There's an awful lot of red, especially around the dripstones and the layered mouldings that were so cunningly arranged by the medieval builders to channel the dripping and sluicing of rain and melting snow. These stones are expendable features known as 'sacrificial stones', employed where conditions are toughest – on the parapets, string courses, hood moulds, sills and buttress slopes, all the surfaces that receive and shed water. The top band of the gable end on the Lady chapel, says Lee, has thinned by four inches since its construction in medieval times, the sacrificial stones shrinking as their surfaces have been sloughed off by weathering.

If you don't know your stone, you store up trouble for future folk. When Sir George Gilbert Scott renovated the cathedral in the 1860s, he used a lot of Chilmark stone that had been dug out, but then left in the quarry by the medieval masons. 'There was a good reason for them rejecting it,' Lee remarks. 'It wasn't good enough. Now it's giving trouble – lots of cracking and shearing off.' There are problems, too, with the dark, decorative limestones. The fossiliferous Purbeck marble can fail when the surface weathers and the fossil shells pop out; Ashburton marble with its swirly patterns, often used to replace rotted Purbeck marble, can shear across and fall. As for the spire . . . it moves, naturally, with winds and heatwaves and cold snaps. The medieval lime mortar moves with it, and so tends to last longer at its task of binding the stones together. But Victorian repairers used cement, and that has proved more rigid and prone to cracking and failure. The ironwork they inserted to clamp one stone to another expands with heat, forcing the stones apart. The wet gets in and the iron rusts and rots, leaving a flaky gap. It all adds up to a mess of trouble for Lee Andrews and his crew.

Next to the masons, the cathedral's glassworkers pursue their dedicated craft. Vicky Burton shows me a complete rectangular window panel from the chapter house, first made in 1266. It's propped against the wall, repaired and ready to be reinstalled. It's 'grisaille' or greengrey glass, intricately segmented by its leadwork, patterned over with three-headed stiff-leaf. Backlighting reveals vivid blue, dark green and two shades of red – a dusky mauve and a deep, glowing crimson. Potash, lime and sand, heated to 1,350 °C, were used to make the glass. Apprentices roughed out the stiff-leaf shapes, and then the master painter took over to complete the painting freehand. The paint would be mixed with ground glass, water and wine or vinegar, then painted on and fired at about 690 °C to bond it to the glass. Vicky spins the panel round to show me the reverse or outward face, its surface deeply pitted by chemical reaction to moisture. Rain and condensation have dissolved tiny pockets of potash and lime over the years, leaving behind a mass of pockmarks.

Who discovered the secrets of this intricate process, and how, remains a mystery. What they found out, says cathedral glazier Sam Kelly, still underpins the craft today.

'Well, I wanted a job that wasn't in an office. I did a five-year apprenticeship back in the 1970s. Back then they paid you bugger-all and kept you at it twenty-four/seven, and there was plenty of work. Nowadays, the problem for younger people who want to start is that there aren't many jobs going, and there have been some problems with poor skill levels in recent years, especially in the basic craft areas. It is a craft; the art side of it doesn't get much of a look-in with ordinary glaziers. Probably never did.

'There are a number of different sides to the craft, from making lead lights through to conservation of medieval windows. Some of those will require good artistic skills and others won't. It's up to individuals which side of the trade they're more involved in. But it's a trade that requires a wide diversity of skills. It's very much a team game.

'The Victorians were technically very clever craftsmen, I'd say, as well as artists. Nowadays new work can be a case of design by committee. If I have a design I'd like to do, I have to have it passed by English Heritage, by the Church Buildings Council, by the cathedral fabric committee. That's just a fact of life.

'Practical experience, attention to detail and dedication is what makes a good glazier, nothing else. And it's a craft that hasn't really changed all that much. If a medieval glazier walked in here now, he'd be a bit amazed at the lighting, the gas torch and electricity, but other than that – well, he'd be able to get to work straight away.'

Salisbury Cathedral's east window of five slender lancets was installed in 1980 in order to bring more light and colour into the building. In fact its huge swirls of deep Chartres blue, studded with deep dusky scarlet, cast a sombre mood, unsurprisingly considering its subject matter: 'Prisoners of Conscience', a very twentieth-century pre-occupation of many cathedral artworks. The window was made by French father and son glass designers Gabriel and Jacques Loire, actually in Chartres itself, world famous for blue glass. The three central lancets show aspects of the Crucifixion, flanked in the outer lancets by prisoners' faces, some strong and resolute, others racked by doubts and inner torment.

In the centre of the nave stands an artwork that lifts the spirits, a font of ever-flowing, softly trickling water, shaped like a cruciform leaf, the very beautiful and imaginative creation of water sculptor William Pye. Here is modern art linked to the Christian faith and to natural forces. The font still shows on each of its four sides a cross-shaped stain of holy oil, administered in 2008 during its dedication by the Archbishop of Canterbury. It's like a bronze infinity pool, the mirror-black water contained only by surface tension, eternally pouring from the downturned lip of each corner into a drain below. Lay reader and visitors' chaplain John Singleton sees me admiring the font. 'There was a cry of distress one day,' he says. 'A Japanese tourist had put his camera down on the water, which he took to be a marble table, only to see it sink. It was the smoothness of the water that fooled him.' The chaplain smiles. 'During long services, elderly men such as myself can find the sight and sound of that constant trickling of water quite . . . well, *difficult*, shall we say. I try not to sit too near it, myself.'

'Art', says Canon Treasurer Robert Titley, receiving me in the chapter office, 'is absolutely fundamental to a cathedral. I'm very keen indeed to see more art in Salisbury Cathedral – creativity of all kinds, in fact. It's what this place is about: moments of creative surprise.'

What is a canon? I don't know, and have never asked until now. A canon, says Robert Titley, that's simply a priest who works in a cathedral. And a canon treasurer? 'I'm responsible for the fabric of the cathedral, for the furniture, for the craftspeople who work here. And for the possessions – including the artwork. I hope you've sought out some of it. Modern art in an ancient place: that disturbs some people, the very thought of it. But cathedrals are all about expressing worship, and welcome, in many ways.

'Salisbury has a special role as a tourist destination in its own right. You might call it a signature cathedral. We get just under a third of a million people dropping in every year, as well as those for whom the cathedral is a scheduled stop-off on their tourist itinerary. They say, "We'll do Stonehenge, and we'll do Salisbury Cathedral." Only one of those two places connects with Christianity, but both are numinous places. I think that's absolutely true.

'The cathedral's an ancient place of prayer, but people come here with every kind of motivation. There are believers, who will recognize God here; and there are non-believers, and we hope they will meet God here – one of those moments of creative surprise. It's a place of pilgrimage, which is a phenomenon very much on the increase. We get explicit pilgrims, completing a journey of faith and prayer. And we get implicit pilgrims, people who come to find something or complete something, even if they don't know what it is they're after – perhaps nothing formally religious.

'One afternoon the last visitors had left our Magna Carta exhibition in the chapter house, and a young man with a baby in a pushchair suddenly appeared. I said, "I'm very sorry, but you're too late," and he looked tremendously upset and said, "But I am Romanian, and I've come all the way here from my country just to see this Magna Carta, because it's so important to all people." That was a journey of faith, a pilgrimage.

'And then the cathedral attracts all sorts of people who are homeless, or angrily despairing, or disturbed – some of them deeply disturbed. Reading parts of the Bible such as the Book of Revelation, without appreciating the allegory – that can be a very dark theme park.'

*

On 4 March 2018 the sleepy little cathedral city itself morphs suddenly into a very dark theme park. The name of Salisbury is rocketed to centre stage by the world's news media when the former Russian spy, Sergei Skripal, and his daughter Yulia are discovered incapacitated on a bench in the city centre. They have been deliberately poisoned with a very rare chemical weapon, the military-grade nerve agent Novichok. Suspicion immediately falls on the Russian state – Russia is the only place the poison is known to be manufactured, and Russian president Vladimir Putin has previously issued threats against Sergei Skripal. Vigorous denials from Moscow follow, as Britain and her allies expel Russian 'diplomats' and consign the country to the international deep freeze.

Salisbury is a small place. The bench where the Skripals were found and the restaurant and pub they went to beforehand are all in about a hundred yards' radius at one side of the town centre. The parish church of St Thomas stands only fifty yards away. St Thomas's is the obvious place for people to walk into, the natural focus for anyone wanting help or a place for prayer or information, rather than the more distant cathedral.

The Bishop of Salisbury, the acting dean and their staff grasp the need to respond sensitively and tactfully to this crisis. They do not want to barge in and take over these responsibilities from the parish church. But Salisbury Cathedral and its spire are, inescapably, the chief symbols of the city. During the following weeks the world's media jockey for camera positions, not outside St Thomas's, but in the Cathedral Close, the iconic spire prominent in the background. Over Good Friday CNN do a twenty-four-hour broadcast to America, and they set up in the Cathedral School grounds with the floodlit cathedral as their backdrop. Print media get in on the act, too. *The Week* magazine commissions a cover featuring John Constable's famous painting *Salisbury Cathedral from the Meadows*, a bright yellow 'Toxic Hazard' warning notice stuck in the foreground with Vladimir Putin's head in place of the skull.

'Salisbury has been portrayed as a toxic place,' Acting Dean Edward Probert tells me down the phone, 'especially to the Americans. Trading in the city has dropped like a stone after the attack, and so have tourist visits. It's affected everyone, including the cathedral of course – we're the biggest draw in the city, our largest stream of income is from tourists, and visitor numbers at the welcome desk have dropped dramatically. Numbers attending our Holy Week and Easter services were a long way up, however. That's to be expected – people look quite naturally to the cathedral as the place to come and share their shock or fear, or their desire to be together with each other at such times.

'We've been praying for the victims at each of our services, and for the wider community that's been so badly affected. There has been a lot of behind-the-scenes work for us, too – a visit by the Home Secretary to our Good Friday service, not official, but still requiring a lot of arranging and security; accommodating the needs of the world's media; attending meetings of the recovery coordination group that's been set up, and so forth. But the cathedral hasn't laid on special services or anything of that sort. We have consciously taken a step back on that. The prayer and social work aspect of this incident is very much focused on St Thomas's, and they don't need us claiming precedence or getting in their way.'

Dudley Heather gathers his tower tour party crisply together. His is a brisk, no-nonsense manner, as befits an ex-RAF man. Facts and figures spill out. The spire and upper tower consist of 6,500 tons of stone, 350 tons of lead, 3,500 tons of oak. The spire leans about 34 inches out of true. The whole cathedral weighs upwards of 100,000 tons. It's founded on a bed of gravel 27 feet thick, through which river water flows. Really? 'Yes, really – and it has to be kept flowing, too, by various ingenious sluices. The gravel mustn't be allowed to dry out. If it did, it would crumble, and so would the cathedral. Any questions? Right, up we go.'

As we ascend the spiral steps in their narrow chamber, from above comes a powerful ear-battering vibration as the wind drums in the tower. From below drift the squeaks and squawks of musical instruments tuning up. Soon we emerge in a gallery overlooking the west end of the cathedral, with the foreshortened figures of the multicultural Chineke! Orchestra directly below, at practice on Mozart's Symphony No. 29. From on high we survey the narrowboat of the nave. 'It was basically used as a commercial market till the 1780s,' remarks Dudley.

Up we go, into the shadowy, timber-braced loft space above the nave. The wind roars, grinds and booms. The sarking boards that strengthen the roof are braced either side by immense rods of timber, sawn in half longitudinally, each as long as a ship's mast – perhaps they were once just that. The ribs and upper works of the nave roof beneath our feet are encased in a thick coat of slaked lime and crossed by board walkways. At the far end we step into the tall stone box of the original tower, braced all round with fourteenth-century iron rods. Five hundred years later George Gilbert Scott added the massive iron bracing bars that cross the space, literally pulling the stone walls tightly together.

Up a spiral wooden stair, then a stone one into the bell chamber. No. 6 bell is huge, its rim lettered: 'Caroli R XIII. Anno Domini 1661'. (That XIII was a canny piece of loyalism – for good sound Royalists, discounting the vulgar irrelevance of the Commonwealth years, 1661 was indeed the thirteenth year of Charles II's reign.) The half-hour strikes, and the bell chamber clangs and hums.

Up more wooden stairs to the top of the tower chamber, added in the early fourteenth century as a foundation for the spire. Here sits a great wooden windlass, fifteen feet across, thick cordage coiled around its drum. It takes half an hour for this brute of a device to raise a ton of stone from the nave floor to the tower top.

We are right under the spire now, looking up into the octagonal cone and its crazy cat's cradle of timbering. The original bracing timbers were removed after the spire was completed – imagine the bated breaths! What we see now is timbering reinserted after storm damage in 1360. 'But look carefully,' urges Dudley. 'Notice anything?' With a bit of prompting, I do – none of those braces and beams actually reaches the stonework. Apart from the massive kingpost, it is all a sham, no more than a great suspended climbing frame supporting the ladders up which the clerk of works has occasionally to climb the 150 feet to the weather door on the north side of the spire.

Three months ago the papers carried a story about the spire that gave me goosebumps, if not the screaming heebie-jeebies. Photos showed the cathedral carpenter Richard Pike and his colleague Gary Price, clerk of works, four hundred feet above the ground, roped up and clinging to the tip of the spire. They were changing light bulbs – the red ones that warn off aircraft. They were both wearing safety helmets, not much use if things had gone wrong, but necessary adjuncts to health and safety. They'd had to ascend all the tower stairs, followed by the ten wooden ladders suspended inside the spire, then squeeze out of the weather door (eighteen inches by twenty-four) before climbing a via ferrata of metal rungs on the outside of the spire to the tip. It was Richard Pike's first climb to the top in his twenty-seven years of service to the cathedral.

'I'm the only person who knows how to do it,' explained Gary Price, 'so it's nice to pass my knowledge on to Richard. It's a bit like being on a space station; every process takes longer than it would on the ground. We were also battling the wind up there; it does get a bit chilly, so try-ing to use your fingers becomes harder. The view from the top is incredible; you can see for miles. It's my fourth time now, and I still get nervous getting out the weather door.

'It's incredible – you think, How did they build this seven hundred years ago, when it takes us two hours just to change four light bulbs today?'

In one corner under the spire a black-and-white television is flickering. 'Nest-cam,' says Dudley. We're looking at a scene just beyond the wall, outside in the violent wind, where in a wooden box spattered with guano a peregrine chick is huddled, its face and chest squeezed against the stonework. It's as fat as butter in its suit of white fluff. The three siblings that hatched alongside this survivor are gone, fallen to their deaths, probably. The remaining chick has scooped the lottery, and is so corpulent from over-feeding that it can't sit upright, but slumps back on its stumpy tail, its belly distended before it like a clubman in an armchair after dinner. We coo and cluck as we watch, wondering when the absent parents will be able to force a passage through the wind barrier. Next time we look, the female peregrine is back with her chick – in fact, half-smothering it as she protects it from the wind. Her slate-grey back feathers ruffle like sea waves as she squats against the stones, the chick flattened beneath her with its head and neck extended among white cobbles of guano, her face towards us. Her fierce yellow eyes are unblinking as her stare passes through the wall, through the spectators, across the spire and out to who knows where?

4

Chichester

Dressed Overall

THE CITY OF CHICHESTER lies low on the gravelly littoral that spreads seaward from the feet of the South Downs. Its silver-grey cathedral lies low, too. Like Salisbury, it is the spire that gives the cathedral away, a beautiful tapering arrowhead pointing into the sky, a landmark for all the country round about, from the Sussex Downs behind the city and from far out at sea as well. In fact Chichester is the only English cathedral that's visible from the sea, and there is something indefinably maritime in its atmosphere – perhaps it's just the proximity of the sprawling, salt-scented creeks and mud-flat peninsulas of Chichester Harbour.

Chichester Cathedral, though, can be elusive from near at hand. The town is close-packed around its basic Roman layout of North, South, East and West Streets, running to the cardinal points of the compass from the central Cross. The biggest building for many miles becomes hard to spot when you are down in the streets. The classic prospect is of the cathedral's east end from West Street, a magnificent blaze of pale silver stone and tiers of tall narrow Romanesque windows under green roofs and that dominant spire, the bows of the building pushing the long extension of the Lady chapel before them.

Today I approach from South Street through an arched gateway, and am ushered into the presence of the cathedral by a succession of handsome flint and brick medieval buildings with ecclesiastical windows and crooked ridges – the Deanery, the Chancery, the Bishop's Palace – that stand around Canon Lane like courtiers.

Now one sees the south side of the cathedral looming high, its spire rising over all. You enter through St Richard's Door, the 'Door of Mercy'. Inside, all feels light and lively. A double tier of Romanesque arches rises on either side of the nave. A third tier above looks newer, picked out with shining black columns. Simple rib vaulting crosses the roof above, the intersections tied with bosses of crimson and gold. Modern art blazes at you from behind the altar, from the windows and the side chapels, swirls and stabs of colour against the pale stone. There's a lift of the spirits and a palpable sense of excitement.

A scarlet-robed doorkeeper glides politely forward at the west end. Can he help me? A tour? Certainly. How did it all start? Well . . .

Ten miles south of Chichester lies Church Norton, a tiny hamlet on the muddy tidal shore of Pagham Harbour. A little Saxon chapel stands in a graveyard here, all that is left of Chichester's original cathedral. The cathedral formed part of Selsey Abbey, a monastery founded in AD 681 by the Northumbrian bishop and holy traveller St Wilfrid. Selsey was a remote location, some not-very-good marginal land granted to Wilfrid by Aethelwealh, King of Sussex. The bishopric of Selsey was soon established by the sea, and for the next four hundred years existed in greater or lesser prosperity. By 1066 it was in a sorry state, one of the poorest in the country.

Right from the outset of the Norman Conquest, King William I wanted his subjects to know exactly where they stood in relation to their new lords and masters. The conquerors and God were to be seen as allies, strong, judgemental and inescapably present, right at the heart of things. William wanted the new flush of cathedrals to stand tall in the centres of population. So in 1075 the down-at-heel bishopric was moved from the lonely Selsey shore and set up in proper style in the thriving old Roman town of Chichester, with its fifteen hundred inhabitants and three hundred dwellings.

No local stone was good enough for building the Norman cathedral at Chichester. At first the builders brought Isle of Wight stone across the Solent, and then beautiful light Caen stone from Normandy. In winter, the unfinished walls were topped with thatch to prevent frost damage and left till next spring saw the resumption of work. Winter was always tough on cathedral builders. Masons could continue their work on breaking and shaping stones for the new season, carpenters on carving and preparing wood. Other skilled and unskilled workers would go back to their farms, or the farms of others, or disperse to wherever they could pick up work to feed their families, fragmenting a tight-knit team which would have to be laboriously pieced back together come springtime, the gaps filled with strangers who would have to be taught the new skills and would take time to bed in.

Chichester Cathedral's vicissitudes were those of so many of its sister cathedrals. Fires ravaged it, a particularly bad one in 1187 necessitating a complete rebuild. Towers collapsed and collapsed again, wobbling to destruction on their gravelly foundations. The magnificent spire is a Victorian reconstruction; the original crashed spectacularly to earth in 1861. Yet once inside, as always, there's the feeling of being cradled in the belly of an enormous upturned ship, ethereally structured yet as solid as a rock.

I wander in and out of these ancient stone ribs and deckings, but all the time the presence of a new-made world is at my elbow in wood, glass, plastic resin, stone and metalwork, the harvest of contemporary imaginations fertilized by the Christian message. Chichester, like Salisbury, stands out from the crowd of its sister cathedrals in its embracing of modern art, with two figures in particular to thank for this: Bishop George Bell, and Dean Walter Hussey.

George Bell (born 1883, Bishop of Chichester 1929–58) was a highly coloured figure, a poet and art-lover, attracting attention and controversy. Before the First World War he worked in the Leeds slums; during that war he worked for the welfare of war orphans and POWs. After the war he became a great advocate for ecumenism and a supporter of the trade union movement – 'Brother Bell' to his fellow NUPE members, and a well-known friend to unemployed victims of the Great

Depression. Around the time of the rise of Nazism in Germany he became friends with Pastor Dietrich Bonhoeffer, and gave his support to Nazi opponents and Jewish Christians in particular. The Second World War saw him backing and helping displaced persons, conscientious objectors and members of the clandestine German resistance. Bell was a vocal opponent of what he saw as the barbarian and illegal practice of area bombing. He was a public thorn in the flesh of Sir Arthur 'Bomber' Harris and Winston Churchill, whose disapproval extended after the war and may have helped block Bell's path to becoming Archbishop of Canterbury. Post-war he was a nuclear disarmer, advocating European reconciliation and a rapprochement with the German people.

Bell was a life-long supporter of the arts, knowledgeable and passionate. As Dean of Canterbury in the 1920s he instigated the Canterbury Festival, attracting such luminaries as Poet Laureate John Masefield, playwrights Dorothy L. Sayers and Christopher Fry, and poet-playwright T. S. Eliot. Eliot's classic *Murder in the Cathedral* was written for the 1935 festival in response to a commission from Bell.

After Bell was appointed to the Diocese of Chichester, he championed some fine modern work in the churches under his care – a swirling, airborne Christ in Glory at St Mary's at Goring by German-Jewish refugee Hans Feibusch; wonderfully coloured murals including the four seasons and the Wise and Foolish Virgins by Bloomsbury darlings Duncan Grant and Vanessa Bell at Berwick Church, East Sussex; and icon-like murals by E. W. Tristram in the chancel at St Elisabeth's, Eastbourne.

Walter Hussey (born 1909, Dean of Chichester 1955–77) was friendly with Bell, and it was on Bell's recommendation that he was appointed dean. The 1960s and 70s became golden decades for contemporary art in Chichester Cathedral. Dean Hussey was a devotee of modern arts, and he set the cathedral awash with colour and challenge. The strongest colour splash of all that he commissioned was John Piper's tremendously vivid *Holy Trinity* tapestry of 1966, a controversial piece that got every tongue wagging. Sited behind the high altar, it snaps at one's attention like a great clap of the hands. God the Father blazes as a round ball of light shaped like a tambourine, God the Son is represented by a tau or headless cross with whorls of blood where hands and feet should be, and God the Holy Spirit sears through the air in a great curling sheet of flame.

One of Walter Hussey's boldest commissions was right at the end of his tenure, and it echoes the sensitivity to Jewish culture and art that was so strong in both dean and bishop. When Hussey engaged Marc Chagall to produce a work using the vivid techniques of stained glass, the artist was over eighty and couldn't speak a word of English. Chagall had lived in France most of his life, but he was Russian by birth and a Hasidic Jew by tradition. The window that Chagall designed for the north choir aisle is not large, but its blood-red glass and leaping, joyous figures could not be more expressive of Psalm 150, which inspired it:

> *Praise ye the Lord . . .*
> *Praise him with the sound of the trumpet: praise him with the*
> *psaltery and harp.*
> *Praise him with the timbrel and dance: praise him with stringed*
> *instruments and organs . . .*
> *Let everything that hath breath praise the Lord.*

Musically speaking, it would be hard to top the piece that Hussey commissioned from Leonard Bernstein, the red-hot American composer's *Chichester Psalms*, first performed in the cathedral in 1965, sung entirely in Hebrew, the orchestration all crashing, tinkling, rattling New Yorkisms – a syncopated and jazzy modern masterpiece. Shallow and slick, reckoned one critic, but just about everyone else loved it.

As for paintings, the Chapel of St Mary Magdalene houses a remarkable work by Graham Sutherland, *Noli Me Tangere*, painted in 1960. Christ on Easter morning strides vigorously up an open staircase in a white sleeveless vest and gardener's straw hat. He has halted mid-step, one hand pointing upwards and onwards, the other thrust out to bless and also to warn off an imploring Magdalene, who kneels by the stairs in a low-cut green dress, looking up at Jesus in an attitude of wonder and supplication.

The dynamic tension between man and woman in Sutherland's painting is palpable, as are Jesus's dominance and Magdalene's sub-missive attitude. This clicks into sharp focus when I come across a piece of art in the south aisle of the nave that was made eight centuries be-fore, a pair of early-twelfth-century Romanesque carved stone panels showing the miracle of Jesus's raising of Lazarus from the dead. All the figures depicted have a wide-eyed look of amazement, owing in part to the removal of the gemstones that once filled their eye sockets. The first panel shows Mary and Martha, the sisters of Lazarus, one standing, one on her knees, their hands clasped, their round faces bearing expres-sions of unguarded desperation as they implore Jesus to revive their dead brother. Christ stands over the sisters, a huge figure twice their size, dominant, calm and absolutely in control, while the disciples gog-gle in wonder over his shoulder.

The second panel depicts the moment of Lazarus's raising. The emotions etched on to the main characters' faces are not at all what one would expect. Lazarus has been successfully awoken from the sleep of death, and looks understandably solemn as he rises from the grave. But the outsize Jesus, looming overhead, wears an expression of pain rather than elation, his brow knitted in stern concentration as he blesses the reanimated corpse with two outstretched fingers. Martha and Mary, meanwhile, look frankly appalled, their foreheads drawn agonizingly tight, their faces with downturned mouths shaded by a hand apiece as they turn away in what the artist must have intended for awe and dis-belief, but which, accentuated by those saucer eyes, appears to the modern onlooker more like an access of pure horror.

Burlesque relief is provided by a pair of knee-high workmen, small and grumpy, in conical hats, digging the perpendicular grave with what look like peat spades. One bares his teeth in a comic grimace: 'What, I've dug through all this bloody rock, and now you tell me he won't be needing it?'

In St George's Chapel, dedicated to the Royal Sussex Regiment, fourteen plain wooden panels are let into the walls, each as tall as a coffin lid. Opened, they reveal twenty-eight tall white boards, each containing the names of about 160 men – over four thousand soldiers of the regiment killed in the First World War, from Lieutenant Colonel A. J. Sansome to Drummer E. Haffenden.

One name stands out, that of Brevet Lieutenant Colonel G. E. Leachman, CIE, DSO, 'murdered in Mesopotamia 1920'. I've never come across the rank of 'Brevet' before. Later I find out that it's rather a token gesture – an honorary rise in rank for gallantry or meritorious conduct, without conferring the authority or pay of an actual promotion. Wikipedia has quite a little section on Gerard Evelyn Leachman, I discover. He was a British intelligence officer, an explorer, adventurer and tribal expert in Arabia before the First World War. His featured photograph has him in disguise as a Bedouin, long-faced and dark-skinned. 'With his dark, Semitic looks and skill at riding a camel,' says the entry, 'Leachman was easily able to pass as Bedouin and often travelled incognito.' All the camel-riding skills and fancy dress, however, couldn't save Leachman from a deadly bullet in the back in 1920, consequence of a dispute with the son of a local sheikh.

I find it impossible to walk by the sonorous monuments of a cathedral without stopping to look, to wonder, to pass my hand across marble feet or little stone lapdogs. My own feet, latest of many million, pass across a slab in the south aisle whose scuffed-out legend hints at a poignant story: 'Eliz. Ye wife of Thomas Cole, with Two Children. She Departed this life March the 12th 1723 aged 22 years.'

Nearby in the baptistery, a memorial to the eighteenth-century poet William Collins tells of a fall from the sublime to the benighted. The marble medallion shows the Chichester-born odist slumped in dejection, a scrap of poem curled where he's cast it on the floor in despair. There can rarely have been an epitaph as downbeat as his:

> *Tho Nature gave him, and tho Science taught*
> *The Fire of Fancy, and the reach of Thought,*
> *Severely doom'd to Penury's extreme,*
> *He pass'd in madd'ning pain Life's feverish dream;*
> *While rays of Genius only serv'd to shew*
> *The thick'ning horror, and exalt his woe—*
> *Ye walls that echoed to his frantic moan,*
> *Guard the due record of this grateful stone . . .*

William Collins had severe mental problems. He sold few poems in his lifetime, and failed to generate any great interest in them. Samuel Johnson knew Collins quite well, and didn't think much of his work, finding it harsh, laboured and self-conscious. 'His lines commonly are of slow motion, clogged and impeded with clusters of consonants,' the doctor opines in *Lives of the Poets*. And the picture he paints of Collins's day-to-day existence is of a life of misery, plagued by debt, drink and depression.

> His disorder was not alienation of mind, but general laxity and feebleness, a deficiency rather of his vital than intellectual powers. What he spoke wanted neither judgement nor spirit; but a few minutes exhausted him, so that he was forced to rest upon the couch, till a short cessation restored his powers.

Reading that, I wonder whether William Collins suffered from ME. Whatever his ailment, by his early thirties the poet had been locked up in McDonald's Madhouse in Chelsea. His sister rescued him, and took him to live with her in Chichester until his death in 1756.

I reread the excruciating epitaph of this obscure poet whose name

I've never heard before. A sad, horribly painful life? Evidently. I burrow the Internet and find Collins's 'The Passions: An Ode for Music'.

> *First Fear his Hand, its Skill to try,*
> *Amid the Chords bewilder'd laid,*
> *And back recoil'd he knew not why,*
> *Ev'n at the Sound himself had made.*
>
> *Next Anger rushed, his Eyes on fire,*
> *In Lightnings own'd his secret Stings,*
> *In one rude Clash he struck the Lyre,*
> *And swept with hurried Hand the Strings.*

It seems flouncy, florid stuff to me. A 'bad poet', justly forgotten? Not at all, apparently. The Poetry Foundation hails him as 'one of the most skilled eighteenth-century lyric poets'. He is praised for bridging the gap between Alexander Pope and the Romantics. An entry by Edmund Gosse in the *Encyclopaedia Britannica* states of Collins: 'He divides with [Thomas] Gray the glory of being the greatest English lyrist of the 18th century.'

So much for my ignorant judgement. And huzzah for the endless fascination of the real-life stories behind cold marble monuments.

I step outside to shake off the melancholy shade of poor Collins, and raise my eyes to where the cathedral's spire points into a hurrying grey sky. Here is a tale of two cities, etched in silvery stone. Between 1310 and 1330, fifty miles to the west, Salisbury Cathedral's epic 404-foot steeple rose in stages beside the River Avon. A little later in that century, no doubt motivated by the fabulous spectacle and its effect on the rival cathedral's visitor numbers, Chichester began its own spire, a 277-foot needle of creamy silver Caen stone atop a tower built some two hundred years before. The original Salisbury steeple has tottered and lurched over its seven centuries of existence. It has survived many lightning strikes and windstorms, but still stands proudly today. For five hundred years Chichester's spire, too, appeared to be standing up to everything that man and the natural elements could throw at it; but deep in the structure of the tower that supported the spire, all was not well.

During the latter half of the fifteenth century a magnificent Caen stone screen was installed by Bishop John Arundel across the chancel arch. After the Reformation this 'Arundel Screen' had an organ placed on top of it in lieu of the rood screen. Decorative wrought iron was added later. All this embellishment had the effect of blocking off any view of the choir from the nave. In 1859, when Dr Walter Hook had just been appointed Dean of Chichester, the decision was taken to reposition the organ and remove the Arundel Screen so as to open up the main body of the cathedral for public worship. The following year the carved stones and wrought iron of the screen were dismantled and carefully stored in numbered segments. What they had concealed now came to light: an enormous crack in the pier of the western arch, five feet deep, caused by the crushing weight of the spire that had gradually been bending and breaking the stones of the tower below.

Wooden 'shores' or props were rushed into place, and shoring work continued all through the summer of 1860. In November, more fissures were seen to be opening up. More shores were inserted over the New Year. By the end of January 1861, the walls were beginning to bulge. More cracks appeared in the piers that supported the tower. Transept arches and walls began to lean out of perpendicular. Timber splints were applied, metal bolts inserted. It was no use. The piers, each bearing a weight of about 1,400 tons, were no longer up to the job. The weakened stonework of the tower, hitherto hidden – and perhaps held together – by the Arundel Screen, was too far gone to be saved.

On Wednesday 20 February, a day of high winds, dried sandy mortar began to pour from the cracks. It became clear that spire and tower were about to fall. Next day the workmen left the cathedral for their lunch break as usual. They were forbidden to re-enter, and the final act of the drama unfolded quite quickly. Around the cathedral groups of local residents watched in grim fascination as the steeple leaned slightly, then fell straight down and 'through itself' like the 9/11 towers, collapsing into the church and hurling the capstone of the spire to the far end of the nave.

The *Illustrated London News* reported:

> The crushing and settlement of the south-west pier had caused a serious pressure on the top of the south-east and north-west piers, the entire separation of the church walls from the western supports of the tower had become evident, heavy stones burst out and fell, the core of the south-west pier poured out, crushed to powder, and the workmen were cleared out of the building, and the noble spire left to its fate at a quarter past one. Not more than a quarter of an hour later the tower and spire fell to the floor with but little noise, forming a mass of near 6000 tons of ruin in the centre of the church, and carrying with it about 20 ft. in length of one end of the nave, and the same of the transepts and choir. The spire, in its fall, at first inclined slightly to the south-west, and then sank gently into the centre of the building. The appearance of the fall has been compared to that of a large ship quietly but rapidly foundering at sea.

Within ten days of the disaster the Duke of Richmond, the Duke of Norfolk and Lord Leconfield had met for a working breakfast and 'settled the matter' of financing a reconstruction. Fifty thousand pounds was raised through contributions throughout the county, planning and building went forward with typical Victorian energy under architect *du jour* George Gilbert Scott, and the original weathercock vane was restored to its pinnacle in 1865 by Scott himself. At the re-opening of the cathedral in 1867 the sermon was preached by the Bishop of Oxford, Samuel Wilberforce – 'Soapy Sam' to one and all, having been characterized by Benjamin Disraeli as 'unctuous, oleaginous and saponaceous'.

The spire sails against the clouds today, a symbol of serenity. A small dark form in the shape of a cross detaches itself from one of the cathedral's southerly turrets and shoots along the roofline. No one else happens to be looking up, but I see it for what it is: a peregrine, one of those that habitually nest in the turret. It cuts straight through a panicking flight of pigeons, taking not the smallest notice of them, a sleek black privateer amid a convoy of fat merchantmen. The peregrine executes a sharp turn to port, and disappears behind the spire in a fizz of energy and magnetism.

WELLS
Looking east to master mason William Joy's beautiful solution – the ingenious scissor arches that saved the tower from collapse in the 1340s.

WELLS

Above: The great west front of the cathedral, a Gothic masterpiece, sails ship-like over Cathedral Green at the heart of the tiny city of Wells.

Left: Bishop Peter Hancock, like his predecessors, has the eight-hundred-year-old Bishop's Palace as his residence.

LINCOLN

Below: Contemporary controversy: Paul Ellis's startling 'greedy skull' carving is his caustic comment on the greed of bankers.

Lincoln

Above: Looking from high on the west front, a medieval prospect over the fourteenth-century Exchequergate to Lincoln Castle beyond its stout curtain wall.

Left: Master stone-carver Paul Ellis applies his 'rough style' expertise to a piece of stiff-leaf.

Salisbury

Below: Ancient and Modern: William Pye's infinity-pool font stands centre-stage within the Early English symmetries of Salisbury's nave.

SALISBURY

Above: How they did it – this model by James Mogford gives a fascinating insight into the skills and trades involved in building the cathedral.

CANTERBURY

Above: 'Good medieval glass lights itself in luminous colours. It throws a brilliant luminescence.' Léonie Seliger, Director of the Stained Glass Conservation Department, admires a medieval glass portrait alongside its modern counterpart.

CHICHESTER

Above: A contemporary photo shows the mass of rubble after the steeple collapsed in 1861.

Right: Marc Chagall's ecstatic 'dancing window', one of Chichester Cathedral's modern art treasures.

CANTERBURY

Above: A striking view of Canterbury Cathedral from the east, where the extensive ruins of the monastic buildings hold the grave of St Augustine, pioneering Christian missionary in sixth-century England.

YORK MINSTER

Left: The beast with seven heads runs rampant, part of a remarkable depiction of apocalyptic horrors in York Minster's Great East Window, painted in 1405–8 by master glazier John Thornton of Coventry.

Below: Cat's cradle: a thicket of thirteenth-century timbers holds up the chapter house roof.

YORK MINSTER

Above: Modern lighting relieves the subfusc daylight filtered into York Minster through its medieval glass.

DURHAM

Top right: 'Sanctuary! Sanctuary!' – medieval fugitives from justice begged admittance by banging the cathedral's demonic-looking door knocker.

Right: Prick and pounce: the specialist techniques of the cathedral's Broderers produce exquisite embroidery.

Below: Sandstone of the north wall, sculpted by wind and weather.

ELY

Above: Light and grace: musical angels serenade Christ in Glory in the fourteenth-century Lantern, a unique masterpiece of ingenuity.

Right: Pre-Raphaelite Heaven – Ely's spectacular nave roof paintings of the 1850s.

Below: Christ ascends into Heaven, leaving his Apostles to stare after his disappearing feet.

ELY
Western aspect of Ely Cathedral. The northwest transept fell into ruin in the fifteenth century and was never rebuilt, leaving the cathedral endearingly lopsided.

5

Canterbury

The Holy Mutineer

OF ALL THE CATHEDRALS I VISIT, the preliminaries for Canterbury are the trickiest, the most bureaucratic, and the least coherent. There are more preparatory hoops to jump through. There's a long, stern form to fill in, talk of fees payable to each interviewee. It doesn't seem that I can just rock up and have a look-see, or fix up a walk-and-talk on the sort of informal basis that obtains at, say, Lincoln or Salisbury.

Canterbury wears a different face from the other cathedrals, colder and more strait-laced. It's very much the Mother Church of the worldwide Anglican Communion, a massive international tourist attraction, a commercial enterprise that has to maximize its bottom line in order to cope with all the attention and the sheer number of visitors. It has to stay on top of repairs and improvements, to keep ahead of the game. The 'Canterbury Journey' is the somewhat aspirational name given to the current big project: to restore and enhance the western end of the cathedral with repairs to the west towers, nave roof and Christ Church Gate, and with landscaping designed to improve access, as well as building a new Welcome Centre with a community space. The cathedral is a World Heritage Site, so they can't just dig and build away as they please. It has cost, currently, some £25 million – £13.9 million from the Lottery, £10.9 million from the Canterbury Cathedral Trust, £250,000 from the Friends. That's a vast amount of money to raise and to justify.

There are huge demands on the staff's time and tempers, and once I appreciate this I can better understand the 'all business' attitude. As it turns out, only one interviewee actually presents a bill, and the atmosphere on the ground is less stiff than the preliminaries would suggest. As usual, meeting people melts formalities.

The story of Canterbury Cathedral is the story of Christianity in these islands, in all its social, political and religious struggles. It also contains a tremendously gripping drama, the soap opera of pride, anger and sundered brotherhood, of passion and defiance, sin and redemption that is the Thomas Becket saga. Becket 'made' Canterbury as a pilgrimage destination, not as a milk-and-water saint with meekly folded hands, but in the public imagination as a funky, feisty rebel, a red-blooded mutineer with the crew behind him against the arrogant captain King Henry II. The fact that the mutineer's red blood was splashed on the cathedral floor – his brains too; we have all the gory details from a first-hand witness – set the seal on the deal, as did the humbling, the public whipping, the self-abasement, the barefoot *via dolorosa* of remorse undertaken by the man who loved him and who ordered his murder.

The outline plot: Thomas Becket, born a merchant's son in London's Cheapside in *c.* 1120, is only a mediocre student, and not very good at Latin, but he has diplomatic skills. His employer, Theobald Bec, Archbishop of Canterbury, is impressed by the way the bright young clerk carries out a couple of missions to Rome, and gets him a grounding in canon law, the rules of Church government. Becket secures various benefices that bring him a good income, and by 1155 he has risen to be Lord Chancellor, political and spiritual adviser to the newly crowned King Henry II. He's a bit of a bon viveur, ostentatious in his dress, enjoying his riches, a proudly self-made man who drives himself to excel at his job as the king's first lieutenant. He fosters the king's oldest surviving son Henry in his own household, and shows him a fatherly love that the king himself never displays. When old Archbishop Theobald dies in 1161, Thomas is the only man that Henry II will tolerate as his successor.

On 2 June 1162 Becket is ordained a priest; the very next day he's consecrated as Archbishop of Canterbury, the most powerful Church position in England. Trouble starts immediately. The king has misread his friend and ally. Thomas is not going to toe any royal line; instead, he resigns his chancellorship, dons a hair shirt as token of his new asceticism, and starts resisting Henry's attempts to assert the power of the throne and the courts over the Church. In 1164 Henry puts him on trial for contempt of the Crown and for various irregularities during his stint as Lord Chancellor. Becket flees into exile in France, where he remains for the next six years, stripped of his income and his influence. The wrangle between king and exiled archbishop festers and spits, both claiming the moral high ground.

In May 1170 Henry has his son crowned as heir apparent by the Archbishop of York in Canterbury Cathedral. That provides the break-through; Becket's pride can't take the snub, and he negotiates a return to England. As soon as he's back, he excommunicates several enemies, including the Archbishop of York and the Bishops of Salisbury and London. When King Henry hears of that, he can't believe his ears. In fury and frustration, he snarls about nurturing drones and traitors, being kicked in the teeth by a man he's raised high, and getting rid of a turbulent priest – accounts vary. Whatever the king comes out with, it is enough to send four of his knights galloping off to Canterbury, where on 29 December 1170 they hack Archbishop Becket to death in his own cathedral.

Henry is distraught – he 'didn't really mean it'. Becket becomes an instant martyr, popular hero and symbol of resistance to royal oppression. The murderers are excommunicated and banished to the Holy Land to eke out their lives in penitence. The Pope orders various punishments and acts of reparation for Henry. They culminate on 12 July 1174 in a public barefoot penance and whipping for the king at the tomb of the newly canonized Thomas. The shrine of the holy mutineer becomes the most popular object of pilgrimage in these islands.

*

'The Becket story resonates with contemporary issues,' says Canon Christopher Irvine, pouring coffee in his medieval flint-built house in the cathedral precinct. 'It's the story of a power struggle, the little man versus all those powerful forces. A nobody who challenged all the somebodies. That story resonates in all eras, doesn't it?

'I'm fascinated by how this unlikely opportunist son of a draper and friend of the king ended up a saint. In exile he changed. It might have had something to do with travelling from one monastic community to another on the continent, to places of safety, reflection and prayer, unlike the dangerous games of power politics he'd been used to. He returned to England on 2 December 1170 a changed man, and four weeks later was dead.

'It was remarkable, the rapidity with which Becket became an international saint. By about 1180 his fame had spread incredibly far, north beyond the Arctic Circle, south to Sicily, west to Spain, east to Esztergom, the capital of Hungary. Partly through monks – the manuscripts containing accounts of the Becket miracles spread from one monastery to the next, and were copied and travelled onwards. Partly it was Henry II's daughters marrying into foreign nobility and taking the stories with them. These stories spread like wildfire. In 1220, when Thomas's body was translated from the crypt to its new shrine, a huge mass of people of all sorts came from all over. He was a true celebrity, at the centre of a worldwide web of adoration, literally.'

Before I set off to walk around Canterbury Cathedral, Max Kramer the precentor (organizer of the liturgy or public worship of the cathedral) has a word, suggesting what to look out for. 'The cathedral is deliberately laid out to *make* you walk around it in a certain way, to take you on a particular journey. You start at the southwest door, up the south aisle, then north through the tunnel under the quire to reach the Martyrdom, site of Becket's murder. Then further east, and clockwise round the ambulatory to reach Becket's shrine. You never actually see the whole thing from any one point – pillars and angles of stonework are in the way. So to get the whole picture you have to do the walk, the internal pilgrimage.

'As you walk through the cathedral, you actually climb towards the light – by the time you've travelled from the west entrance to reach the shrine of St Thomas with its candle, you've climbed so many steps that you've reached the height of the west end window, twenty feet up. Rising up towards the light that you saw from far off at first, right at the end of the journey.

'Sight, I think, is so important in pilgrimage. The pilgrims' object, the end of the odyssey, not being some vague idea, but a physical object that comes into view, like a shrine. This kind of journey is a practice that goes across an incredible diversity of cultures and religions – the need to make pilgrimage is obviously something very deeply rooted in the human spirit.'

A gaggle of Canterbury Christ Church University students in mortar-boards and academic gowns, along with flocks of parents in their Sunday finery, swarm in the cloisters, the tunnels and passages leading to the nave. It's the university's graduation convocation. Stern-faced security men guard the Cathedral Gate. A mass of clanking scaffolding is going up around the west end of the cathedral; workmen in hard hats trundle up and down in skeletal lifts.

The building is a true Tardis. From the outside, for all its bulk, it appears low-built, almost humble. Once inside, it seems massively, and magically, spacious. The first thing the guide calls to our notice is how uneven the cathedral floor and steps are, how worn down and scuffed out of true by centuries of pilgrim feet.

He elaborates some of the early history – King Aethelbert of Kent donating a disused Roman building to St Augustine for use as a cathedral, when that pioneering missionary arrived in Kent in AD 597 to convert the Angles, heathen islanders, to Christianity; the flourishing of learning and culture at St Augustine's Abbey as the monks and cathedral clerics settled in under benign royal patronage. Then the misery of Viking invasion and waves of attacks from late in the eighth century onwards. The guide describes a siege of Canterbury as late as September 1011. The Danes burned the cathedral and captured Archbishop

Alphege, or Aelfheah. He was their prisoner for seven months, stead-fastly refusing to let his friends pay the ransom the Danes demanded. At Greenwich on 19 April 1012 his murder foreshadowed that of Thomas Becket. The *Anglo-Saxon Chronicle* reported:

> The raiding-army became much stirred up against the bishop, because he did not want to offer them any money, and forbade that anything might be granted in return for him. Also they were very drunk . . . They seized the bishop, led him to their assembly on the Saturday in the octave of Easter, and then pelted him there with bones and the heads of cattle; and one of them struck him on the head with the butt of an axe, so that with the blow he sank down and his holy blood fell on the earth, and sent forth his holy soul to God's kingdom.

In 1067, the year after the Norman Conquest, fire destroyed the rebuilt cathedral. The old Anglo-Saxon archbishop, Stigand, was deposed, and the new Norman incumbent, Lanfranc, built yet another cathedral. But fire, that persistent enemy of cathedrals, attacked the building four years after Thomas Becket's martyrdom.

The great blaze of 1174 started outside in the city. Unnoticed by the monks, sparks blew into the roof space and started a conflagration. Molten lead from the roof began raining into the quire, and destroyed it. In a way, the burning of the old cathedral and most of its images did the monks a huge favour, almost like an insurance fire. The ground was cleared in time to celebrate and to honour the brand-new saint with a brand-new cathedral in the new style. Canterbury's quire is the earliest example of Gothic work in these islands. Guillaume de Sens, the master mason engaged to build the new quire, brought the style with him from France, but had the bad luck to injure himself on the works. In 1178 the scaffolding he was working on suddenly collapsed and he was hurled to the floor of the nave, where he broke his back. Fellow master mason William the Englishman completed the works.

In the cloister we admire a boss high in the vaulting that depicts Henry Yevele, England's chief master mason of the late fourteenth century. In 1377 he's recorded at work on another nave, hugely high, with flying buttresses outside to support it. The boss in the cloister shows an actual likeness of Yevele with furrowed brow, bearded but with a clean-shaven upper lip, framed in heavy curls of hair; a strong face, thoughtful and confident.

'Talking of cloisters,' says the guide, 'the monks of St Augustine's weren't as bad as they were made out to be at the Reformation.' Far from lolling in silken luxury, in fact, the monks possessed just three items of clothing – one habit and two sandals. Every day a chapter of the Rule of St Benedict was read to the prior and monks in the chapter house – hence the name. Some parts of the Rule were more concerned with practical matters than others, e.g. Chapter 30 on the underwear of monks making a journey:

> Those who are sent on a journey shall receive underdrawers from the wardrobe, which they shall wash and restore on their return. And let their cowls and tunics be somewhat better than what they usually wear. These they shall receive from the wardrobe when they set out on a journey, and restore when they return.

Actually the Canterbury monks enjoyed excellent hygiene arrangements, including a fifty-six-seater necessarium. The mental image causes me to wonder just how many mass outbreaks of tummy trouble there were. In the Black Death epidemic, only two of Canterbury's monks died. They had a bronze tank in a water tower, fed from a spring two miles away. A plumber's plan from 1160, now preserved at Cambridge University, shows separate arrangements, all colour-coded, for different qualities of water use – drinking, cleaning and waste.

We pass through the dark tunnel under the quire and emerge in the tall, chilly chamber called the Martyrdom, setting for the saint's gruesome murder. All eyes are on the spot where Becket met his end. 'The jumped-up son of a draper,' says the guide, 'ordained a priest one day and made archbishop the next. He upset a lot of people.'

An account of the murder by a monk who saw it all happen, Edward Grim, has come down to us. One of the four attackers, Reginald Fitz-Urse, told Becket: 'You're a dead man,' to which Thomas retorted, rather splendidly: 'Get your hands off me, you pimp!' Then the knights lost whatever control they might have had, cutting off the crown of Becket's head and smashing his skull.

> As to the fifth, no knight but that clerk who had entered with the knights, that a fifth blow might not be wanting to the martyr who was in other things like to Christ, he put his foot on the neck of the holy priest and precious martyr, and, horrible to say, scattered his brain and blood over the pavement, calling out to the others, 'Let us away, knights; he will rise no more.'

The guide leads us on round the broad curve of the ambulatory, designed to accommodate enormous flows of pilgrims, to the shrine of St Thomas. The original shrine was smashed to pieces at the Reformation. Thomas's bones disappeared. Canterbury Cathedral has resisted the current fashion, as at Hereford and Worcester, for an eye-catching rebuild. In the shrine of St Thomas today, a furrow on the floor shows where countless million supplicant knees have bent against the flagstones. One plain candle, burning on a sea of stones, is all that remains of the 'Big Reveal', the culmination of the greatest medieval pilgrimage in Britain. It seems enough.

The medieval stained-glass windows in the ambulatory and its chapels that tell the story of Thomas Becket are some of the most striking I've seen. The depth of colour, the humour and extravagant artistry are quite remarkable. They pass by in a blur of blues and greens on the short guided walk to the shrine, and I make myself a promise to revisit them. By the greatest good luck Léonie Seliger, Director of the Stained Glass Conservation Department, is free to point the way.

I'm bidden to the stained-glass workshop in the cathedral precinct. Downstairs in the long, light building, conservator Joy Bunclark is working on a panel of protective glazing, which will create a thermal buffer between the old glass and the wind and rain. Joy trained at Lincoln Cathedral. She uses a mixture of ground glass and iron, copper, lead oxide and vinegar – a metallic glaze that subtly tints the glass. 'We want to dial down the brash reflection of modern glass,' says Léonie Seliger. Joy buffs the glass with a cloth, dusts it with fine brushes, and paints the glaze on. The attention to minute detail, the concentration and craftsmanship, are striking.

Léonie expounds on the fragility of the medium they work in. 'Transport of glass was a massive problem in former times,' she says. 'Before canals and railways and smooth roads, people packed glass in straw and shipped it along rivers and across the Channel on barges.

'We have no glass that's really contemporary with Thomas Becket. He died in 1170; four years later the cathedral burned, and all the early-twelfth-century glass was probably lost then. The glorious medieval glass of the cathedral now dates to the late twelfth century onwards. Victorian replica glass tends to be dull and dead, but good medieval glass lights itself in luminous colours. It throws a brilliant luminescence into the building.'

Upstairs Léonie indicates a piece of glass, salvaged from a window for restoration. It dates from about 1180. The side that faced outwards towards the weather is tremendously pitted; holes and tunnels are driven into it, as though weevils have been at work on some animal's hide. There is a faint, blurred suggestion of foliage. 'This sort of old glass has a slowly decaying surface. In Victorian times there was a gasworks right outside the window, and the sulphur in the air reacted badly with the potassium in the glass, increasing its rate of erosion.'

Léonie places the dull, pockmarked fragment on a light box, turning it carefully over so that the interior face is uppermost. 'We don't like to take too much apart,' she says. 'If you take the trouble to look, you can see what remains within this eight-hundred-year-old glass.' She flicks the switch. Glowing colours spring into life. Smoky dark blues and reds, a muddy purple, faded gold. The stalks and veins of a stiff-leaf design show out sharply in thick, tarry black.

Apart from fire and careless handling, the medieval glass of the cathedral had few threats to its integrity until the iconoclasts arrived during the Civil War, hot with holy zeal and self-righteousness. 'In December 1643,' says Léonie Seliger, 'we suffered the rage of Richard Culmer – "Blue Dick", iconoclast and window smasher.'

Nehemiah Wharton, himself a Puritan soldier and a letter-writer, described Culmer as 'odious for his zeal and fury'. Blue Dick refused to wear clerical black, hence his nickname. He was a Puritan minister who became a 'Commissioner for the demolition of superstitious monuments'. Culmer needed soldiers to protect him as he set about destroying the glass, statues and carvings in Canterbury Cathedral. He had to keep Parliament informed of his activities, and his 1644 report, 'Cathedral Newes from Canterbury', still survives. Its spiteful, frothy-lipped fanaticism comes clearly across the centuries:

> Saints were battered in pieces there: St. Dunstans Image pulling the Divel by the nose with a pair of tongs, was pulled down, Devill and all. When the Cathedrall men heard that Ordinance of Parliament, against Idolatrous Monuments, was to be put in execution, they covered a compleat Crucifixe in the Sermon-house windows, with thin boords, and painted them, to preserve the Crucifix, but their jugling was found out, and the Crucifix demolisht. And as the monuments of Idolatry are in great part taken out of that Romish Cathedrall: So that Cathedrall nest of Prelaticall Hornets, is almost dispersed and gone; God hath scattered the proud . . . All the Cathedrall rabble at Canterbury, may (without knocking up their Cathedrall Porter) pack away with all their Cathedrall Bagg and Baggage, and Prelaticall Popish Trinkets.

Local parishioners hated Blue Dick so much that he was refused various livings. In 1645 he tried to take up the living of Minster in Thanet, but on his day of installation found that his parishioners had locked him out of the church. When he tried to break in, they seized and beat him. The parish refused to pay tithes to him. But he retained his position as a minister till the Restoration, and died shortly afterwards.

We commence our private tour of the stained-glass windows. On the north side, the side of darkness and the past, the depictions in the oculi or large round windows are of Moses and the Old Covenant. On the south, the side of light, they are of Christ and the Evangelists. Together the windows of the ambulatory make up the earliest surviving large ensemble of glass in England, telling the story of Becket and his miracles, and giving an intimate, detailed picture of the clothes, hair, accessories, tasks, obsessions and social interactions of medieval people.

The miracle windows were all completed by the time Becket's remains were translated from the crypt to their shrine in the Trinity Chapel in July 1220. How did the windows survive King Henry VIII's 1538 decree that all images of Becket be removed from churches? How did they escape Blue Dick's attentions a century later? Testimony to preservation by monks or citizens, thanks to Becket's enduring popularity, perhaps.

Of the actual life of Becket, few depictions remain. A tall lancet window holds later roundels telling the story in a vertical descent – Henry and Becket on adjacent thrones, the king red-bearded and morose, his friend making an expansive gesture; two knights pushing at the cathedral door while a third looks furtively round in a classic cloak-and-dagger pose; Henry praying at Becket's shrine; Becket himself seated Christ-like in glory, his sombre glance averted.

The miracles are better represented. Here is Mary of Rouen, a bipolar woman, shown madly dancing, clapping her hands, guarded by men with sticks, falling to the ground, and crushed in the depths of despair. Men wielding birch scourges seem to threaten her. Her hair is wild, her body contorted, though gracefully, as though the artist could not help himself. Cured, she abases herself at Becket's shrine, depicted as a low stone box with two oval portholes into which arms and legs could be pushed to touch the healing relics.

Two roundels show the healing of Mad Henry of Fordwich. In the first, Henry in yellow leggings and bedraggled red cloak is dragged to Becket's shrine, hands tied behind his back. He's being given tough love by his two carers, who are beating the devils out of him with upraised rods. In the second roundel, Henry is restored to sanity. His cloak neatened, he prays at the tomb. The ropes that bound him, the rods that chastised, lie cast before the shrine as votive offerings. The 'carers' clap their hands, and the attendant monk smacks his forehead in amazement.

Other windows, of biblical scenes, are of equal vigour and liveliness. The medieval blue glass is startlingly intense, with a lambent glitter. The Old Testament is well represented. A ponytailed, barechested and bare-legged Adam digs a stony plot of ground. A sexy Queen of Sheba sashays in a clinging purple dress. A sailor in a short-sleeved green shirt solicitously pulls Jonah out of the mouth of a dolphin-headed whale. The city of Sodom is shown collapsing in a terrible jumble of ruins, fire and brimstone raining down from Heaven, while a pair of angels urge Abraham's nephew Lot and his daughters onwards in their flight into the hills. But Lot's nameless wife has stopped to look back at the destruction, in contravention of angelic orders. She is stuck like a statue, as white as salt, her body poised to flee, her face forever turned towards the doomed city.

New Testament windows include the Three Kings lying asleep together (still wearing their crowns) in a comfortable-looking bed, a cloak folded over the bedhead, the hand of one of the kings thrown back behind his head in a very natural posture. The parable of the sower shows a glum-faced peasant in a green tunic and red cloak, broadcasting seed from a cloth knotted round his neck while blue, green and golden birds peck it all up from the ground. Nearby in another roundel a fellow sower, bald and brown-faced, releases showers of grain from a basket, the grain lying thickly in newly turned furrows of chocolate-coloured soil.

'Yes, these colours are truly wonderful,' says Léonie Seliger at my side. She sees painted glass, handles it, judges and works it every day of her life. Yet here and now, like me, she can only stand and stare in pure admiration.

The fabric of Canterbury Cathedral is covered in the graffiti of ages, from masons' marks to pilgrim crosses, dashed-off signatures and complicated line etchings. The hotspots, naturally, tended to be out of the eyeline of the clergy. No one has taken them seriously as worthy of study until now, but they have proved a hit, when pointed out, with the visitors who keep the cathedral's finances afloat. Hence their recent in-clusion on tours of the building.

'Mary' and 'Henry' are deeply incised in old Gothic writing, beauti-fully cut with time and care some hundreds of years ago, on either side of a doorway. Below them, yesterday's felt-tip scrawl: 'Natty & Ivan'. 'Graffiti are the memorials of those who couldn't afford chantry chapels and big monuments,' says Nathalie Cohen, the cathedral's archaeolo-gist. 'You might be poor and ordinary, but you could come in here and make your mark, put your name and a date down as a marker of your existence.'

In the crypt the atmosphere is at a constant temperature. It's a stable environment, a cool and dark space. Graffiti spring to life in the light of Nathalie's torch: a horseman; a bow-bladed knife; an axe; another horse; disembodied hands, faces, noses. The cave paintings of Lascaux come to mind. A pillar capital shows elaborate strapwork, and a carving of a long-eared demon grasping two beasts by the muzzle, one in either hand. This superbly detailed work, today's masons agree, was done not with hammer and chisel, but, somehow, with the clumsy blade of an adze.

At the east end a pagan symbol adorns a pillar – an apotropaic design, supposed to ward off evil spirits. A circle or mesh made up of a diamond in the middle of complicated petal shapes, it's a snare to trap a witch in. Witches and demons are pretty stupid, says Nathalie, and they'll follow a line if they happen to chance on one.

Back upstairs in the main body of the cathedral, Nathalie points out a row of horseshoes deeply gouged for good luck on the outer face of the north wall of the quire. Descending the steps leading down from the south side of Becket's shrine, she indicates another graffito incised into the wall. It's a long-nosed face with a glum expression, the eyes shut, the small mouth turned down at the corners. An elaborate crown adorns its brow. I lift my phone flashlight and another face springs out behind and above the crowned head, a long face with huge sad eyes, its brow caught in a great radiant halo. It looks as though this second figure is cradling the crowned head on its breast, as St John rests on Christ's breast in the iconography of the Last Supper.

I draw Nathalie's attention to this background detail. Could this be King Henry II, full of woe and remorse, seeking solace and forgiveness in the bosom of Christ, or even of his sanctified friend and enemy, Thomas Becket? 'I don't know,' she says, 'it's possible.'

As I go out of the south door, there's a blare of trumpets from the nave as the latest batch of university graduates is formally hatched. Cheers! Huzzah! Outside in the sunshine there's the clickety-clack of running high heels on flagstones, a flurry of mortarboards sailing into the air, and a faint sweet smell of incense where someone has left a joss stick smouldering in a crack of the cathedral wall. Its shaft is pushed into a hole bored in the stonework. I look more closely. The hole is one of four salient points of a tiny cross, blurred almost to invisibility, cut into the wall by some nameless, unknowable pilgrim, some day long gone and forgotten.

6

York

Long Hard Haul

Unlike lincoln cathedral on its ridge or Chichester Cathedral with its beckoning spire, when I try to spot York Minster from afar I find myself baulked. Once I'm up on the narrow walkway that ribbons along the 700-year-old city walls, the layout becomes clearer. This belt of medieval stone is drawn tight around the centre of York, and the walkway points forward like a ghostly white finger to where the pale stone ship of York Minster rides amid a snaggle of narrow old streets with bulging frontages, cobbled lanes, needle's-eye yards and snickets.

The minster, close to, is a fortress of a place, most of it railed off, the way to the entrance hard to find across the green lawns of Dean's Park. At the south door I glance around. A dishevelled young woman sits on a bench nearby, her back against a nailed door in the minster close. Surrounded by bags and backpacks, she drags hungrily and deeply on a roll-up, shivering and twitching, one of those lost in the dark theme park that Canon Robert Titley talked about at Salisbury Cathedral, staring through me at some private Hell of her own.

Perhaps it's the way these trapped eyes bridge the space between outside and inside that makes the interior of the minster feel at first impression like a cage of stone, enclosing and channelling thoughts that the architecture ought to set free to sail to every corner of earth and sky.

Down in the half-lit bowels of the minster lurks a vision of Hell to terrify the least imaginative. Under a spotlight in the crypt, impossible to ignore, the chunky limestone slab of the Doomstone bears a terrifying depiction of what awaits sinners: a giant cauldron, stoked by demons with simian grins and huge pitchforks, above which a finely dressed woman and two men weighed down by their own money bags are being lowered into the flames. Toads, magical symbols of evil, gnaw the face of one victim. The whole scene appears to writhe and twist, so vigorous is its execution; and the carving is so clean-cut that the Doomstone must have spent most if not all of its thousand years sheltered from weathering inside successive cathedrals on this spot. You can't imagine a more graphic way to plant the message in uneducated or disordered minds: behave, or else.

Until 1829 the existence of the crypt had been forgotten. In that year John Martin, a religious obsessive who harboured a grudge against the Church of England and who had escaped from several lunatic asylums, became fixated on a faulty note in the organ. Late at night he set fire to a pile of cushions and books in the quire. The organ burned, as did the quire woodwork and roof. When the ceiling fell, the wreckage broke through the quire floor, revealing the presence of carved stones underneath. It was the minster's crypt, undiscovered till then.

History is to be read in stone down here beneath the minster floor. The clues lie under and around your feet, a maze of angles and shafts, holes, cobbles and cornerstones. With the guidelines of the subterranean 'Revealing York Minster' exhibition to steer me, I learn all over again how wind and weather and the imperfect engineering knowledge of successive eras can tease apart the most massive works of man. The minster's 233-foot central tower had already collapsed once before, in 1407, when the original thirteenth-century structure folded down into its own foundations. The 'new' tower that replaced it stood undisturbed for well over five hundred years, but in the 1960s concerns began to be expressed about its safety. It was reported to be tottering on a crumbling base. Contemporary black-and-white photos record cracks spreading across arcades, gaps between stones widening. Investigation showed that the piers of the twenty-thousand-ton tower were precariously footed on the jumbled remains of Dark Ages and Roman buildings, underpinnings that were never designed to carry even a fraction of such a weight. In 1969 Bernard Fielden, Surveyor of the Fabric, issued a dramatic warning that a single stone dropping out of the tower could set off a chain reaction which might cause the entire structure to collapse.

Excavations revealed a huge Roman basilica buried in the foundations – not a church as such, but the *principia*, the great stone-built assembly hall of the Roman garrison of Eboracum, built on the spot nearly two thousand years ago. In fact the stonework of the *principia* extended only under the southwest corner of the tower, which was slowly sliding sideways, most of it founded on nothing more substantial than a thick layer of mud.

The area under the central tower was dug out to a depth of sixteen feet, opening up in the process a new undercroft for the minster. Three thousand sandbags were inserted. New concrete underpinnings were fixed to the ancient foundations, Gothic and Norman, by a forest of steel rods. The tower was saved, at the cost of £2 million and five years' work. And as the engineers secured the tower, the archaeologists worked alongside them, digging twelve-foot trenches by night through the newly created undercroft to the sound of the minster organist practising above their heads. They hoped to hit the original Anglo-Saxon cathedral built in the 630s by King Oswald of Northumbria. In fact they never did. But they explored and uncovered the Roman remains that visitors peer into today.

Permanence and indestructibility are all in the Ozymandian eye of the beholder. Everything shifts; everything changes. In my mind the thousand years that have passed since the Norman Conquest seem an incredibly long stretch of time, yet York had been the chief city of the north lands of Britain for a thousand years before the Normans arrived. In York those two thousand years are telescoped, magically. The Romans sited their fortress of Eboracum between the rivers Ouse and Foss to give them access by inland waterway to the sea. We walk their Via Principalis under the name of Petergate, their Via Praetoria in the guise of today's Stonegate. And in the crypt under York Minster we stare down through a hole in the floor, past the massive stones, green with damp, of an early Norman church, to a circular slice of stone six feet further down, the base of a column that once embellished a military commander's house in the garrison of Eboracum.

An open stone-lined channel four feet deep runs through the exhibition space. It's a Roman drain from the garrison city, its floor twinkling with coins chucked in by modern visitors acting on a hard-wired impulse to propitiate someone, or something. On show nearby are cloak pins, an iron spearhead, foxed glass, a belt buckle, a soldier's amulet – items familiar enough to our generation raised on clever modern archaeology, the trimmings of everyday life two thousand years ago. This exhibition is a palimpsest in ancient stone and ultra-modern glass floors, in Roman brooches, Saxon silver coins and the polished ivory Horn of Ulf, a thousand-year-old elephant tusk fabulously carved for a Viking thane.

The Romans left; the Angles and Saxons came. In AD 627, only thirty years after St Augustine's epoch-making arrival in the Isle of Thanet reintroduced Christianity to England, King Edwin of Northumbria converted to the new religion and immediately built a wooden minster or monastic church in York. His successor Oswald followed suit ten years later with a stone version. In AD 741 that church was destroyed in a fire, then rebuilt. Vikings invaded and seized the city in 867, renamed it Jorvik, and held it for the next hundred years. Fortune ebbed and flowed, but thanks to the spread of Christianity among many of the Vikings, the stone-built minster survived in use throughout the Scandinavian occupation.

Three years after the Normans' arrival in Britain in 1066, King William I stamped his authority on the rebellious northern segment of the island with the campaign known as the Harrying of the North, a rolling, genocidal application of fire and sword. The Anglo-Saxon minster was badly damaged and burned during York's subjugation. It was repaired, then razed by the Danes in 1075 when they launched a final attempt to retake the north. Five years later Thomas of Bayeux,

Archbishop of York, set about building a minster to reflect the power and presence of the new order, a statement of Norman permanence, a building that nobody would dare to damage or degrade. 'We're here now, and this is our might and right,' said the new minster that rose above and across the Roman street pattern. It was very up-front and visible, the white plastered walls squared with red lines – partly a waggle of the archepiscopal willy in the direction of Archbishop Lanfranc of Canterbury, himself very recently the builder of a brand-new Canterbury Cathedral, with whom Thomas of Bayeux enjoyed a bitter rivalry.

Massive tub pillars, deeply incised with zigzag and diamond, remain from that Norman minster. A fire ravaged it in 1137. Archbishop Roger Pont l'Évêque remodelled the minster's west end. In 1220 or thereabouts, as Bishop Richard Poore was starting to build his great all-of-a-piece cathedral from scratch at New Sarum down in Wiltshire, Archbishop Walter de Gray was remodelling York Minster in the new fashionable Gothic style. The pointed Gothic arches could bear more weight than the rounded Romanesque. Walls could be taller, windows larger. Those stylish arrowhead arches looked lighter, too, less blunt and brutal – the mailed Norman fist still present, but only implicit within the elegant Gothic glove.

A great wide nave with a wooden roof was built, a chapter house, many chapels. Wonderful stained-glass windows were installed. The central tower was rebuilt following its collapse in 1407. Finally in 1472, almost four hundred years after Archbishop Thomas of Bayeux began his political fortress of a cathedral, the Gothic minster with its old wounds and burn scars, new limbs and rickety footing was declared finished, and consecrated.

Time and fate had not done with it yet, though. Iconoclastic smashers came through after the Reformation and during the Civil War. Jonathan Martin was hounded by his psychosis to set fire to organ and quire in 1829. In 1840 the nave and south aisle roof burned to ashes. In 1984 a lightning strike set the south transept roof on fire and caused the stained glass in the 700-year-old rose window to crack into more than forty thousand pieces. Amazingly, the glass itself stayed in situ. Under the direction of master craftsman Peter Gibson of York Glaziers Trust – a modest man, who refused to sign his own work – it was removed, panel by panel, by people precariously perched at the top of scaffolding. The multiple thousands of glass fragments were glued back together, sandwiched between clear glass sheets, re-leaded and remounted. Looked at from floor level nowadays, you can't see a sign of anything amiss.

Against the western crypt wall stands a massively solid Roman sarcophagus. A plain, rough stone box, it was shaped by some nameless mason a thousand years before the questionable life and death of its last occupant, the minster's dubiously miraculous saint of convenience, St William of York.

Thomas Becket of Canterbury was the gold standard for saints capable of attracting crowds of pilgrims and streams of pilgrim money. All the medieval cathedrals were desperate to find a good credible miracle worker who could compete with Big Thomas. The Archbishops of York, in particular, nursed resentment of their southern rivals, forever winners in the Pilgrim Stakes and the Archepiscopal Supremacy Handicap. York had its ancient history, its ancient minster and its large sprawling diocese. But the city and its minster lacked a saint until the canonization of Thomas Becket in 1173, and the resulting fame and fortune that poured in on Canterbury, sharpened the necessity of finding one.

About four years after Becket's ascension to sainthood, with excitement running wild over Canterbury as a pilgrimage destination, there came a sudden spate of miracles at the tomb of Archbishop William Fitzherbert in York Minster. William had died in 1154 of drinking communion wine poisoned by an enemy, rumour said – a sort of quasi-martyrdom, if one stretched credulity. Shortly before William's death a lot of people had had a lucky escape when a bridge over the River Ouse collapsed as huge crowds packed on to it to welcome the archbishop to York. Some saw that as miraculous. Later William's tomb was accidentally broken open; his body was found uncorrupted, and sweet smells issued from it. But nothing dramatic in the miracle line occurred until the Feast of Pentecost in 1177, when all sorts of amazing events took place in a rush at the Fitzherbert tomb: sight restored to a man blinded in a duel, speech to the dumb, a woman cured of dropsy on the spot, another vomiting up a poisonous frog that she had unwittingly ingested. Also 'three dead people brought back to life', according to William's *Vita*. Quite a lot of question marks over William's life – undue influence exerted by his kinsman King Stephen to get him the Archbishopric of York, perhaps some bribery by William or his father, political chicanery – were rubbed out, and after further delay and a papal investigation of miracles, William Fitzherbert was canonized on 18 March 1226.

York had finally got a saint for its cathedral. The minster was under-going a Gothic makeover under Archbishop Walter de Gray at the time. A big elaborate shrine for the relics of St William was built at the west end – and pilgrims and their money came pouring in.

Down at the foundations of the minster, pondering the undercroft exhibition and its 2,000-year-old story, I feel my nose rubbed again in the fact of another cathedral church as a living, ever-changing entity. These giant, delicate buildings move. They wobble. They bend and break. Like the fable of the human body renewing all its cells every seven years, a cathedral is in constant flux, bits dropping off, bits being renewed. What it is *not* is an eternally solid, standfast fixture in the landscape. A speeded-up film of York Minster's thousand-year existence would show it leaping about, its outline bending and flowing, towers rearing and tumbling, spires pricking up and falling, windows shuddering in and out of colour, walls a shimmer of falling fragments like flakes of skin sloughing from a body – a continuous process, flowing over every inch of the structure. If cathedrals are ships, they are ships forever in rough seas, hulls creaking as they expand and contract, upper works blown into rags, in frequent need of having their barnacles scraped off.

*

Under the arch of the minster's stoneyard in Deangate, beyond the east end of the cathedral, John David, master mason, is waiting for me – a tousled man of great enthusiasm, his words tumbling about like his curly hair. He slaps his hand on a square-cut block of stone, one of a load waiting to be worked on.

'Magnesian limestone, from the quarry we use at Highmoor near Tadcaster. All made of the bodies and shells of tiny creatures that died in a warm, shallow tropical sea, in the Permian era – maybe two hundred and fifty million years ago. See the black flecks in it? That's manganese oxide. All kinds of building stone have been used on the minster in different restorations over the centuries, but magnesian limestone in these thick blocks is excellent – it cuts as clean as marble, but it's much easier to work. Most stone nowadays is cut thin and used for cladding. A lot of quarries are closing. It's only cathedrals that need such a quantity and quality of stone.'

Upstairs in the setting-out room, a jumbled and cluttered loft, among old-fashioned dividers, a clatter of zinc templates, drafting calipers and clippers, John unrolls a plan of an external buttress of the south quire, on which a team of fourteen people has been working for a year and a half. The buttress is crumbling, in both its early-fifteenth- and eighteenth-century stonework. During the eighteenth century wrought-iron cramps were inserted into repairs to help hold them together. Now, as at Salisbury, three centuries of rain and frost have rusted and buckled the cramps, forcing apart the joints in the stone. 'This pinnacle . . .' John indicates the offending part on the plan. 'It was about to slip off sideways and fall on to the vestry roof. You can't remove a whole pinnacle just like that – you'll disturb the stones below. You have to do it bit by bit. So we're dismantling it, taking out the cramps and rebuilding it a piece at a time.'

In the masons' workshop, masons Pete and Harriet are working on separate sections of the new pinnacle, Pete shaping a square block into the geometric planes he'll then carve, Harriet already at work carving the curls of the crockets on her section. They tap the chisels delicately with round-headed mallets, shaping the stone one flake at a time. When finished, their two blocks will fit together, flat face to flat face, to form one course or horizontal row of the pinnacle. Nearby, Lee is carving a fox-headed prelate with a staff, using as his model an eighteenth-century grotesque that needs replacing. Three centuries of exposure to rain, wind, frost, pollution and the shifting of the building have reduced it to a headless and handless torso, blurred by erosion. I run my hand over the smooth flesh-like surface of the new carving and the rough, granular flakes of the old. It's a continuous process of re-birth. Two hundred and fifty years ago this fox-priest replaced a predecessor, perhaps an early-fifteenth-century original. 'Mine'll be up there for a good few years, hopefully,' says Lee, 'but someone else's will follow it, that's sure.'

Their boss is pragmatic about the work, which by its very nature starts the process of its own dissolution the moment it is hoisted high and left to the wind and rain. The natural deterioration of the minster's stonework took a sharp turn for the worse during the Industrial Revolution, especially after York became a railway hub, with a dramatic decline in air quality thanks to increased amounts of sulphur and soot in the atmosphere. The Clean Air Act of 1956 and the phasing out of steam on the railways saw things improve, but climate change is reversing these gains. 'Climate change', says John David, 'will bring more wind and more rain to rot the stone. But on the other hand, as we clean up our air there'll be less pollution for the stonework to contend with. Our carvings, the shape and form they take, the way they're held together, all reflect the changing atmospheric conditions. We don't think short term here. We think in terms of several hundred years – at least.'

Off to one side of Deans Park stands the Old Palace, now the minster's library. The custodian produces a long cylinder which he unrolls with quiet formality – a fabric roll or list from 1399 of the payments and materials associated with the minster. On its linen backing it resembles a map of a strange archipelago, with outlying islets of parchment fragments and watery, pale lines of medieval penmanship in Latin.

Poring over the rolls, you can tease out snippets of information about long-gone individuals – scribes, recorders, masons, carpenters, illustrators. Another fabric roll of 1370 details the fearsomely ordered lives of the stonemasons. From Michaelmas till the first Sunday of Lent they were obliged to clock into the workshop as soon as there was enough light in the sky to do an honest day's work with no skiving ('yai sall stande yar trewly wyrkende ate yair werke all ye day aftyr'), and they must not knock off till it's too dark to see. The orders also stipulate how long they get for lunch break, for drinking and for sleeping. Any slackers or bad eggs are to have their money stopped at the discretion of the master mason, and the curse of 'ye Goddy's malyson and Saynt Petirs' is invoked upon persistent offenders.

Inside York Minster's chapter house, I get a funny feeling. Something's odd about this octagonal chamber, but I can't put my finger on it for some time. Then I realize there's no central pillar. The chapter house is seventy feet high and sixty across, a huge open space. How did the masons of AD 1290 keep the ceiling up? 'Look closer,' urges Geoff Green, our guide on this tour of the 'Hidden Minster'. I can't see the secret. 'It's made of wood, not stone,' says Geoff. My God, he's right. All those narrow, intricate wedges and interlocking sprays of ribs – wooden, the lot of them, so much lighter than stone that a central pillar wasn't needed. The builders simply made what amounts to a wooden dome, hanging suspended from an invisible cat's cradle of timbers hidden in the roof above. Staring up through binoculars I can now see the points where the wooden ceiling ribs take over from the stone ones springing from the walls below. These stone-to-wood joints are endearingly rough and clumsily executed, a curiosity in a space so meticulously realized.

The coloured windows of the chapter house diffuse a dusky light.

Ranged round the walls in conversational clusters, the forty-four seats of the College of Canons are separated by slender pillars of shiny black Purbeck marble. The pale stone canopies that roof in each seat are pimpled with carvings, hundreds of them. Their rude humour has visitors chuckling as they walk round clicking cameras and phones at gurning monkeys, pigs, lions, priests, nuns and a great quantity of grotesques pulling their own eyes, noses and mouths out of shape. Many are expressive of pain and mental distress, human heads howling soundlessly outwards at the bottom of a cage of spandrels. I have a flashback to the tormented face of the girl outside the south door. Other grotesques are slyly hidden, as though positioned on purpose to distract a seated canon in the midst of his solemn deliberations – an almond-eyed Green Man peeking from a swirl of leaves on the base of a spandrel, a muckle-mouthed nun grimacing on the reverse of a canopy.

Geoff is a vastly experienced guide. His colleague Sandra is rather nervous; this is only the second Hidden Minster tour she's guided. The two of them show the tour group a model of the chapter house roof timbers, and try to explain the strains and stresses, which beams do what. Heads are scratched in puzzlement. Maybe we'll understand when we get a look at those timbers from close up.

In the vestibule entrance to the chapter house we turn our backs on the crowds and slip through a narrow door. A spiral stair winds away above us, and we shuffle up its wedge-shaped steps to reach the mason's loft. In medieval times the master mason was to all intents and purposes the chief architect too, and he needed a large, quiet space where he could fiddle and dream and try out designs in private. The mason's loft is an L-shaped room, clapped on top of the single-storey vestibule some time in the early fourteenth century, a few decades after the chapter house was built. The loft builders provided the master mason with a large fireplace and his own private thunderbox or garderobe, a signal luxury at that date. They also incorporated a portion of the chapter house's external wall into the room, and it's remarkable to see a line of thirteenth-century stonework heads and floral decorations, originally made to embellish that outside wall, looking almost as sharp as the day they were carved, thanks to their incarceration away from the storms and pollutions of seven centuries in the still, cool air of the loft.

Over the loft floor, bunches of wooden Victorian design templates hang from long frames like desiccated fruit bats. The roof is of massive, barn-like timbers, installed unseasoned by the carpenters. The wood was easier to work while still moist, and as each timber matured and dried the tenon or tongue at its end would twist in the mortice slit of the neighbouring timber, gripping it more tightly. Large windows pour light in on the working space, a wide tracing floor of plaster of Paris trodden down by children wearing socks (and here are the imprints of their little feet) until the texture of the surface was to the master mason's satisfaction, not too hard and not too soft. It formed a giant doodling pad on which plans could be etched, smeared away and re-etched in fine spidery lines. The floor could be brushed with soot to highlight the mason's plans, like a medieval Etch A Sketch, for the benefit of visitors, most likely clerics or other rich benefactors keen to see how their money was going to be spent.

We sidle along a gangway built out over the tracing floor, craning our necks and twisting our heads to get the light to shine on the 650-year-old incisions in the plaster below. With the help of Geoff and Sandra I make out clover leaves, ellipses, arrowhead arches and convex curves that shadow out the stone tracery of a window. It's a recognizable piece, too, one of the aisle windows in the Lady chapel. That building project took place over a twelve-year period between 1361 and 1373, and the tracings would have been sketched out pretty early on in the process. Thanks to the excellence of the York Minster archives, we know the names of the successive master masons whose incumbencies covered that period: William de Hoton Junior and Robert de Patrington. I squint along the faint sunlit lines of the tracings that one of them must have made – probably William, as Robert didn't take over till 1368 – and feel those two particular names come a little more alive.

Up another spiral stair and out into the wind. We pass across the enclosed parapet of the chapter house roof, at the base of the octagonal cone whose sheets of lead cladding converge skywards over our heads. Into a doorway, under a stone arch and on into what Geoff the guide has described as one of the most extraordinary spaces we will see in our lifetimes. And Geoff has not oversold it.

Whoever designed the miracle of timbers that hold up the chapter house ceiling and support the leaded cone above must have had his fair share of mad genius. The whole wonderful structure centres on a king-post consisting of three oak trees spliced together, their base marked by a beautifully carved boss in the centre of the chapter house ceiling immediately below. From the kingpost radiates a spiralling, whirling cat's cradle of roughly shaped timbers, some dropping down or shooting up at steep angles to meet fellow beams in a mortice-and-tenon embrace, others reaching out on the level to butt up against the boarded interior of the cone. These wooden slats and the lead roofing sheets they support are pierced at various points with tiny triangular vents, to let out the flammable gases that can build up in an underventilated space. As in a sailing ship, everyone dreads a fire in the timbers; oak can smoulder and reach tremendously high temperatures before bursting into visible flames.

'We've had three major fires,' remarks Geoff. 'One in 1829 – that madman Jonathan Martin, who didn't like the sound of the organ, or much else to do with the minster, and set fire to a load of cushions and books. He burned the quire, and the organ too, so he did what he set out to do. Then another in 1840, that was William Groves, a clockmaker, who left a burning candle in the tower by accident – that did for the nave roof. And of course the fire of 1984, a lightning strike that damaged the rose window. So we've had our share.'

The mast-like kingpost rises to a peak in the shadows beyond the geometric wilderness of timbers. The nautical feeling is compounded by the eccentric ladders – single spars with foot-pegs protruding either side to serve the function of ratlines – that slant up into the canopy of the roof like fat oaken rigging. You can imagine Horatio Hornblower's salty sidekick Captain Bush scrambling up one of those in a jiffy, wooden leg or no.

'The trees that made this kingpost', Geoff informs us, 'were felled in 1288.' We murmur admiringly on cue. 'And see that crossbeam there, the one with the mortice holes cut in it? The carpenters must have recycled it from an even older structure when they built this roof. We bored into it and took a core, carried out a dendrochronology test on it, and found out that the tree that made it was felled more than a hundred years before the Normans came to Britain – in AD 954; they can be that precise. My guess is, it was part of the previous cathedral, the Anglo-Saxon one. But' – he shakes his head – 'you can't get massive English timbers like these any more. So many of the great oaks were felled to build the navy's ships in days of sail. They took all the best ones.'

A dry American voice cuts across Geoff's exposition. It's one of our tour group, a rangy man who drawls with an engineer's authority, 'Well, you're going to need some more of 'em from somewhere.' He points to one of the dozens of interlocking timbers, then another. 'I'd keep an eye on those stretchers if I were you. They're not doing their job.' All eyes swivel to the offending timbers. 'And those two bracing beams that are missing over yonder . . .' He gestures towards a discoloured indentation. 'Put 'em back, would be my advice.' Geoff and Sandra exchange glances. There's a general impulse towards the exit, and the American smiles with quiet satisfaction. He's done his party piece and fluttered the hen coop. I follow him down the spiral stairs, thinking of the timbers inside Salisbury spire and their sham status as architectural supports, and wondering how many more Ships of Heaven have unsuspected trouble in the rigging.

The guidebooks tell you that the Great East Window in York Minster is the size of a tennis court. They declare that it's one of the world's largest, and greatest, works of art in stained glass. But nothing prepares you for the great blaze of colour and hyper-realism at the east end of the minster. In fact Heaven seems a rather pallid notion when one looks upon the thunder and fury of the artist's vision of some six hundred years ago. Wonderfully lifelike, the window's idiosyncratic figures and faces are portrayed in pin-sharp clarity, the skilful use of lines and shading giving them individual expressions. The details of their medieval clothes and possessions are so finely drawn that you have the impression you are looking at a portrait of those times, quite as much as with a Bruegel painting.

This gigantic window was designed, and largely hand-painted, in 1405–8 by John Thornton of Coventry, a master glazier very well known across Britain for the brilliance of his work. Two former Bishops of Coventry were instrumental in commissioning Thornton – Richard le Scrope, Archbishop of York, who invited Thornton to tender for the work, and Walter Skirlaw, Bishop of Durham, who paid for it. Scrope and Skirlaw knew the master glazier's work of old, and both were convinced he was the man for the job. His contract stipulated that Thornton was to be paid four pounds a week, with a yearly bonus of a hundred pounds, 'to finish the same within 3 years from the Date hereof; and obliging himself with his own hands to portraiture the said window to the Historicall images & other painted work in the best manner and form that he possibly could and likewise paynt the same where need required'.

The subject matter of the east window is set out in 311 panels of glass, arranged in three storeys. God sits at the apex, the Saved occupying the arches immediately below. The subject matter of the rest of the window could hardly be more ambitious: it is a depiction of Alpha and Omega, the beginning and the end of times. The story of the Creation and Genesis normally fills the upper half, but today I find it a blank. The original has been removed for restoration, and a great sheet of transparent glass is in temporary occupation, wriggling with spidery black lines which outline the individual pieces of the design.* An

* Restoration of the Great East Window was completed, and the whole window reinstated, early in 2018.

exhibition alongside shows some of the missing masterpiece: the Creation, with toothily grinning fishes curvetting through royal blue seas, a sky full of swans, a horse and a beaver freshly made for Adam's delight; God's hand in a flash of scarlet light creating a Garden of Eden full of tempting fruits; Adam and Eve in silvery white nudity as a golden-haired angel points them out of paradise.

The lower half of the window, already restored to full colour and reinstated, depicts the Apocalypse as described in Revelation, a really astonishing compilation of images, terrifying even to the modern mind. I spot St John, author of the Book of Revelation, at top left, boiling away in a barrel of oil, then in a sailing ship on his way to exile in Patmos. After that it's all horror and destruction, the number seven repeating like the beating of the drum of doom: the Son of God with seven candles and seven stars; seven angels with seven trumpets; a fantastic battle in Heaven, a blood-red dragon against a grinning Beast whose seven heads are crowned with seven diadems. Babylon falls with riotous calamity; men and women abase themselves before the Beast, which turns on them with thorn-like teeth; angels tip up the vials of the wrath of God, pouring out blood into rivers and over towns.

Lower down we see a series of seven books with seven seals. As each seal is opened, a new set of catastrophes is unleashed. John Thornton spares no detail of what the wicked world is loosing upon itself. Men cast themselves on the ground, blocking their ears, holding out their hats to shield their faces, as angels zoom across the sky pouring floods of fiery wrath out upon houses, towns and rivers. Over all the sun burns madly, its rays as thick and solid as spears streaming out to blast all life on earth.

The nearest thing to which I can relate these terrors is the scenario in Peter Watkins's 1965 docudrama about a nuclear apocalypse, *The War Game*. When I first saw that in an art cinema in Brighton shortly after its release, it chilled me and shocked me in equal measure. Now I stand marvelling under Thornton's masterpiece window, and imagine its impact when first unleashed on medieval minds.

The glass has cracked and broken over its six hundred years of existence. It's been damaged by dirt, pollution, fire, vandalism, clumsy repairs and the movements of the building itself. Moisture is the main enemy – weather attacking the glass from outside, condensation from inside, corroding the glass into bubbles, pits and eventually holes. Accumulated dust and dirt compound the problem, trapping moisture like a sponge against the glass – as does linseed oil, which was applied to protect the glass in former times. The stonework of the window frame is likewise vulnerable to moisture, to pollution-borne chemicals, to freezing rainwater and bad repairs and the acids in birdshit.

A ten-year project to conserve the Great East Window started in 2007. It takes about six hundred working hours to restore one glass panel, and there are 311 panels in the Great East Window. Two hundred thousand working hours, give or take. Restoring it will cost £11.5 million, a massive bill partly subsidized by the Heritage Lottery Fund. John Thornton, master glazier and visionary artist, ended up being paid fifty-six pounds for his masterpiece six hundred years ago.

As well as restoring the glass, two thousand stones around the window frame have had to be replaced. All the glass has been taken out in stages. As in the present case of the Creation, replacement panels of clear hand-blown glass have been inserted pro tem, the jigsaw pattern of the missing pieces outlined in lead.

Once a panel of glass has been removed to the glaziers' studio, the conservators photograph it and make a rubbing to record the position of all the lead lines. The old lead is removed, and the medieval glass is cleaned with soft brushes or cotton buds dipped in de-ionized water (no minerals), and perhaps a scalpel too. Some of it is found to be beyond saving and has to be replaced. The actual technique of painting the glass hasn't changed much. Iron oxide mingled with ground lead and ground glass is pounded into a powder, then mixed with a flux, mostly lavender oil now, but vinegar, gum arabic and urine have been used as fluxes in the past. It's painted on to the glass, and fired to make it adhere.

Medieval plumbers, inserting the lead strips that hold the glass pieces in place, laid them on thinly. Lead was expensive and heavy. But repairers over the years have tended to run half-inch strips across cracks in the glass, gradually diminishing the area of the illuminated panels. During the current project the width of all the lead has been drastically reduced, allowing the window to reclaim its original light and colour. Also, the advent of modern adhesives has allowed some of the cracked pieces previously joined with lead to be edge-bonded or glued together.

Once the restoration work is complete, the panel is photographed in all its new glory and put back where it belongs. Spaces are left in the window frame for air to circulate, reducing the condensation that's the biggest corrosive enemy of medieval glass. And exterior glazing is inserted with each panel to protect it from the weather.

The glaziers that John Thornton employed may have worked anonymously, but they left signs of their individual presences all over the window, detectable at close quarters under workshop lights by the sharp eyes of today's restorers – mostly thumb prints, and tiny fibres of medieval clothing. Later restorations attracted other signatures, such as the graffito 'Thomas Clarke, plumber and glazier, July 4 1794' incised by the fourteen-year-old Thomas on the backside of a horse in the Apocalypse half of the masterpiece. I scan the window with my binoculars, all the way up to God the Father seated at the very apex. Are those . . . no, too sacrilegious, surely. I twiddle the lenses. They are, you know.

Right across the Almighty's forehead, scratched there by some forgotten dismantler anxious to see the Lord of Hosts restored to his rightful place, two words come into focus: 'Top Senter'.

Daylight begins to fade in the minster. Choral evensong is under way. I stand looking up at John Thornton's great embodiment of creation and destruction, as the Psalmist's poetry weaves its own visions of an earthly paradise, and the long hard haul required to attain it.

Thou makest the outgoings of the morning and evening to rejoice.
Thou visitest the earth, and waterest it, Thou greatly enrichest it;
The river of God is full of water: Thou providest them grain, when thou
    hast so prepared the earth.
Thou waterest its furrows abundantly; Thou settlest the ridges thereof:
Thou makest it soft with showers; Thou blessest the springing thereof . . .

Psalm 65

7

Durham

The Phantom Helmsman

I CATCH MY FIRST SIGHT of Durham Cathedral, today as fifty years ago, from the train as it slows to rumble over the viaduct at the top of the town. Back then, arriving for my interview at the university, I'd been struck by the perfect placement of the two principal objects in view, stumpy castle and many-towered cathedral, juxtaposed on a high saddle of ground above the clustered roofs of the city. They dominated their surroundings, seen through a haze of smoke that drifted from a thousand chimneys. As I walked down from the station into the town I was greeted by the smell of coal smoke and the sight of serried ranks of back-to-back brick houses, their dividing lanes hung with drying washing and dotted with sacks of the free coal to which miners were entitled. Durham might have been a university town, but it was also a coal-mining one, a fact of everyday life one couldn't ignore.

Castle and cathedral stand on a high peninsula of rock, a narrow, ship-like prow stuck out into a tight loop of the River Wear. It's a spectacular site, made by nature for defence and display. If any Ship of Heaven sails high and handsome, it's Durham Cathedral. There's only one way to approach it as far as I'm concerned, and that's on foot along the river, trailing the edge of the peninsula to Prebend's Bridge with its calendar photo-view of the twin towers at the cathedral's west end. Then up the cobbled South Bailey, past the heavy front door of my former college, St Cuthbert's Society, and on to where the cathedral looms up suddenly on my left hand, impossibly huge and all-pervasive.

Cuthbert, as a name, was a bit wet. That's what I thought when I managed to sneak past the interview and scrape a place at St Cuthbert's Society. But I soon learned to think differently about this saint whom the locals seemed to regard familiarly, like a friend. They talked of him as they did of local celebrities who'd done all right. On the sitting-room wall of my digs the landlady had a picture of St Cuthbert looking out of a cave. 'Our saint, you see,' she would say. In one of the city pubs a china eider duck sat on the chimneypiece. 'A cuddy's duck,' said the old men, taking pity on the ignorant student. 'Cuddy, short for Cuthbert, Saint Cuthbert, y'knaa. He looked after the cuddy's ducks up in Holy Island, wouldn't let them wild buggers up there touch 'em.' The landlord indicated the china eider and gave a phlegmy laugh: 'Canny work for a saint, y'knaa. That's why we keep that bugger sat up there.'

York and St William Fitzherbert, Canterbury and Becket, Lincoln and St Hugh – these are examples, more common than not, of cathedrals already built that had to cast around for a saint to bring in the pilgrims and the money. Durham, by contrast, is the story of a saint that gave rise to a cathedral. St Cuthbert died four hundred years before the current Durham Cathedral was built. The monastic community that had settled here did not need to seek a holy worker of miracles. The pilgrims were already coming in such numbers that they had to build the cathedral to cater for the crowds.

The monks of St Cuthbert brought their own saint with them when they arrived in AD 995 on the peninsula in the River Wear where the cathedral now stands. By that date the community had been leading a nomadic existence for more than a hundred years, ever since the threat of Viking raids had forced them to leave their monastery on Lindisfarne or Holy Island, a tidal island off the Northumbrian coast. They had faithfully carried the body of Cuthbert, miraculously uncorrupted, in his wooden coffin from place to place, temporarily settling here and there, but always moving on in search of a fitting place to enshrine their beloved prior and saint for good and all. In 995 they were on their way north from Ripon when a Heaven-sent vision diverted them to Durham, the 'place of the dun cow'. Here on the rocky peninsula they stayed, and here they built a succession of ever grander and more solid shrines as pilgrims flocked to the spot.

Was it the tale of these monkish wanderings, the obvious devotion of his followers, that so attracted people to Cuthbert? Was it the miracles, the healing of the halt and lame? Or did folk admire the character of Cuthbert, a struggler and battler against demons both outside and within, a modest man who shied right away from fame and adoration? By all accounts, the Venerable Bede's especially, Cuthbert was a bit of a lad in his youth, until a vision sent him to join the monastery at Melrose. He became a fiery itinerant preacher and converter of heathens, until settling at the island monastery of Lindisfarne. He became prior there in AD 664, but his desire to be alone with God ate away at him. He retreated to Hobthrush, a tiny blob of a tidal islet off Lindisfarne (then, as now, a great gathering place of cuddy's ducks), and then further offshore in 676 to the windswept volcanic shelves of the Farne Islands.

Here Cuthbert lived in absolute solitude, poverty, hunger and hardship, fighting off demons and scraping his food from the rocks. He might have been dismissed as a pure madman, but Cuthbert's was a charisma that never faded. Eight years after his self-imposed exile on Inner Farne, the Synod of Twyford elected him Bishop of Lindisfarne. The picture on my student landlady's wall recorded the moment that Cuthbert was brought this – for him – bad news by Trumwine, Bishop of the Picts, and Ecgfrith, King of Northumbria. This heavyweight delegation was rowed across in person to Cuthbert's retreat to beg him on bended knee. The hermit, according to Bede, found their pleadings impossible to resist: 'At last he came forth, very tearful, from his beloved hiding-place and was taken to the synod. Very reluctantly he was overcome by their unanimous decision and compelled to submit to the yoke of the episcopacy.'

Cuthbert didn't last long ashore; within two years he had resigned his bishopric and was back in retreat on Inner Farne, a sick and worn-out man, to die there on 20 March 687. His body – found to be undecayed when 'elevated' to its coffin eleven years later – lay in its tomb on Lindisfarne for the next two hundred years, working miracles, visited and venerated by pilgrims in their thousands, until Viking raids prompted the monks to carry it ashore and commence their restless pilgrimage. His coffin was opened, and opened again, over the centuries. Kings and bishops peered in. Trinkets were put in and taken out. The lid was sealed and resealed. Everyone wanted a piece of Cuthbert, a cure, a tangible reassurance that he really was in that modest wooden coffin. What supreme irony for this humblest of hermits, who only wanted to be left alone with his Lord, the sea ducks and the lonely islands. He is the Phantom Helmsman, invisible and untouchable in spite of all, who still steers this great Ship of Heaven that was built in his name.

There's a circus setting up outside Durham Cathedral. That's how it looks as I climb the slope of Dun Cow Lane and emerge on to the open lawns of Palace Green. The buildings around this large open grass square are of beautiful old sandstone, pitted, eroded and honey-coloured. A spacious, dignified scene, in contrast to the congeries of pantechnicons, catering vans, outside broadcast units and snakes' nests of cables. Chocolate-munching riggers and vaping cameramen loll around on their breaks. What's going on? 'Avengers infinity war,' says one. Um . . . I'm sorry – would you mind . . . ? 'Filming inside,' he elaborates. 'Paying a packet for it. *The Avengers*, you know. The new one – *Infinity War*, it's called. You're not supposed to know that, by the way.'

Cathedrals need money. This one's sandstone parapets are crumbling. Scaffolding sheaths the central tower, singing in the wind, a soft aeolian fluting as I walk the walls. Durham Cathedral is mighty, but plain. It is a giant monolith, the archetypal Norman statement of presence and permanence. Four storeys of round-headed Romanesque arches run undeviating along the north face. Nine hundred bitter northern winters have eaten the sandstone walls into holes, hollows and tunnels. Some blocks are pitted like coral, or caves in a miniature cliff face; others are all a-swim in multicolours of purple, ochre, gold, black, as dictated by the exposure of random layers of minerals. Weathering has moulded every stone individually. I walk the walls in fascination. Abstract and beautiful shapes made without any human artistry unreel like a silent film as the walls go by – whorls and swirls, futuristic curves, calcite burrows sealed by silica spider webs, slanting bands of petrified rain. In the shallow trench at the foot of the wall lie crumbs, flakes, powder and chunks of sandstone, falling in a steady, invisible shower from the disintegrating parapets and dripstones a hundred feet overhead.

There's a demonic head adorning the north door, the main entrance into the cathedral – a bronze mask with a boozer's nose and staring, hollow eyes. Its grinning jaws are clamped on a semi-circular knocker ring. Rays emanate all round the face, rays with tightly curled tips like octopus tentacles. It's a faithful copy of the twelfth-century sanctuary knocker which fugitive traitors and murderers would bang, calling out 'Sanctuary! Sanctuary!' for admittance to the temporary safety of the cathedral. I remember laughing at this verdigrised Punchinello fifty years ago as a student, and it hasn't lost any of its air of menace or its power of freaky humour.

Looking down the cathedral nave, there are no ceiling bosses, nothing to relieve the severity of the zigzag vaulting in the roof – the first pointed arch shapes to be used in Britain, designed to bear the weight of the stone roof. The aisles are blocked out with interlaced blank arcading. The pillars of the nave were built twenty years or so after the Norman Conquest. They are massive, twelve feet thick, heavily and commandingly carved with decoration of chevrons, lozenges, flutings and spirals. These patterns are deeply cut into the stone as though with a broadsword. It's a heraldic, militaristic stone forest. The eye is frogmarched rather than invited forward down the nave, shouldering a couple of screens aside to bump up against the east end and its great rose window. The only figurative decoration is a line, on either side of the nave, of staring, monstrous heads, some with demonic ears and bared teeth.

It is almost as though you have to brave this intimidation and bombast to win through to the tranquillity of the chapels at either end of the nave where Durham's saint and his saintly biographer lie at rest.

I tag on to guide Margaret Tindle's tour. She points out a modern window donated by the Durham branch of Marks & Spencer to celebrate their centenary in 1984. To me it looks like thirteen cabbages on a chopping board. No, says Margaret, it's the Last Supper, and we call it the Daily Bread window. 'Just as appropriate for M&S really,' she says with a small smile. Later I find a poignant, indignant article written by young journalist Caitlin Allard in the student newspaper *Palatinate*, inspired by the window and by the rash of expensive student accommodation and style shops currently infesting the city. 'Marks and Spencer is shutting down,' writes Caitlin:

> Some believe that this is insignificant, but a company that has donated a window in a building that has stood at the centre of a community for a millennium, has at least some standing in Durham's status as a community. M&S Director Sacha Berendji stated the change was 'vital for the future' of the business, but it cuts community ties. There has been much upset, particularly for the elderly who don't have a car or can't drive . . . Durham is losing basic resources needed by residents. Partly as a result of this, it is losing its sense of community that the window donated by M&S was meant to represent. 'Daily Bread' is beautiful and captivating, and will act as a reminder of when both Durham's economy and community were thriving and functional.

The piece concludes: 'The Cathedral itself remains a place of community, but elsewhere, life is becoming more and more of a struggle.'

The Galilee Chapel is temporarily closed to the public, Margaret regrets. I sneak a look in anyway over the shoulder of a ponytailed roadie. A marvellous cave of zigzag arches, slender columns and traces of coloured frescoes, the Galilee was built in the 1170s as a Lady chapel, a place where women could make their offerings at Our Lady of Pity altar. Cables snake across the floor, technicians mutter, cameras trundle, bright lights shine down. Can I see Tom Hiddleston? Ooh, is that Scarlett Johansson? Much of the circus outside on Palace Green has been transferred in here with the shade of the Venerable Bede, whose shrine this is. So how much will Durham Cathedral make from allowing *Avengers: Infinity War* to be filmed in Bede's resting place? Margaret doesn't know.

'Bede,' she says warmly, as though she's speaking of a personal friend, 'now he was a bright lad, one of those with a restless enquiring mind – you know the sort. He thought the world was round, which was quite an advanced idea for the time. Do you know that his *Life of St Cuthbert* is still in print, thirteen hundred years after he wrote it?'

I look it up on Amazon. Bestsellers rank – 33,736. Hmmm, better than most of mine. Two and a half review stars only, though. I hope they can't log on to Amazon reviews in Heaven.

The Venerable Bede (AD 673–735) spent almost his whole life in a monastery at Jarrow on the River Tyne. He made no mighty journeys, preached no memorable sermons, converted no savage heathen warlords. Yet this quiet, broad-minded scholar and linguist lies in the Galilee Chapel at the west end of the cathedral, a place of honour second only to St Cuthbert's, not exactly venerated and prayed to, as is Cuthbert, but loved and respected down the ages as no other Dark Ages monk has been. Bede wrote hymns and biblical commentaries, a history of the world, and *The Ecclesiastical History of the English People*, which is still a major source of knowledge about the very early Christian church in Britain. Everyone who knew him seems to have loved him, and that sentiment continues today. The hermit saint at the east end, his gentle biographer at the west: these two, at any rate, give the cathedral a sense of balance.

Margaret mentions others dead and buried in the cathedral, especially the remains of Scottish prisoners who died in the aftermath of the Civil War. After the Battle of Dunbar in 1650, three thousand Scots prisoners were marched south and temporarily incarcerated in the cathedral. Of those, nearly a thousand died in this makeshift POW camp. What to do with such skeletons as are unearthed? These men died less than four hundred years ago. Repatriate the remains? Or rebury them reverently in a cemetery in Durham? It's a moral and practical problem, neatly resolved when the remains of about twenty-eight men, almost certainly Scottish prisoners, are discovered behind the university library on Palace Green. They are placed in a communal coffin and interred in soil brought from Scotland, in a simple ceremony conducted in a sunny glade of Durham's Elvet Hill cemetery by one of the cathedral canons and two ministers from Scotland.

In the south aisle stands the Miners' Memorial, a black ornate slab supported by coal-black angels. The inscription says: 'He breaketh open a shaft away from where men sojourn. They are forgotten of the foot that passeth by. Job 28.4'. A solemn and poetic reminder of the dangers and loneliness of the collier's life, and of the as-yet-unbroken bond between the local community and their cathedral. The Memorial Book is open at the page that commemorates the Easington Colliery disaster on 29 May 1951, when eighty-three men died during and after a gas explosion at the pit on the Durham coast. It's humbling to realize that the deadly dangers of coal mining do not belong to some Dickensian past, but were still very much present in my own lifetime. Some of the pits around the city were still working when I came to live here in 1968. Remembering that, I picture the men in their Coal Board donkey jackets walking home after a shift, some with coal smears still visible. Also the tremendous crowds of miners and families parading with pride and emotion through the city behind their silver bands and lodge banners in July, sunshine or rain, on the day of the Durham Miners' Gala, always known locally as the Big Meeting.

'This cathedral will be full with local people, standing room only, next Gala Saturday, that I can guarantee,' says Margaret. 'They still feel that connection to the pits and to the cathedral. But times change, don't they? When I take a party of schoolchildren round these days and we come to the Miners' Memorial, I can no longer talk about "your grand-fathers who worked down the mines". In fact I hesitate to say "your *great*-grandfathers", it's getting so far away.'

I have an appointment with the Broderers. This team of expert embroid-erers, working diligently and quietly behind the scenes, produce many of the cathedral's fine embroideries. At present they have a great collab-orative project on hand, the Cuthbert Cope, a fabulous garment of damask, silk and gold, to be embellished with sixteen scenes from the life of Cuthbert in appliqué round the hem. For now it is only partly off the drawing board, and I can't persuade the Broderers to let me have a sneaky peek.

Cheryl Penna, neat and precise, has been a Broderer for ten years. 'There are fifteen of us now. I joined when I retired,' she tells me in the long room near the Great Gate where she works under bright ceiling lights. 'I always sewed and embroidered, but didn't have any formal training till I studied for my City & Guilds and the Royal School of Needlework Certificate and Diploma.'

Today Cheryl's working on an embroidery of St Aidan of Lindisfarne, seventh-century Irish-born pioneer of Christianity in Northumbria. A large piece of cloth lies flat on the table, the saint half finished upon it. Who designs such things, and how? 'Tracy A. Franklin, the Broderers' leader, a specialist professional embroiderer – she'll design it and draw the actual-size pattern on paper. Then we'll trace the design out on to thick tracing paper, then tissue paper. After that, to transfer the outline of the design on to the fabric, we might use "prick and pounce". You prick tiny holes along the tracing line and push specially made pounce powder, which is powdered charcoal, or sometimes cuttlefish powder, through the holes on to the fabric – that's calico as a backing, and linen or silk on top. Or we might tack the tissue paper to the fabric along the lines of the design, remove the pricked paper, and you're left with the design all laid out on the linen. Not as easy as it maybe sounds!'

Aidan is shown simply dressed, though his bible and collar are all embellished with a wonderful, stretchy kind of golden embroidery wire called pearl purl. His deep blue eyes are the only feature of his face added so far. His bald tonsure is framed with side wings of grey and brown silk, like Paulie Walnuts in *The Sopranos*, appliquéd with minuscule stem stitches. 'Hmm, yes,' murmurs Cheryl, 'a few problems I'm having there with fraying silk!' A golden halo surrounds the saintly head. Stitching once round the halo, securing the double rows of golden threads, takes Cheryl about forty minutes. Ten times round and back: seven hours or thereabouts.

Nearby is another completed piece, an Easter altar cloth, a golden crown of thorns whirling like a triumphant sun. The thorns stand proud of the backing; they are of soft kid leather and gold-coloured metal thread, each thorn padded with felt to give a 3D effect and tipped with blood-red threads among the gold, a sophisticated technique known as *or nué*.

Like the cathedral stonemasons, like the carpenters and glaziers up and down the land, the Broderers' techniques are those of their medieval forebears. I marvel at the intricacy, the endless patience and concentration. What brings Cheryl here day after day to expend her fingertips and eyesight on these minute details? 'Well,' she says, 'all of us very much value this cathedral. It's such an important part of our heritage. And of course being a Broderer is very social. You could have five of us working on this piece together. We chat and natter, you know. That's another thing that won't have changed from medieval times!'

South of the workshops and the cathedral lies an open square known as the College, surrounded by the buildings of the medieval priory that administered the cathedral and supplied its needs, a beautiful and ancient assemblage. How on earth did they survive the Dissolution of the Monasteries? Norman Emery, the cathedral archaeologist, a local boy, son and grandson of coal miners, talks me through it. Durham's priory was dissolved in 1539, the same year that St Cuthbert's shrine was raided for its treasures. But instead of being unroofed and abandoned like so many abbey buildings, the institution was simply refounded, with the prior taking on the title of dean and twelve of his monks now designated members of the Chapter. There was no need for mass upheaval in the running of things, no call for destruction of the sturdy, well-maintained monastic buildings.

The monks' dormitory found a new use as a prebendal house (home of the canons), then in the 1840s as the cathedral library. Now it houses the Open Treasury display. The monastic brewhouse is now the masons' workshop. The domestic buildings of the priory became prebendal houses after the Reformation. The canons' stables and the hayloft form the eastern boundary of the square, together with a barn (now the head verger's house). On the south side stands the former office of the granitor or master of the garners – the grain-master. In the southwest corner are more prebendal houses, now the choristers' school – and here comes a neat little line of choristers in blue uniforms, chirping like birds as they leave school for the day. On the west side a gloomy tunnel known as the Dark Entry leads under the old guest hall and out to the precipitous paths of the riverbank. Along from it, the former infirmary (now the archdeacon's residence) offered rest and healing for monks and pilgrims alike. The north side of the square, overshadowed by the massive bulk of the cathedral, is bookended by the Great Kitchen and the Prior's House (now the Deanery).

Standing here contemplating these ordered acres, these comfortable stone and brick houses, the well-appointed facilities, I think to myself that, if you weren't especially bothered about sex, and you didn't mind the early hours, the life of a monk, in brisk spring and warm summer, anyway, might not have been a bad option for a bright local lad.

The Open Treasure exhibition occupies the monks' dormitory and Great Kitchen, abutting the western wall of the cloister. The dormitory, remodelled at the turn of the fifteenth century, is magnificent, a large space under a long roof. Each monk occupied a cubicle off the central corridor with a bed and cupboard, and a window shared with the neighbouring brother. The twelve novices slept at either end of the dormitory where the greater cold and discomfort would purge their sins and do their souls good. Beyond lay the Great Kitchen, under whose floor archaeologists found bones of duck, goose, heron, chicken and porpoise, indicative of a rich and varied diet enjoyed by the monks, or at any rate by their prior and his important guests. A 600-year-old midden, too, full of cod bones. Cod came in fresh(ish) from the North Sea, landed at North Shields; or from Bergen and the Lofoten Islands in the form of stockfish, unsalted, air-dried and capable of storage for years on end. A tremendously wide-ranging trade and network of contacts all across the North Sea kept the monastic cooking pots and larders in fish.

These Benedictine monks were far from self-lacerating hermits like Cuthbert. They operated a brewery, a malting house, orchards, fish traps in the river. They ran a school and lent out their stud bull to the priory's tenant farmers. On the whole they maintained good relations with the city of Durham, and also with their neighbours across the Scottish border, monastic and noble. There were frequent visits, gifts of land and grants of charters – all under the say-so of those 'local monarchs', the Prince-Bishops of Durham. The power exerted by the prince-bishops, lords of the County Palatine of Durham – all the land between the rivers Tees and Tyne – was pretty much equal to that of the Crown itself. The Bishop of Durham appointed his own county officers. He had the right to raise an army, imprison or execute; he could operate his own mint and raise his own taxes, but was exempt from taxation himself. All he had to do in return was stay loyal to the monarch, and keep the turbulent locals in line and the incursive Scots at bay. 'Durham was a buffer state,' as cathedral guide Lilian Groves puts it, 'trying to keep out them up north, to keep safe them down south!'

Durham Cathedral's library of illustrated medieval manuscripts is the finest cathedral library in Britain. Started by St Aidan back on Lindisfarne in AD 635, the priceless collection includes pages from the Durham Gospels of the late seventh century, contemporary with St Cuthbert himself and featuring an amazing Crucifixion scene of a Christ with huge charcoal eyes. There's an eighth-century commentary on the Psalms, and the bible that belonged to Hugh le Puiset, Bishop of Durham from 1153 to 1195, its capital letters bulging with beautifully painted men-at-arms, birds, biblical scenes and foliage. The temporary display in the cathedral's Open Treasure exhibition just now is entitled 'Beasts', and I marvel at magical and mythical creatures from the wilder shores of the medieval mind – wyverns, sea serpents and manticores, along with some gryphon eggs, a unicorn horn, and a gryphon's claw that was the property of St Cuthbert himself.

There's also a wonderful collection of carved stones in Open Treasure, gathered from far and near by William Greenwell, canon at Durham Cathedral, librarian, University College bursar, academic and archaeologist – one of those splendid nineteenth-century polymaths. Roman carved stones include pagan altars unearthed along Hadrian's Wall. A chemist's shop in Hexham, undergoing renovation, yielded pre-Norman carved cross shafts – the shop steps were lifted and turned over, to reveal the carvings on their undersides. Other early Christian cross shafts display deer, horses, birds, beasts and stumpy, wide-eyed figures of Christ and the saints, all laced into a tangle of tendrils. One cross head shows St John bowed submissively over Christ's knee, while the Lord belabours him with what appears to be a soup ladle. I pass from these to a clutch of tenth-century hogback grave markers, Saxon or Danish, of thick sparkly stone carved with muzzled bears' heads. What's remarkable to learn is that after the Romans left Hadrian's Wall, the art of stone carving vanished in Northumbria until the monks, returning from continental travels enthused by what they'd seen, revived the skill in their monastic workshops, whence it spread all over the 'Lands of St Cuthbert between Tyne and Tees', as the territory controlled by the Bishop of Durham became known.

So much beauty, humour and mystery resides in the old stones, but after all they are only the *antipasti* to Durham Cathedral's greatest treasures, the little collection of objects preserved from the much-despoiled and investigated tomb of St Cuthbert himself. These are displayed in the Great Kitchen under modern lighting that emphasizes every gleam, glint, dent and curve. Here is the saint's portable altar, a plain wood slab in a tattered silver casing, along with Cuthbert's own pectoral cross, discovered in position on his breast, made of gold inlaid with garnets, its lower arm broken and mended at some time during his life. His double-sided ivory comb is here, said to have been used by the cathedral's eleventh-century sacrist, Alfred Westou, to tidy up the corpse's ever-growing hair and beard whenever the shrine was opened for Cuthbert to 'receive visitors'. And at the heart of all these treasures, Cuthbert's humble wooden coffin, built to enclose his remains on Holy Island eleven years after his death, now reassembled from hundreds of shattered fragments. Apostles and angels, deeply incised in the wood, stare out from the casket sides with huge, empty eyes and mournful little mouths. Incredible that it has survived all these years, all the carrying and hiding, the shifting of burial places, the parading, the smashing and grabbing, the opening and reopening to satisfy men's eternal insecurity and nosiness.

'Do you know what the average spend of a visitor to Durham Cathedral is?' Rob Matthews, former Clerk of Works to the cathedral, puts the question rhetorically over his cup of tea. 'Thirty-five pence! And the average daily cost of maintaining the cathedral? Five thousand pounds – that's nearly two million a year.

'The wall on the north side along Dun Cow Lane is just the right height to sit on. So people sit on it and they kick bits out of it with their heels. It's needed repairing for some time now, as does the whole cathedral. It's a never-ending process. The cathedrals of Britain have shrunk by about three inches all round. The old way was just to shave off the rotten stone, cut it back to the good stone, but not replace it. That won't do now, partly because as we get more understanding of archaeology and history, we realize how precious these buildings are.

'I am concerned about the quality of the young stonemasons now,' says Rob, and his words remind me of stone carver Paul Ellis's lament at Lincoln, his dream of a national college of the craft. 'Youngsters are coming out of the colleges now with an NVQ which just isn't rigorous enough. They don't have a wider knowledge, or even a knowledge of the basics in some cases. They used to be sent to York for a bit of practical experience, but they weren't learning the theory, and they needed to go to college for that. Anyway, we started the Cathedrals Workshop Fellowship about ten years ago, developing a degree course at the University of Gloucester. Lots of elements – conservation, history of architecture, building in stone, archaeology, engineering, ornamental carving are some of them. The CWF is going a long way to solving this problem of poorly qualified, poorly skilled masons, and that's a legacy I'm quite proud of, especially here at Durham. The fact is, I think of myself as part of this building, and I always will be.'

Back in the cathedral Lilian Groves, eighty-eight years old, sits in a pew to chat. Ex-Vice Principal of the College of St Hild and St Bede at Durham University, she's been a cathedral guide for more than a quarter-century.

'Bede's *Life* made Cuthbert a celebrity. Lincoln, York and the other cathedrals had to find their own saints after they'd been built, but it's Cuthbert, then and now, who's the keystone here. People are *drawn* by Cuthbert – although it's Bede's tomb that tends to draw the Americans. This pilgrimage aspect has just grown and grown. There's a booked tour for pilgrims every month at least, and every so often individual pilgrims arrive. There's been a rise in interest in what they call Celtic Christianity – but I've no time for that. I have been to Santiago, not on pilgrimage as such, but what delighted me was seeing the pilgrims arriving dancing and singing and throwing their hands in the air – pure joy!

'There's been a big growth in long-distance pilgrimage paths dedicated to saints – St Oswald's Way, Bede's Way, St Cuthbert's Way. These saints have had a new lease of life as personalities, as celebrities, you might say.' Lilian gestures in the direction of a glimmering rack of tea lights. 'And I've noticed that the lighting of votive candles has grown over my time as a guide – grown at the same rate as those bunches of flowers at the sites of road accidents. It's a physical act that seals a spiritual impulse.'

She pauses to frame her thoughts. 'People feel lost, I think, and are looking for something. They want to fix something, to have some assurances. Some want to leave something of themselves behind, too, as well as taking something away. It's such a strong impulse. I came on a man weeping by himself in the nave. I pointed him towards the shrine of St Cuthbert, and as I led him there he shouted out: "But I'm a secular man!" In indignation, in amazement – in denial, really, of what he was feeling.

'Anyway, shall we?'

The twelfth-century chapter house is semi-elliptical, boat-shaped, with fine ribbed vaulting. Under the floor lies Nicholas de Farnham, Bishop of Durham 1241–57, his name carved above him. Poor man, he was often sick, but on one occasion he enjoyed a miraculous recovery after drinking a glass of water infused with some bristles from the beard of St Edmund of Abingdon.

In 1796 a reduction in size was planned for the chapter house – the medieval building was too cavernous and tall, its acoustics were poor, and the Chapter didn't care for it. During renovation work under James 'The Destroyer' Wyatt (felt to be far too heavy-handed in his cathedral restorations), the Clerk of Works pulled the keystone out of the eastern arch, and the whole end of the building fell off and into the Deanery garden. A century later the dean was giving a garden party, and someone pushed a stick into the lumpy ground. 'I say! There's something here!' It was the stones of the prior's seat and many others from the old chapter house. They were recycled into yet another restoration, this one more successful than Wyatt's.

Off the chapter house a semi-elliptical doorway, very low and of solid stone, opens into the monks' prison, a cramped chamber hardly big enough to contain a man, with roughly hewn ceiling and walls. Here recaltricant brethren could be locked up for a cooling-off period, generally twenty-four hours, in this medieval version of the naughty step. If seriously out of order a monk could be sentenced by the prior to up to a year's solitary in another, grimmer cell elsewhere.

'See that black line?' says Lilian. It's made of polished Frosterley marble, embedded in the nave floor by the priory monks to indicate the point beyond which women were not permitted to venture. For laymen the barrier was at the quire screen, a little further east. Lilian steps over the line, smiling, and we make our way up to the east end of the cathedral.

Cradling the shrine of St Cuthbert is the Chapel of the Nine Altars, built about 1280 when the constant press of pilgrims round St Cuthbert's tomb had become unmanageable. It gives the east end of the cathedral a curiously blunt look, a squared-off extension, sticking out sideways like the business end of a hammerhead shark.

The chapel is embellished with columns of Frosterley marble, a highly polished carboniferous limestone, peppered with fossils of coral, from quarries over in Weardale. St Aidan's altar is spread with a beautiful cloth, the work of the Broderers. Embellished with butterflies, birds and variegated seaweeds of the Northumbrian coast, it's a salty breath from Lindisfarne where Aidan founded the monastery forever associated with the name of St Cuthbert. A stained-glass window shows Michael Ramsey (Bishop of Durham from 1952 to 1956) with the characteristic tufty eyebrows and cloud of white hair at the back of his head that I remember well from the 1960s when he was Archbishop of Canterbury, a benevolent, saintly First Lord of the Anglican Admiralty sailing in great white lawn sleeves, a figure almost comically at odds with the Swinging Sixties.

There's a modern pietà by local sculptor Fenwick Lawson, two beech trunks transformed into a mournful Virgin Mary lamenting her fallen son who lies curled on the ground at her feet. It was Lawson who carved the exceptionally moving, sombrely dark representation of monks carrying Cuthbert's coffin that now graces the parish church on Holy Island. There's a suggestion of burning and charcoal about that sculpture, and about this pietà in the Chapel of the Nine Altars, too. Close inspection reveals scars and searing on the figures of both Mary and Jesus. In 1984 the sculpture was on display directly below the rose window in the south transept of York Minster. The lightning strike that shattered the window caused molten lead to rain down, deeply scarring both mother and son – wounds that Fenwick Lawson accepted for his sculpture, saying: 'The pietà taught me that there are language systems other than my own which can reinforce the content . . . I never thought of getting a blow torch out, but it added a dimension which is fantastic.'

At last this leisurely wandering through the low light of the cathedral reaches its destination, the shrine of St Cuthbert. After its many vicissitudes, the body of the hermit saint was laid in state in the most magnificent shrine on the completion of the cathedral. When King Henry VIII's Commissioners came in 1539 to strip the shrine of its treasures, they hammered open the iron-bound chest containing Cuthbert's body, breaking one of his legs in the process. The saint's body was reported to be still undecayed, some 850 years after his death. They stripped the gold and jewels off the shrine and departed, having dumped Cuthbert's body into the vestry for someone else to rebury.

In today's feretory or shrine space, all pomp drops away. Three pilgrims kneel in prayer on the cold stone floor around St Cuthbert's grave. It is sealed by a simple, massive slab inscribed 'CUTHBERTUS'. Everything is extremely solid, plain and dignified. The muffled scrapes and clatterings of the cathedral fade into stillness here.

Lilian quietly lights a candle and places it on the slab. 'I do that because it gives others permission to do the same,' she says. 'Sometimes they'd like to, but don't quite know if they dare, if it's against some rule. But Cuthbert isn't simply our saint, Northumberland's saint, is he? He's . . . well, he feels like everyone's.'

8

Ely

The Ship of the Fens

MY FIRST SIGHT OF ELY CATHEDRAL was from the east, on a windy afternoon thirty years ago. It was early summer, and the great church sailed for my delight in a rhythmically waving sea of green barley, the plant tops swishing their bearded heads together with a sea-like susurration. The next sighting I had, a year or two later, was through the dense dark fog of a 'fen blow', very early on an even windier day. The enormous flat fields of black fenland peat around the town were drier than a bone after weeks of drought, and the gale had lifted the weightless topsoil off the ploughland and stirred it into the tides of wind racing invisibly across Cambridgeshire. The cathedral drifted in and out of sight that morning, a ghost ship in a whispering black fog.

On a beautiful still July evening I have returned to find the 'Ship of the Fens' riding a more variegated sea of corn and beet leaves, carrots and dark clay, spuds and floods. Brown hares are lolloping between the beet rows, their coats darkened by rainwater splashes as they brush against the crinkled leaves. I stop by the verge of Quanea Drove, a typically bumpy rollercoaster of a fenland by-road, and watch the hares as the sun sets behind Ely Cathedral.

It is rather remarkable that the Isle of Ely should have a cathedral at all. This almost imperceptible rise of ground, a convex lens of thin greensand over gault clay, stands no more than a hundred feet at its highest above the dead-flat arable Cambridgeshire farmlands. The town that the cathedral shelters is tiny, its situation remote, here in the middle of Fenland. There is no grandeur of location, no proud rock as at Durham or Lincoln. But anyone who occupies this little hummock commands a prospect over all the land as far as one can see in any direction. Before the Fens were drained for agriculture by seventeenth-century speculators, before medieval monks began to control the fen environment, back when it was all swamps and snaky rivers, marshes and carr woodlands, Ely was hard to locate and harder to approach. It was all but impossible to take the occupants of Ely by surprise. They alone knew the ways through the maze of fens and tidal waters. People lived by traps and punts, spears and nets. Food was abundant – eels, fish, wildfowl. The impregnable Isle of Ely, for all its lack of 'civilized' amenities, was actually a desirable holding; and so thought Tonhbert, elderly prince of the south fenlands, when he gave it to his 22-year-old bride Etheldreda in AD 652 as a traditional 'morning gift' on the first morning of their marriage.

The setting sun is a golden ball that reddens and squashes into an elliptical dome as it slides down beside the south wall of the cathedral. I sit and picture Etheldreda, nobly born, a staunch Christian who managed to persuade Tonhbert to let her fulfil her vow of perpetual virginity. When Tonhbert died in 655, she came to live at Ely. Five years later she was married again, this time to the fourteen-year-old Prince Ecgfrith of Northumbria, whose father wanted to establish Northumbrian dominance over the lands that had been Tonhbert's. The teenage prince wasn't quite so ready as Etheldreda's first husband to cede his conjugal rights, but the strong-minded young woman contrived to hang on to her maidenhead through ten years of formalized marriage, even when Ecgfrith succeeded as king in 670 and needed an heir. Etheldreda left the Northumbrian court around 672, having taken the veil. She may in fact not have remained a virgin, but may have proved to be infertile, in which case it would have been a smart move on Ecgfrith's part to release her to be a nun. Freed from his vows, he could remarry and beget the all-important heir.

Some stories say that Ecgfrith pursued Etheldreda, but was frustrated by a miraculous rising of the tide at St Abb's Head from recapturing her as she set off for her island in the fens. There Etheldreda established a monastery for both nuns and monks, and ruled it until her death from plague in 679. Etheldreda's sister Seaxburh succeeded her as Abbess of Ely, followed by Seaxburh's daughter Eormenhild. Werburga, daughter of Eormenhild, later became Abbess of Ely in her turn. The Anglo-Saxon age could hardly show a family dynasty of more capable and commanding women, ordering the lives of both sexes and the affairs of monasteries and their considerable estates. As I watch the sun sink into the ground and the cathedral flush a fiery orange in the afterglow, I can only speculate what happened after Werburga died in about AD 700. History draws a blank on Ely after that, till the Danes made their way here nearly two hundred years later and sent the whole place sky high in flames.

The hares have gone from the beet rows and a cold evening breeze is rippling the leaves. I stretch and yawn, but I can't tear myself away just yet. Tomorrow is for exploring Ely; tonight there's a red and yellow sky to watch, and the odd shape of the cathedral to ponder. Its sunset silhouette is all spikes, turrets, square tower tops and pinnacles at disjointed intervals. It looks massively lopsided. There's a basic shape to all cathedrals that my brain and memory have programmed my eyes to see, and it's based on symmetry: a recumbent cross shape, with a central nave as the main stem, and transepts of equal length composing the arms. Ely Cathedral does not conform. Either part of it is missing, or there's too much of it on the left-hand side. It looks eccentric, multiform and haunting, a ship of the line shattered by broadsides, limping back to harbour after some tremendous battle.

Next morning in Ely town, old sunlit brick walls curve along the streets. Lime trees abound. There are pot plants and vegetables for sale in terraced front gardens – this is the Fens, after all, the most fertile ground in Britain.

Approached from the west in brilliant early-morning sunshine, the cathedral on its green seems somehow both huge and compact.

There's no walled close as such, but a great number of the medieval monastic buildings have survived and surround the church on the south, north and east. The west tower dominates the prospect, pierced by a surprisingly modest door that more resembles a Gothic window, narrowed by a slender central pillar. The whole shape of the cathedral is beguilingly out of kilter. A great three-storey transept juts out from the south side, terminating in twin towers, octagonal and battlemented, a grand design. On the north side there's nothing – just an angled buttress hard up against the tower, its slope crudely sealed with cement. Odd ragged ends of stones stick out of the church wall to show where the entire northern transept, the equal and counterbalance of the southern one, has fallen down or been torn away.

This arm has been amputated, but the cathedral has miraculously sprouted another, much further along its mutilated northern flank – a tall pale stone excrescence of a Lady chapel. Actually I'm put more in mind of a tree, one of those Sherwood Forest giants, that has lost a limb and has budded out another by way of compensation. Ely Cathedral is scarred and lumpy, unbalanced but endearing. Intriguing, too. You can see that this building has suffered a catastrophic injury, and straight away you wonder how and why.

'Someone once came into the cathedral full of delight, saying that they had been stuck in traffic outside the west end and found that they could look in the west door from well outside the building and see all the way down the nave to the colours in the east window. I knew exactly what they meant. There are not many cathedrals you can do that in, and it still brings me pleasure, still thrills me, when the beauties of this building strike someone for the first time.'

Michael White has come to show me around his beloved Ely Cathedral, even though he is officially retired as a guide. A humorous man, full of puns and quips, he's very light of touch. The thirty-five years he spent in the service of the Inland Revenue must certainly have honed his sense of humour. Michael walks the building as though entirely at home, and speaks of characters from the cathedral's past as though they were personal friends of his. Etheldreda is on his mind as we stroll back and forth in the central transept.

'One of the earliest feminists, Etheldreda. She was no man's possession, you know. She made her own decisions about remaining a virgin through both of her marriages, and stuck to her guns. She owned her own property, the Isle of Ely, and had her own personal steward to administer it, so it was her calling the shots.'

On the capitals of the columns at the northwest corner of the transept is a fine carving of the marriage of St Etheldreda to Tonhbert. Beside it is a deathbed scene. 'I always thought that was Etheldreda on her deathbed,' says Michael, 'but when I was up a ladder looking really closely one day, I saw that "she" had stubble. It's actually Tonhbert on *his* deathbed. And just behind Tonhbert's head, what do you think I found? A blue toothbrush, tucked away where no one could see it. Someone cleaning the carvings at some stage had left it there, I suppose, but I rather liked that. Blue for a boy, you know.'

Michael outlines what happened after the Danes destroyed Ely monastery in AD 870. For the next hundred years the isolated settlement in the Fens was left alone by the outside world. Secular priests, unofficial men of God, moved in to cater for the locals' souls, but there was no monastery. Then in 970 King Edgar expelled these makeshift holy men and sanctioned Ethelwold, Bishop of Winchester, to refound Ely with gifts of rents and grants of land, and to build an abbey church on the isle.

King Cnut was a Danish invader and a savage fighter. He was not above cutting off the hands, ears and noses of hostages if it suited him. He came to the throne in 1016 at the age of about twenty-two, and ruled all England with a mixture of sword and diplomacy. Cnut was also, perhaps surprisingly, a devout Christian, and a frequent visitor to the Isle of Ely and its monastery. One wintry story has him sledging to the island across the frozen fen while his tame giant, Brithman, walks in

front to test the ice. Another has the king enraptured by distant chanting across the water as he rows to Ely to keep the feast of Candlemas,
urging the boats forward with the command: 'Nearer, my men, nearer,
so we can really hear those merry monks sing!'

Whatever the truth of that, Cnut died in 1035, and Ely lost royal
favour – particularly after the Norman Conquest, when the remote isle
in the impenetrable fens became a rallying point for rebels. Two centuries before, the Isle of Athelney in the Somerset marshlands had been a
refuge from the Danes for King Alfred; now Ely and its watery wastes,
under the influence of the staunchly anti-Norman monks, sheltered
the Anglo-Saxon leader Hereward the Wake or 'Watchful' in his
doomed guerrilla resistance to the Normans. In 1071 a Norman army
attacked Ely; stories say the great causeway across the fens broke to
pieces as they charged across it. They built a tower and installed a witch
in it to shriek curses at the besieged Saxons, but Hereward fired it, and
her. He thwarted another Norman advance through a reed bed by setting fire to the reeds upwind, then watching his enemies smother and
burn. At last the Normans found a way in via a secret pathway over the
marshes. Was it a treacherous monk of Ely who let slip its existence, as
some stories say? At all events the Normans captured the isle. But
Hereward the Wake was nowhere to be found. Like the Welsh rebel
hero Owain Glyndŵr, this doughty and cunning warrior simply van-
ishes into the mists, never to be captured, never seen again.

In 1082 Simeon, brother of Bishop Walkelin of Winchester, was
installed as abbot at Ely. New cathedrals were being initiated all over
the country as statements of the power and presence of the new rulers,
and Abbot Simeon, at ninety years of age, boosted by the enormous
revenues that rolled in from Ely's far-flung estates, allied himself with
the monks to start the process on the fenland isle. The huge cruciform
abbey church went up in fits and starts, being declared a cathedral in
1109 when Ely broke away from Lincoln and became a diocese in its
own right. The nave was built between 1130 and 1140, from east to
west. And the whole structure was finished by 1189.

The fact that the relics of St Etheldreda and her sisters-in-God were at hand to be enshrined in the new cathedral meant that worship of these Saxon saints, and pilgrimages to them, continued unabated – quite a difficult pill for the authorities to swallow in the new Norman dispensation. 'St Etheldreda's reliquary was a big chest on legs,' says Michael White, 'standing proud of the floor. So if you were sick and you wanted the full medieval MRI scan, you'd be pushed underneath and through the reliquary from one end to the other. It was the focus of extreme devotion – after all, you'd very little other medical help in those days.'

Under the ornate marble floor of the presbytery, just east of the quire, lies the site of the shrine of St Etheldreda – 'Saint and Queen who founded this house AD 673', as the floor slab proclaims. 'Actually,' Michael confirms, 'there's a persistent rumour that her relics, rather than being turfed out into the graveyard at the Reformation as was supposed to have been done, were rescued and walled up somewhere in the fabric of the cathedral. So there's always a low-level buzz of excitement at the cathedral when there's any digging around in the fabric to be done – just in case Etheldreda's relics come to light. She definitely left a mark behind in terms of atmosphere. The fact is that cathedrals do have either a masculine or a feminine feel to them, and in the case of Ely it's very much a female one.'

Vicky Johnson is one of Ely's residentiary canons. When I chat to her later in the day, I'm reminded of the strength and confidence with which St Etheldreda and her spiritual sisters operated in the masculine environment of the Saxon world. That was thirteen hundred years ago, yet women have had to wait until our current generation for the first of them to be ordained priests in the Anglican Church. How have people, men and women both, reacted to Vicky Johnson as a young woman in holy orders?

'Oh, it was that first wave of women who were ordained in 1994 who got a great deal of the flak. They were the pioneers. But speaking personally, I've had very little negative reaction. I was ordained in 2007, and when I was appointed to this job a couple of years ago the publicity was all about "Wow! Ely's first lady canon!" When I arrived there were a few questions along the lines of "What's it like to be Ely's first female residentiary canon?" to which I replied, "I'm just a priest. And by the way, this cathedral was founded by a woman."

'Honestly, it all seems perfectly natural. The cathedral has a girl's choir directed by Sarah MacDonald, and plenty of services with Jessica Martin, my residentiary colleague, or me, reading and presiding – so now you could have a service where all those who are leading worship are women. That's not intentional, but just a sign of how things have changed. We inhabit these roles just as people have always done, and we enter into this tradition bringing all that we are to these vocations.'

Vicky was appointed to the post at Ely from Manchester, where she was a parish priest. 'There are three residentiary canons and four lay canons at Ely. Together with the dean, we make up the Chapter, the governing body of the cathedral. Basically, we oversee the cathedral at every level. They're two very different roles, I've found, a parish priest and a cathedral canon. I think of a parish priest as the captain of a frigate. The ship is light and manoeuvrable, and you have to be, too. A canon of a cathedral is like a senior officer of a supertanker – it's hard to slow or change its course, harder still to stop it and start again, largely because of its size!'

What called Vicky to the priesthood in the first place? 'My parents weren't churchgoers, but they valued church and what it represented. I sang in the church choir as a girl, which gave me a way of contributing to worship. I can remember hearing the priest say the words of the Eucharistic Prayer during Holy Communion and thinking: I'd love to say those words one day. It was singing that really drew me in, the words I sang and heard during worship called to me long before any woman had been ordained and before I could understand what ordination was.

'I did genetics at Leicester University, and then was into my PhD on cancer research at Manchester when I felt the actual call to ordination. But when I enquired, I was told: "Finish your PhD, because the Church likes people who can see things through." So I did that. I moved from science to theology, which to me seemed like a very natural progression.'

I remark on the number of youngsters I've come across who don't know any New Testament stories or parables, and how the biblical allusions people of my generation make as a matter of course are met by blank looks, or sometimes with outright hostility at the very breath of anything religious. Vicky sits and considers. 'Well, yes, I think there is a need nowadays for an apologia, an explanation of Christianity to a secular and pretty cynical society. And sometimes, yes, an apology, too. The Church has to acknowledge its failures and mistakes. There's been some animosity, some online trolling. The Dawkins reaction, you might call it: knee-jerk, ritual negativity. But what I see here is different. This amazing building provokes a different response. Visitors, of all faiths and none, respond with awe to the architecture, to the atmosphere, to the history. Hundreds of votive candles are lit every day. It's a hugely expansive space that's bound to promote wider thinking and contemplation, and the effect on people is shown by their responses in the visitors' book. Nothing blasé about those reactions. They are genuine responses to the numinous and transcendent.'

'We have various sorts of outreach activities, links to the local community. For example, the Science Festival in the cathedral that's just finished. We celebrated science as a gift from a God of all things, so we explored engineering, medicine, technology and much more besides, and as a scientist myself I found that very satisfying to organize. Religion and science are not enemies; both are pursuing truth. And this cathedral is also a place of refuge and sanctuary. There are lost souls who come here in search of peace. The cathedral staff are trained to recognize those in need, and to put them in touch with us. We can't *solve* their problems, and we don't try to, but we can give them a listening ear and a cup of tea, and space and quiet and peace, and if they wish we pray with them.

'As for services,' says Vicky, 'there's different kinds and levels. Pet services, Christingle, Remembrance services, Harvest Festivals, Christmas and Easter are all more and more popular. And for Sunday morning service, the congregation is about three hundred on average. Why this growth in attendance? Well, there's the sheer quality of the preaching and the worship, the tradition, the hospitality. People are made to feel welcome, in a non-judgemental way. And the huge space and large number of people offer anonymity. There's a notable contrast between the culture, as I've observed it, of Roman Catholicism – social, outward and public, a constant flow of people in and out, movement, chatter, a matter-of-factness about religious observance – and the reticent, inward and private culture of Anglicanism. The anonymity of one person alone with their prayers in such a big space – perhaps it speaks to that private aspect.

'But in all of that, I think you're right, I think we are losing the Christian story. Religious literacy is poor. Most people don't know this story any more but they do have a sense of the sacred. Cathedrals tap into these spiritual yearnings that people have. These questions are pressing for the whole Church. We have to think about how these amazing buildings are used so that they can maintain worship and prayer, but also become spaces for the whole community to enjoy rather than crumble to dust. We are stewards of the faith, and it is a faith we need to share.

'As cathedrals become more popular, the flipside is that we may lose the parish churches. They may have to close as congregations shrink and parish priests are stretched ever more thinly and with less time for pastoral work. Do you know that Philip Larkin poem, "Church Going"?'

I don't, but later on I look it up, and find the poet wondering,

> *. . . when churches will fall completely out of use*
> *What we shall turn them into, if we shall keep*
> *A few cathedrals chronically on show,*
> *Their parchment, plate, and pyx in locked cases,*

And let the rest rent-free to rain and sheep.
Shall we avoid them as unlucky places?

Or, after dark, will dubious women come
To make their children touch a particular stone;
Pick simples for a cancer; or on some
Advised night see walking a dead one?
Power of some sort will go on
In games, in riddles, seemingly at random;
But superstition, like belief, must die,
And what remains when disbelief has gone?
Grass, weedy pavement, brambles, buttress, sky.

'I see the cathedrals as centres of stability and reliability,' Vicky sums up. 'Most parish priests can't find the time or opportunity to say a prayer every day in each of their churches. But here we pray every day. At seven thirty a.m. we assemble to pray, all the canons together, and at eight we take Holy Communion together. It reinforces that sense of community and continuity. On a dark February afternoon at evensong, with a congregation of three, with the candles lit and bats flying about, the cathedral feels like a place of continuity. One's very aware that this service has been held here every day for hundreds of years, and will go on being held, no matter what.'

Vicky has to go and get ready to preside at evensong. She gets up and shakes hands. 'Cathedrals are the flagships of the Church,' she says, 'and I think they can be places which inspire confidence in the Church and what it can do.'

And women's role in the Church? 'That can only grow. And these changes, I'm sure, will all take place within the span of my ministry.'

As Michael White and I pace the cathedral I tell him about the sunset view of the cathedral I had last night, and the curiously lopsided look of the building. 'Ah yes,' he says, 'well, that's our tale of the two towers. But first, come and meet my friend Alan.' He leads the way to the centre of the nave. 'Morning, Alan!' he says cheerily, addressing a big blank tomb slab in the floor. 'Dear Alan – my hero!'

Alan of Walsingham's brass has long gone from his slab, its former position marked by a faint indentation. Also gone are the lines of his poetical epitaph, but Michael has them in his head:

> Know that the choir before you exceedeth all others in beauty,
> Made by Alan our brother, Alan the wise master-builder;
> He who of craftsmen the flower, was gifted with strength in his lifetime,
> Alan the Prior, forget not, here facing the choir lies buried.
> He, for that older Tower which fell one night in the darkness,
> Here erected, well-founded, the Tower ye are now beholding.
> Many the houses of God that, as Prior and Sacrist he builded.
> May God grant him in Heaven a seat at the end of his labour.

The sacrist of Ely monastery was responsible for its budget, administration, provisioning and so on. Alan of Walsingham was of the Saloman family, a goldsmith, lawyer and architect, one of a triumvirate of administrators at Ely Cathedral in the early fourteenth century, along with Prior Crauden of the monastery, and Bishop Hotham of the cathedral. 'Alan was a nice man, a likeable man,' says Michael with real warmth; 'he was known as the "Good Companion" and his house was nicknamed "The House of Good Company". The Saloman family were bankers, and one became Bishop of Norwich. Probably a name of Jewish origin, and their Christian descendants rose to prominence at a time when there was great prejudice, and occasional pogroms, against Jews in England. In fact King Edward I issued an Edict of Expulsion in 1290, and it remained in force until the Protectorate of Oliver Cromwell, when Jews were permitted to return – in 1657!'

In the south aisle of Ely Cathedral I've already been captivated by the Babel Window, a vigorous early Victorian portrayal of the Tower of

Babel with builders drinking, arguing, scratching themselves, hauling up buckets by rope and pulley. Roundels depict set square, hammer, spirit level, ruler, triangle, compass, trowel and template. A forest of lolling, wagging red tongues dangles from the skies overhead. The sense of imminent ruin, a *Grand Designs* disaster in the making, is palpable. And as Michael White tells it, the cause of the great tower collapse of 12 February 1322 was as much to do with bad luck as bad judgement.

The monks of Ely had just finished the service of matins, around 4.30 a.m., when the central tower of the cathedral suddenly tottered and fell with a concussion and noise so thunderous that the monks thought there had been an earthquake. The structure collapsed vertically downwards, cleaving a hole in the church floor about seventy feet across. Amazingly, everyone escaped unscathed. The cause of the disaster was unclear, but the year before, sizeable foundations for a fine new Lady chapel had been dug only a few feet to the north, a pit one hundred feet long and fifty feet wide. This new chapel should have been built at the east end of the cathedral, but a pilgrims' hostel already occupied the site. Alan of Walsingham, as sacrist of Ely's monastery, was the prime mover in getting the Lady chapel started, and he may have intuited that the foundation works were at least partially to blame. Certainly he was deeply shocked by the fall of the tower. In the contemporary *Chronicle of the Abbots and Bishops of Ely*, an anonymous monk wrote of Alan: 'He was devastated, grieving vehemently and overcome with sorrow . . . He knew not which way to turn himself or what to do for the reparation of such a ruin.'

In fact it's more than likely that the Lady chapel foundations drained the water from below the crossing, and the greensand underneath just crumbled away as it dried out under the tower. Cracking in the pillars flanking the transept had been noticed as soon as work on the Lady chapel had commenced – that's why the monks weren't holding their services immediately below at the time of the collapse.

Sacrist Alan was not a man to let circumstances overwhelm him for long. The tower had to be rebuilt, and he was the man responsible. He got straight down to it. The same foundations couldn't be used, so he decided to broaden the tower base and use an octagonal, rather than a square shape. Flying buttresses would brace the new structure. Up it went over the ensuing six years, paid for largely by the monastic community itself. By 1328 the octagonal tower was built. The problem was how to cap it off with a steeply pitched roof light enough not to push the new walls apart or initiate another collapse into the fragile greensand substrate. Contemporary engineering couldn't solve the problem of roofing such a structure in stone or lead. It had to be made of wood, a shape and structure so daring that it had never been achieved before, and never would be again.

'Absolutely one of a kind,' says Will Schenck as I crane my neck and swing my binoculars upwards from the crossing floor to follow his pointing finger. 'A work of genius, and there's never been anything else to compare with it.'

Michael White has handed me over to the current specialist in tours around the Octagon. What Will Schenck doesn't know about Ely Cathedral's remarkable wooden crown probably isn't worth knowing. 'The Octagon and Lantern are unique. Nothing like this structure has survived anywhere else. It's a one-off masterpiece of the Decorated Gothic.'

Alan of Walsingham had engaged King Edward III's master carpenter William Hurley to oversee the woodwork of the tower project, and it was Hurley who came up with the idea of making an octagonal wooden lantern, light enough to be suspended inside the top of the hollow stone octagon of the tower on massive oak beams. The roof of the Lantern would form the roof over the crossing, and the upper windows would collect the daylight and flood it down into the cathedral.

Looking up at the crossing roof, it's hard to believe that what I see is all carpentry. The vaulting and ribs, the delicately carved bosses and the elaborate niches where musical angels blow elongated trumpets all have the solid appearance of stone. One expects to see stonework in such a location, so stonework is what one sees. But then I remember the chapter house roof at York Minster, my inability to distinguish stone from wood until Geoff the guide pointed it out, and the focus clicks into place. I follow the painted wooden ribs upwards and inwards to the boss that knits them together, a long-faced and golden-bearded Christ ensconced amid clouds like pink bracket fungi. 'That's the original image, made in 1347,' says Will Schenck, 'though the Victorians touched it up a bit. The Octagon itself was made between 1322 and 1342, and the monastery records even tell us the name of one of the painters, William Shanks – they dangled him on a rope from the Lantern roof to paint the panels of the lower Octagon. The goldbeater was called Ralph. He used a heap of gold coins, rejected because they were blemished, to hammer out the sheets of gold leaf that were needed. It was all done just in time, before the Black Death outbreak in 1349. The population of the monastery fell from about a hundred monks – and hundreds more ancillary staff – to around twenty-five, and work on this sort of thing stopped.'

Will leads the way through a small door and up dusty stone spirals of stairs to reach the octagonal chamber in which the Lantern is suspended. Horizontal spokes dovetail together like a wheel of eight sections. Each of the eight corner posts comprises the trunk of a massive oak sixty-three feet long, ordered from Chicksands Priory in Bedfordshire, bought and stored by Alan of Walsingham, the man of foresight, as soon as the revolutionary design had been agreed. Special wagons, barges and quays on the river had to be constructed to get the tree trunks here. It was another example of Alan's genius for organization.

From the corner posts, 'raking shores' or diagonal beams slope away at forty-five degrees, bearing the weight of the structure. These beams came from trees that were already two hundred years old when they were felled. They carry the wedge-shaped incisions of medieval chisels, scars where splinters tore away, the scuff marks of adze blows.

'Looks like a spider's web, doesn't it?' comments Will. 'But not all these timbers are the original ones. At the time of the Reformation, a couple of hundred years after the Lantern was built, the lead from the roof was stripped off and sold. No money was spent on repairs for two centuries.' He grimaces. 'Bad mistake. The roof leaked like a sieve, and had a standing lake of water that percolated down into the thirsty timbers below. In 1757 the cathedral commissioned a local architect, James Essex from Cambridge, and he reported that eight of the raking shores had rotted and were detached from the structure. The other eight were actually supporting all the weight. Essex was a local man, a joiner's son, who loved and appreciated woodwork. A smarter London architect such as James Wyatt might have just pulled down the whole thing. But Essex copied the fourteenth-century engineering, and inserted extra diagonals – over-engineering it, really, but making sure the Lantern would survive.'

Will circumnavigates the Lantern, opening the long wooden shutters that pierce its façade. I crane out and look up to the fourteenth-century boss where Christ hovers on his mushroom cloud, attended by seraphim, each with three pairs of wings crossed above, before and below. At eye level is a row of calm, strong, asexual faces – Pre-Raphaelite angels, painted on the Lantern's panels. They have long noses and good, firm Victorian chins. They hold an array of medieval musical instruments, as mentioned in Psalm 150.

> Praise him with the sounding of the trumpet,
> praise him with the harp and lyre,
> praise him with timbrel and dancing,
> praise him with the strings and pipe,
> praise him with the clash of cymbals.

The trumpeting angels are obliged to blow their instruments straight up into the sky, in order to squeeze them into the narrow panels. There are censing angels, too, swinging thuribles over their heads. All wear robes of pastel hue – pink, blue, green, peach, mauve. They were painted, and the boss and vaults repainted, in the 1860s by Thomas Gambier Parry, who merrily destroyed the work done by the dangling William Shanks, five hundred years before, by painting over it. Parry's angels are beautiful creatures, but there's something odd about them – odder, that is, than the simple fact of being angels. As you stare, it becomes clear. Their torsos are too short, their legs too long. As with the stone kings and bishops on the west front at Wells Cathedral, these angels have been unnaturally stretched out to counterbalance the foreshortening perspective when viewed from far below.

On the ledges of the Lantern lies a drift of poppy petals, remnants of those that were let fall last Remembrance Sunday in a blood-red shower that floated down to cover the altar below. There are Second World War graffiti on the backs of the panels. 'L, D, P, T & C Tunnell – Brothers', says a pencilled note. 'That last C stands for Cedric,' says Will. 'He was the youngest, just a child during the war. We got him up here in his seventies, staggering up all those stairs. It was the first time he'd climbed up to the Lantern, and when he saw his name written there, and knew that his brothers had included him along with them all those years ago . . . that was a special moment.'

I'm still keen to know about that torn-off limb, the phantom northwest transept whose absence gives the cathedral such an unbalanced appearance. In this matter, Will Schenck's guiding colleague Mark Bradford is the go-to man. We meet him under the Octagon. Mark marches us to the west end of the cathedral, and bids us look up.

'This was the last bit of the cathedral to be built. It was finished by 1189. In the first thirty years it shrank by a foot or more, thanks to the poor quality cement they used. After the central tower collapsed, a four-storey belfry was built on top of the west tower as a substitute bell tower, but it caused trouble ever after. It made the tower lean sideways. In 1404 they inserted extra arches under the tower to take the weight, but it didn't help other vulnerable bits of the structure. Familiar story! Within a hundred years the northwest transept had fallen down, and the mess was never properly tidied up, as you can see. It was just left as it was, a rough slope.'

Under the west tower a little boy of five or six is running delightedly round in half-circles, just inside the west door of the cathedral. He's trying to follow the windings of a labyrinth inlaid in the floor by George Gilbert Scott during nineteenth-century restorations. 'The west tower's two hundred and fifteen feet tall,' Mark remarks, 'and George Gilbert Scott made the journey round that labyrinth exactly two hundred and fifteen feet from the edge to the centre.' The little boy has a long way to go yet, but his giggles echo in the space under the tower.

Mark's pointing finger draws our attention to the five-sided barrel ceiling of the nave, painted during the 1850s restoration with twelve brilliantly colourful Pre-Raphaelite scenes from the Creation through the Flood to the Nativity and to Christ in Glory. 'Henry Styleman le Strange was the squire of Hunstanton, a gentleman artist and a friend of Dean George Peacock. He started on the tower ceiling and then the nave, painting on to a boarded false ceiling from scaffolding. When he got six bays down the nave, he died, and Gambier Parry finished it off for free. It didn't hurt Parry, as the good work he did helped him get the commission for the Lantern painting a couple of years later.'

We climb the spiral stairs to the tower roof, where we blink in the daylight. Here is a carved head with heavy brows and a contemporary look about it – not quite contemporary, in fact, with its generous sideburns and mullet. 'John Bradford, foreman of the restoration works and master mason, 1973–4', says the plaque. A satnav beacon is clipped to the parapet – the company rents the space, another dribble in the torrent of Ely Cathedral's income. There's a very fine view of the medieval town and cathedral close, the monastic range, the great monastery hall (now the Bishop's Palace), and two curiously dimpled, inverted cones of brick – water-catchment reservoirs in the roofs of the twin south towers. Beyond, a thirty-mile prospect stretches from the spires of Cambridge to the sugar-beet factory silos at Bury St Edmunds.

'By the Second World War the cathedral roof's lead was several hundred years old,' says Mark as we lean on the parapet. 'It had become very white, and would shine in moon and starlight. It was unmistakeable in this flat Cambridgeshire countryside – there was no disguising it. If they'd wanted to bomb it, the Luftwaffe could have. But it was more valuable to them – and the RAF – as a waymark in the night.'

Part of the triforium or arcade along the upper walls of Ely Cathedral incorporates the pleasingly ramshackle Stone Store, from whose waist-high railing you look down into the body of the cathedral. The Stone Store is a chaotic lumber room where the clutter of the ages has drifted to rest. A Victorian wheelchair stands with its woven cane seat rotted out. There are carved stone window stops and wooden choir-stall pinnacles, one depicting St Etheldreda, robed and bland-faced. A stout crane on rails anticipates its next cargo of stone. Two straw men left over from the flower festival sprawl in sinister abandonment across a pile of stone blocks. The Wise Men wait for the Christmas crib. A dead bat lies on the floor in a little tarry pool of corruption. I lean on the rail and look across the nave to the opposite compartment of the triforium, through a crooked arch supported by a wonky pillar (the effect of settlement early in the cathedral's history), to what appears to be a heap of roughly carpentered coffins for giants – the dusty and mighty bass pipes of the organ.

Down in the Chapel of St George I recognize a pilgrimage site, a shrine to the dead of the First World War. The chapel's walls are lined with panels, each one closely inscribed with the names of 'The Men of Cambridgeshire and the Isle of Ely who gave their lives for the country in the Great War of 1914–1919'. I glance down the lists, the lines of hundreds upon hundreds of names, horrified at the sheer numbers. A. H. Bryant of Abington Piggotts, R. Starling of Borough Green,

W. Wedd and S. Wedd of Kneesworth, F. L. Strapps of Ely, A. Diggins of Wisbech St Mary. Real names, real men.

Gradually the realization dawns that every panel bears a little button handle. I pull the hinged boards of names out from the wall, and there underneath are twice as many names, thousands on thousands. C. W. Farrow of Dullingham, J. Stubbings of West Wratting; T. Elsegood of Chettisham, the only man from his parish to die; and the seven Ankers of Whittlesea: A. S. Anker, J. Anker, F. Anker, C. J. Anker, another J. Anker, E. W. Anker, P. J. Anker.

A whole forest of men cut down in their prime; thousands of individuals, of whistlers and fiddlers, of eel catchers and ploughmen, of humorists and miserablists, of lovers and sons and grandsons.

A remarkably complete medieval range of monastic and ecclesiastical buildings skirts the cathedral – the old Bishop's Palace in red brick, the patchwork walls of the southwest monastery range, the gold ironstone gatehouse and the Great Barn beyond. The Queen's Hall, Prior Crauden's private chapel, the infirmary, the Black Hostelry where visiting monks would be put up. The Reformation put paid, technically speaking, to all that aspect of the cathedral's life in 1539; St Etheldreda's shrine was broken up, images smashed and treasures appropriated by the Crown; but in practice not much really changed. The monastery's prior became the cathedral's dean, three of the monks who weren't pensioned off became canons, and it was a case of 'keep calm and carry on'.

So I've always imagined; but a conversation with cathedral guide Barbara McGowan changes my understanding. 'You have to think of the effects on ordinary people,' is her comment. 'The Reformation wasn't just a theological revolution or a liturgical one, it was also a matter of small details. Most people didn't understand what on earth was going on. The new religion didn't just arrive fully formed – it took time to be accepted. It didn't make for an easy picture, socially. All very well for theological scholars, but what about the ordinary Joe Bloggs in the fields with his plough? Now the Catholic priests and the monks were abolished, who was going to mediate for him with God and the powers that be? Don't forget that the monastery was the NHS of the day, the social security. The infirmary was gone, the monks were gone, the food, the distress relief – all gone, along with the income that poor men had earned by working for the monastery. Everything the monks used to import to Ely by river, all the labour they employed: all dried up.

'Then Queen Mary succeeded in 1553. Back came the Catholics, out went the Protestants. Seven of the eight newly appointed canons were "relieved of their duties". Bishop Goodrich, who had become Lord Chancellor, lost his job, although he managed to remain Bishop of Ely. All change! As you were! Up with the graven images! Five years later, Queen Elizabeth I came to the throne. Was she another Protestant? Better hide those rosaries and that statue! Back came the canons. They built walls round the monastic houses they had taken over, and made them into private property. Ordinary people were scared, deprived of income and in the most frightful muddle, and Elizabeth had to introduce a Poor Law to mitigate the effects.'

If religious sail-trimming in Tudor times proved a scary muddle for ordinary folk, so did the desperate upheavals of the Civil War a hundred years later. Cathedrals and churches up and down the land suffered the kind of demolition job at the hands of Puritan zealots that Blue Dick Culmer carried out with such vindictive glee at Canterbury. But Ely was fortunate. A few hundred yards from the cathedral's west front stands a black-and-white house, whose occupant in those internecine years carried more clout than a dozen Blue Dicks – local boy Oliver Cromwell.

The tombs of the family of Cromwell's mother, Elizabeth Steward, stood in the south quire aisle of Ely Cathedral, a fact which may have made the Parliamentarian leader more protective of the 'family cathedral' than he might otherwise have been. 'Old Ironsides' was a stern disciplinarian, but he was well aware that his Roundhead soldiery could get out of hand. On one occasion they interrupted a cathedral service to object to the liturgy being used, returning the next day to break some windows and pinch the pipes of the already dismantled organ, which they blew derisively as they marched through Ely 'making a loud noise'.

When Precentor Canon Hitch insisted on mixing worship with music in January 1644, Cromwell sent him a note intended to forestall trouble. 'Lest the Soldiers should in any tumultuary or disorderly way attempt the reformation of the Cathedral Church,' said Cromwell's letter, 'I require you to forbear altogether your Choir-service, so unedifying and offensive.' Canon Hitch, undaunted, carried on chanting his responses, whereupon Cromwell and a party of soldiers, hats on heads, marched into the cathedral and confronted the cleric.

'I am a man under Authority,' Cromwell said loudly, 'and am commanded to dismiss this Assembly.'

Hitch paused for a moment, and then bravely started chanting again from the pulpit: 'As it was in the beginning—'

'Leave off your fooling, and come down, Sir!' Cromwell barked.*

Canon Hitch took stock of his angry Puritan opponent and the soldiery primed for trouble, thought better of singing on, and led his whole congregation out of the cathedral, leaving Cromwell victor of an empty battlefield.

In the passage to the Lady chapel mills a gaggle of middle-aged choristers from St Mark's Episcopal Church in Berkeley, California. Dressed soberly in black cassocks, giggling and joking quietly together, their heads and arms are lost in a cloud of billowing white starched surplices that float and flutter as they don them. There's an atmosphere of holiday and half-suppressed schoolyard hysteria as they ready themselves for

* *Supplement to Oliver Cromwell's Letters and Speeches* by Thomas Carlyle (Chapman & Hall, London, 1846).

their great moment. Half an hour later, grave and intent, they are singing like so many angels at choral evensong. Canon Vicky Johnson presides. The congregation, outnumbered three to one by the choristers, occupies the choir stalls, a lit candle flickering at every place. My stall has an arm-rest stop carved in the likeness of a man with a fringe, pulling a face, both hands tugging his mouth into a grotesque leer. I have his ugly mug, smoothed by six centuries of clerical palms, cupped in my hand as I sit back to hear the choir sing Psalm 99: 'The Lord reigns, let the nations tremble; he sits enthroned between the cherubim, let the earth shake.'

Here stalks the mighty God of the old dispensation, called to life in the plummy modulations of Californian mouths. I know what Old Ironsides would have made of this, and I smile to imagine Vicky Johnson sending him about his business. The smile becomes a yawn. These harmonious voices are so soothing at the end of a long day. I think of King Cnut and the merry monks of Ely. With eyes shut I float up and away on the royal sleigh, following the footsteps of the giant Brithman across the icy fens.

9

Worcester, Gloucester and Hereford

'Commend our bones to Davy Jones,
our souls to Fiddler's Green'

I WOULDN'T SAY I POSSESS a particularly savage breast, but the music of Hereford Cathedral's choir at evensong is certainly effective in soothing it. This sublime singing has been polished and perfected over the three hundred years that the Three Choirs Festival has been going. What started all those years ago as a cosy singsong among clerics from Worcester, Gloucester and Hereford soon became a monster celebration of music and song, rotated between the three sister cathedrals of the Anglo-Welsh borderlands. Soon there were choruses of two hundred singers or more blocking the cathedral crossings, piled up in tiers with the rearmost row halfway to the roof.

The cream of composers and musicians have always been drawn to this celebration. Purcell, Handel, Haydn, Mendelssohn; then local boys Edward Elgar, Gustav Holst and Ralph Vaughan Williams; Arthur Sullivan, William Walton, Benjamin Britten; Constant Lambert, Peter Maxwell Davies, Richard Rodney Bennett. You couldn't wish for a richer stew of music, and the public goes on lapping it up today. The Festival Society, the cathedral choristers, the large voluntary choirs; the local shops and eateries, the cathedral coffers: it's a shot in the arm for business, as much as it's a source of pride and excitement for the three cities. Especially, perhaps, for Hereford, smallest of the trio. Hereford is a low-key sort of place in the comparative isolation of the Welsh Borders, one of the most modest of England's county towns with half the population of Worcester, less than half that of Gloucester, and notably fewer amenities. The Three Choirs Festival and its fabulous music have become a cornerstone of Hereford Cathedral, and a bedrock for the community out here.

This evening at evensong the choristers of Hereford Cathedral sing a blues of a psalm, number 6:

> Have mercy upon me, O Jehovah; for I am withered away:
> O Jehovah, heal me; for my bones are troubled.
> My soul also is sore troubled . . .

Bones and the soul: how those two elements preoccupy the Psalmist. The soul – fair enough. But what is all this about bones, troubled bones? I catch the phrase and hold it for a while; then I let it slip as the choir begin to sing the Nunc Dimittis with really unearthly beauty. I close my eyes and swim where their voices lead me. But after the service, walking out into the town, a ripe old sea shanty, 'New York Girls', comes unbidden to mind. After being shanghaied in San Francisco and wrecked in the ice-cold North Sea, having eaten their grub from a salt-horse tub and taken a glass with a Chinese lass in a houseboat in Canton, the shantymen with their straw-stuffed beds and aching heads take a last long look at land, and make a final request of the landlubbers they're leaving behind: 'Commend our bones to Davy Jones, our souls to Fiddler's Green.'

That's it, exactly. Our worn-out bones to Davy Jones's locker at the bottom of the sea, our souls to the sailors' paradise of Fiddler's Green where doxies and dances come free, the barrel never runs dry, and the music flows like Nelson's blood. Give or take a subtlety or two as to the tune, and perhaps a question mark over the vision, there flies a fitting signal from the three Ships of Heaven of the Three Choirs Festival. Bones and souls is their theme; bones, souls and the outer edges of man's aspirations.

A brisk cold autumn Sunday morning, with a convocation of dozens of swans and their cygnets in the River Severn around the bridge at the centre of Worcester. The Severn is slow-flowing, copper-brown. The wall along the river path is a patchwork of the stones and bricks of many centuries. Worcester Cathedral stands guard over the low-rise red roofs of the town, a big bulk and presence. There's no better view from a county cricket ground than Worcestershire's on the opposite bank, looking across the Severn to the great east window and central tower of the cathedral.

A handsome sandstone gateway arch with a mock portcullis leads to the cathedral's south side. A low tunnel burrows into the cloister past a row of bells. The choir is practising for sung matins somewhere nearby, the warbling of a solo voice and disjointed snatches of harmony echoing along the passage. The duskiness of the sandstone diffuses a warm half-light through the cloister. The ceiling's heavy ribs are joined by carved bosses, of which dozens are Green Men – mostly the sort with faces enwrapped in leaves and leafy twigs.

'Do you like these sandstones?' enquires my godson Andy Harrison, who's been waiting patiently for me. He runs his hand across the squared stones of the cloister wall, some pale green, some dusky red. 'Nice chequerboard effect, don't you think?'

A geologist by training and through personal passion, Andy has offered to show me the bones of Worcester Cathedral – a geological tour of the rocks from which the place is made, how these stones relate to the shape of the land, what formed them hundreds of millions of years before the quarryman's pick exposed them and the mason's eye marked them down for use. 'The greyish-green stuff's from Highley, up on the Severn a few miles north. Hard as anything.' I knock the pale stone of an archway with my knuckles. He's right. It's coarse and abrasive, but solid. 'Three hundred and forty-five million years old. These rocks were deposited under tropical conditions, in the deltas of shallow lakes and rivers flowing over low-lying floodplains.' The words bring it all alive. I can feel the sticky tropical heat, and see those river deltas branching in the floodplains. 'You can see the cross-bedding, those different layers at different angles as the current or the wind pushed ripples up the inclined bed in the shallows.'

Andy pushes his finger into a hole in an adjacent block of red sandstone. 'Bromsgrove sandstone from quarries up at Hadley, a bit nearer Worcester – on the Severn, too, so that's how they'd have brought it down to use on the cathedral. Early Triassic, maybe two hundred and fifty million years ago, so younger than the Highley, and quite different. It isn't marine; it's basically compressed sand deposited by an ancient river that flowed through the Worcester basin.' He picks out a dark red flake. 'Softer, too. See how crumbly it is, how ready to weather into holes?'

I poke at the Hadley stone. It's far softer and smoother than the gritty Highley stuff, leaving a faint pink shadow on my finger. Hard and soft, older and younger, lake delta and river: these differences would be hard for an untrained eye to spot in these two stones similarly shaped, side by side in the apparently haphazard chequered patterning, result of later repairs to the original fourteenth-century cloister wall. On the west side we find a place to perch, a narrow, knee-high shelf with a groove along its length, the water trough of the monks' lavatorium, human touch in the cold stone.

So what's the story, Andy? A quick flip back to set the scene, please.

'You see it better from the cathedral tower, but Worcester sits in a shallow basin between the Cotswolds in the southeast and the Malverns to the southwest. The Black Country to the north and the Mendip Hills to the south have minerals and coal, but the Worcester basin that lies between them is made of Mercia mudstone of the late Triassic period, maybe two hundred million years ago. The rivers had gone by that point, replaced by an arid environment, and the basin was occasionally flooded by the sea, which then dried out into coastal swamps, leaving depositions of salt from the evaporated seawater. Some of that salt was up to two miles down, but it got hoisted up by subterranean movement and later erosion by glaciers. You know the brine springs that produce Droitwich salt? They're from those deposits.

'Anyway, layers of muds and sands built up in the basin from the Jurassic era onwards. Then during the last Ice Age an ice barrier blocked the northward flow of the Severn into the Dee estuary. The river forged a new channel in the opposite direction, south through the Worcester basin, bringing with it rubble and silt and sand washed down from higher ground. Layers of sands and gravels got spread by floods along the river terraces of the Severn. So you had good soils and a nice wide river for drinking, irrigation, transport and so on. A perfect place for settlement, really, and Neolithic farmers soon established themselves on the high ground where the cathedral stands.'

I sit on the monks' water trough and picture the tale, the laying down of the landscape's bones, the sea inundations, the salty swamps; then the smashing power of the Severn's breakthrough and the sweeping floods along its terraces. The Romans discovered a shallow ford across the Severn here, says Andy, by which they could get across the river into Wales. They founded a fort and farmed the silty soil. The Saxons followed suit, taking over the old Roman settlement. The Severn became a commercial highway. The mudstone and alluvial gravel were great for farming, but a very shaky foundation for any building as massive as a cathedral. A Saxon monastery was founded, nevertheless, and on its remains St Wulfstan, Bishop of Worcester from 1062 to 1095, built the first post-Conquest cathedral.

Down in the crypt we are in Davy Jones's locker, deep beneath the floor. Here we find Wulfstan's earliest work – arcade pillars, columns, a labyrinth of quiet side chambers and chapels, all of creamy stone. 'Oolitic limestone,' Andy pronounces, 'quarried near Bath and in the Cotswolds, and brought up here along the Severn. From the Jurassic era, so very roughly fifty million years younger than that red Hadley sandstone.' The walls are infilled with crudely shaped and unshaped stone rubble, glued together with rough cement. They are seamed with tension cracks, evidence of the shaky underlying layer. Telltales or glass plates have been cemented across the fissures; they will fracture if the cracks widen any more, a simple early-warning system.

Andy and I 'perambulate' Worcester Cathedral, as Sir Nikolaus Pevsner would have said. Towers have fallen, walls collapsed, fires and floods ravaged the building over the centuries, a familiar tale to me among the Ships of Heaven by now. The architecture is remarkable, every kind of Norman and Gothic variation from Bishop Wulfstan's plain and deep-sunk walls to the beautiful and intricate Chantry Chapel of Prince Arthur, a three-storey palace of prayer, elaborately fretted and pinnacled. Poor wee Arthur Tudor, heir to the throne of King Henry VII, is buried here, having died in 1502 when he was only fifteen, leaving equally disconsolate Catherine of Aragon as a widow of sixteen. If only he hadn't died! His younger brother, handsome Henry, would not have married Catherine, and might never have acceded to the throne. Even if Henry had become king, with another wife he might have engendered a son and heir, might not have forced the break with Rome, initiated the Dissolution of the Monasteries, started that whole farrago of quick-change Protestant and Catholic switches outlined by Barbara McGowan at Ely Cathedral. I fast-forward through the Tudor dynasty, merrily rewriting history, until the coarse voice of realism says in my inner ear: Yes, and your auntie would be your uncle if she'd a pair of . . .

We perambulate here and there, Andy expatiating on the geological feast laid out on every hand. The twelfth-century chapter house, banded with smooth grey-green and abrasive yellow sandstone. The steps that lead up to the shrines of St Oswald and St Wulfstan, of polished black limestone dotted with fossils – sponges, corals, devils' toenails, brachiopods. The pillars of King John's Quire, in honour of the king whose tomb stands there now, of Purbeck marble the colour of tar, dotted with the platelets of crinoids or sea lilies. Sir George Gilbert Scott's florid Victorian pulpit with a body of pink mottled alabaster, a dark crimson waistband of Cork marble, a base of grey carboniferous limestone and green serpentinite legs.

William Ward, 1st Earl of Dudley (1817–85), has green serpentinite legs to his tomb, too, a great box of red mottled alabaster with a granite base. This Black Country coal-owner, lying in godlike white alabaster effigy, was a tremendous benefactor to the cathedral, on whose 1860s restoration he poured out money like water. We overhear a guide putting another gloss on Dudley's reputation. 'Oh, he disapproved of secular music and tried to have it banned in the cathedral. He stopped one of Elgar's first performances. Oh yes, all the shopkeepers of Worcester draped their windows with black crepe in protest.'

Sated with stone, Andy and I climb the cathedral tower. I count 247 steps up and 236 down, so there's definitely some magic at work. Up to the hexagonal clock room with a magnificently ticking and whirring mechanism hoisted on high in its own glass case.

On up narrowing wooden treads to squeeze out of a goblin door on to the tower roof, whipped by wind and spattered by showers. The view reels round as a geological frame for the cathedral, now that I know what to look for – the breccia hummocks of the Clent Hills to the northeast, the sandstone and basalt summits of the Clee Hills far to the west, the rich alluvial farmlands of the Vale of Evesham out east, a curve of the limestone Cotswolds further southeast, and close across the River Severn in the south the dragon humps of the Malverns, ancient crystalline volcanic caps perhaps a thousand million years old, half in sunlight and half in deep blue shadow.

A spitting autumn day, and the tall slender tower of Gloucester Cathedral with its four corner pinnacles drifts across the flatlands as I approach the city.

I haven't been to the cathedral more than a couple of times since I used to mooch around Gloucester as a teenager in the 1960s. Back then it was the girls who worked at the sack factory on the docks that preoccupied me. I wanted to get a holiday job there, but was terrified and fascinated by these foul-mouthed viragos in tight, sweaty singlets with their husky voices and wholesale contempt for a nice young boy such as myself. To that teen psychodrama Gloucester Cathedral was no more than a backdrop, a bristle-topped tower occasionally glimpsed above the roofs of the city. From time to time my parents would come home humming with delight after one of the Three Choirs Festival concerts in the cathedral, but I wasn't interested in that soupy sort of singing. If it didn't have an electric guitar with it – forget it.

Now I thread the narrow alleyway of College Court, past the low shop-front that Beatrix Potter featured in her *Tailor of Gloucester* illustration, with Simpkin the tailor's cat padding through the snow. Under the archway, and out into . . . Well, here's a turn-up for the books.

The cathedral looks wonderful, a decorated palace of silver-white stone. But things have changed. The clogged old car park that always disfigured the view from this south side has vanished. Diggers, cranes, bleeping klaxons, plastic toilet huts and blokes in hi-vis jackets have invaded its space. A notice explains what's going on: it's Project Pilgrim, a ten-year, £6-million plan to provide a less ugly approach, to become greener by adding solar panels, to create a new entrance area that will make the cathedral more welcoming to people of every faith and none – and, while they're at it, to brush up the fast-crumbling fifteenth-century Lady chapel, inside and out. Hats off to the Heritage Lottery Fund, the Trusts and individual donors who are stumping up the money, says the notice.

The rain sweeps away, intense sunshine spotlights the cathedral against slate-grey clouds, and she is revealed as the archetypal Ship of Heaven, riding high in dry dock while shipwrights and chandlers, caulkers and coopers fuss about her. A flotilla of chapels clusters round her east end like spiky little tugs, adjusting her lie in relation to the safety fences and the piles of carefully shaped paving stones in creamy white that wait to be laid.

Harry Potter is a modern-day saint. He may not actually exist, but then neither does Fiddler's Green. Young pilgrims flock to his various shrines. Many believe fervently in him. He can do magic, if not miracles, and he is a money-spinner for anywhere with a claim on his persona.

Gloucester Cathedral has been the setting for many of Potter's most dramatic appearances on earth. In the year 2000, at the behest of film-makers, the fourteenth-century cloisters were magically morphed into Hogwarts School of Witchcraft and Wizardry. They are a location scout's dream with their long, dimly lit perspectives where hundreds of pillars rise like witchy tree trunks to sprout into a maze of fan vaulting, the first of its kind in the world, forming an intricate, interlocking forest canopy of mellow gold stone. When Warner Bros came to Gloucester Cathedral to shoot three of the films, *Harry Potter and the Philosopher's Stone*, *Harry Potter and the Chamber of Secrets* and later *Harry Potter and the Half-Blood Prince*, they hid the electric light switches, the inscribed tombstones in the floor, and whole flights of stone steps. In the stained-glass windows the saints lost their haloes, and Adam and Eve gained a few more clothes. Potter and his chums dodged angry trolls, hid in the loo and sought the entrance to the Chamber of Secrets. And a generation of youngsters pestered their parents to take them to church – à la Hogwarts.

I enter the cloisters, and it's the liveliest part of the great stone building, full of colour and chatter and movement. Dozens of children on their half-term break are down on their knees on either side of a long strip of paper, so long that it runs the full length of the west cloister. Designed by architectural artist Amy Jane Adams, this 'colouring-in carpet' is printed with a pattern of fan vaulting, and the kids are embellishing it, some with wax crayons and broad expressionist scribbles, others absorbed in filling every tiny nook and cranny of the delicate lacework with felt-tip pens. Some have added wizards in pointy hats, flights of bats, round-faced boys with round spectacles. Potter is definitely on these young minds. Every so often, says a woman kneeling with a fistful of crayons, her daughter has been glancing up to check the fan vaulting on high for magical owls bearing letters, or looking about a little nervously for bloody messages appearing on the walls. 'Harry

Potter's real to them,' she says, indicating the long double line of children. And is this a sort of pilgrimage to him? 'Well, don't know if I'd go that far . . .' she ponders, 'but yes, I suppose it is, isn't it?'

Down among the bones I go, into the crypt beneath the cathedral. When the Norman monks began their abbey church under Abbot Serlo shortly after the Conquest, they grounded it on a long-vanished Anglo-Saxon monastery that had been founded by King Osric in about AD 670 and run by his sister (or maybe great-aunt), Abbess Kyneburga. As with St Etheldreda and her religious house at Ely, Gloucester's was a double monastery for men and women, and as at Ely the first three persons-in-charge were all women.

The church of the Benedictine monks lies below the east end of the cathedral, and it's an unpolished piece of work with a plainly vaulted ceiling and squat, rough-hewn tub pillars. The dogtooth carving of the rounded arches, clumsy and cracked, is probably the amateurish handiwork of the monks themselves. It's all simply built, much of it dominated by the huge square buttresses that were inserted to bear the extra weight of the enormous east window when that was installed in the 1350s.

The undercroft is built over a ditch dating back to the Roman city of Glevum. Even back in 1089 an extra layer of arcading had to be put in to hold things up. Each pillar stands in a hole. 'Look down there,' urges the guide, and we see our faces reflected in water – that's how near the floor is to that wet old Roman ditch.

Abandoned here in Davy Jones's locker stands the font designed for the cathedral by Sir George Gilbert Scott. This grand object proved unpopular with the customers; it's made of unyielding granite, and Victorian mothers were worried in case some butterfingered cleric should bash their baby's head on the rim.

During the Second World War a mystery item, impenetrably wrapped, was brought from London and smuggled into the crypt. Rumour and conjecture ran wild. In fact it was the Coronation Chair from Westminster Abbey. Half the glass from the east window was stored here too, meticulously labelled. The air was so damp, though, that all the labels fell off. After the war, heads were scratched as to how to reassemble the multi-thousand-piece jigsaw, till someone remembered a shop in Westgate that had sold picture postcards of the cathedral. One turned out to be of the east window, and the restorers used that as an aide-memoire.

Up above in the Lady chapel, all is scaffolding, ladders and lights of the ongoing restoration. The floor is a dusty confusion of tools, plans and snakes of electric cable. Two men in hi-vis work clothes are reassembling the floor tiles in a frame, puzzling over a colour-coded plan as they ease each tile back into its rightful place. 'Cleaning stonework, we are,' says one, 'cleaning the glass, lifting the tiles, relaying them. Installing underfloor heating in here, too – did you hear us when you were down there in the crypt? Well, some of the work we're doing is only a couple of inches above the ceiling down there. But once we've finished, look, you'll never know we were there at all.'

In the nave, the light falls peachy soft. All the north side pillars lean outwards, at quite a startling angle once you become aware of it. The pillar bases are a rosy pink colour – when a great fire consumed the wooden roof in early Norman times, the burning timbers fell and piled up round the pillars, literally baking their nether regions.

The thought of baked nether regions sticks in my mind and will not go away as I stand in the quire, ruminating on bones that some took to be holy. Under a beautiful alabaster effigy lies King Edward II, done to death – some say disgustingly at the end of a red-hot poker – in the dungeons of Berkeley Castle a few miles down the River Severn. His screams could be heard in Gloucester, we were told as children. Even if such a story is pure tosh, that's a nasty image to carry around. After his death Edward's remains were offered to monasteries at Malmesbury and Bristol, but both declined, deeming possession of them too dangerous until it was known which way the political wind would blow. The Prior of Gloucester, however, saw the chance to spin the king as a saint and a martyr worthy of pilgrimage, and that turned out to be a shrewd move. Within six months Gloucester's monastery had made enough money to rebuild the monks' church.

Robert Curthose, Duke of Normandy, William the Conqueror's eldest son, lies on a tomb chest outside the quire, his head crowned, his legs crossed at mid-thigh as befitted a crusader. Poor Robert! He quarrelled with his brothers (they emptied a chamberpot over his head; he punched them), he rebelled against his father and was cursed by him, and he had his clothes stolen by pranksters while he lay snoring in bed with a whore. King William, judging him a weakling and fool, left the kingdom of England to Robert's younger brother William Rufus in 1087, and their youngest brother Henry succeeded Rufus on the throne in 1100. Robert the Crusader had the humiliating experience of being captured by Henry in 1106, and kept a prisoner for the rest of his life until he died nearly thirty years later, a very old and sad man.

I lift the misericord seats in the quire and chuckle at the skittish images created there some seven hundred years ago. A medieval wood carver's guess at an elephant with horse hooves and tail, trotting with a howdah on its back. A recumbent traveller in great boots, cradling a donkey. Someone riding backwards on a goat; someone galloping a horse through a flock of birds. A herd of pigs having a shoving match under an oak tree, while a squirrel polishes off the acorns. Bruegelian allegories, now irretrievably lost? Or just the carver having a bit of fun as he practised his skill?

A covey of Chinese and Far Eastern youngsters swoops down in a gaggle of thirty. They crowd round, giggling at the carvings, snapping selfies. Then with a mighty twitter and a massed gasp – 'Ah! Harry Potter!' – away they rush at the imperative of someone's iPhone to seek out the next ten-second pilgrimage spot in St Potter's paradise.

My first impression of Hereford Cathedral is of a building perfectly suited to its surroundings. It's invisible if you approach from the town centre to the north, and if there are signs pointing the way, I fail to see them. Only when I have practically reached the churchyard do the crocketed pinnacles of the central tower slide up and into view above the surrounding roofs. I look up at the building through a skein of plane-tree boughs. The whole impression is of a manageable, even cosy cathedral. It is not a lofty ocean liner, but a familiar day-to-day transport.

If the story of the Ships of Heaven is condensed in any one cathedral, it's Hereford. Shadows of the indignities that communities can suffer at the hands of soldiers are here in the monument of brave Sir Richard Pembridge, hero of Crécy and Poitiers – Scots mercenaries fighting for the king and billeted in the cathedral during the Civil War broke off his hands and his right leg. Yet John Maine's *Ascension*, a modern monument to the SAS, shows how proud the town is of its pet regiment. The installation features an arc-shaped grotto of beautiful blue stone, Brazilian syenite, flecked with dark spots and melded with a glow of white from the side like an image of deep space. Above it a tall window ripples with three thousand flames of blue and white glass, flickering skywards, lifting the eye from dark to light, a beautiful metaphor.

In the Romanesque arches one can read the soaring architectural vision of the cathedral builders; in the collapse of the western tower and west front on Easter Monday 1786 their often unsuccessful struggle against the forces of nature and geometry. The smashed faces and hands of the Twelve Apostles round the font express all the tight intolerance of past bigotries, while the irreverently gurning Green Men of the twelfth-century Herefordshire School of Sculpture confirm that man's desire to cock a snook and burst the bounds will always sneak in somewhere.

The bones of Hereford Cathedral are many. Those of St Thomas of Cantilupe are well scattered among churches and abbeys, having been separated from his flesh by boiling after his death in 1282. Thomas was a popular Bishop of Hereford. People admired his sincerity (he wore a hair shirt next to his skin, and welcomed the lice that bit him as reminders of the sufferings of Christ) and his generosity. By contrast his predecessor-but-one, Bishop Peter d'Aigueblanche (1240–68), was a Savoyard who never bothered to learn a word of English and seldom set foot in his diocese, but gave lucrative local livings to his cronies and family members. Peter's memory 'exudes a sulphurous stench', wrote monkish chronicler Matthew Paris. Although John Peckham, Archbishop of Canterbury, excommunicated Thomas shortly before his death after a series of disagreements, there was a strong desire to have him canonized, not least among the secular canons of Hereford Cathedral who knew the potential for monetizing a saintly shrine. It took a little while, perhaps because the excommunication had not officially been annulled; but on 17 April 1320 Thomas of Cantilupe was canonized. Various bones claimed to belong to Thomas had already been enshrined in the cathedral, and these were now removed from their original shrine and reinterred in a new and more splendid one, where they soon attracted enough money from pilgrims to rebuild much of the cathedral. At the Reformation this shrine was destroyed, leaving the disregarded original still intact. And that original has recently had a makeover, rather a flashy one in pink and purple.

I pass under angels, under dragons and Green Men. Some scowl, some glare, some bare their teeth in mirthless laughter. Cloaked and naked men ride upon lions. A ram with vast curled horns menaces me with pop eyes. A demon with scaly legs stares me out from under a wooden seat. No modern sensibility would conjure for a cathedral what the medieval mind conceived as suitable for placement in a house of prayer. But then the medieval mind was a questing organ every bit as curious as our own. And it was at large in a world mostly unplumbed by western Christian explorers, a world where angels and devils and rooster-faced basilisks seemed not at all improbable. Rumours of strange lands, when they filtered back, were hard to distinguish from fact. That did not matter much, with Christianity installed at the hub of all things, when the Lincolnshire monk Richard of Haldingham set out seven hundred years ago to map the known and the unknown world.

*

For a funny, cartoon-like, accessible snapshot of the medieval mind at work upon the shape of the world, Mappa Mundi is hard to beat. Unscientific, unfactual, playful, it is crammed with tall stories, bar-room speculation and fake news.

Mappa Mundi hangs in a beautifully lit display space off the cloister. The map's original board frame hangs opposite, the pin hole at its centre corresponding to the hole in the centre of the map where Richard of Haldingham placed his compasses to draw out the circle of the world. Dendrochronology tells us that the trees whose wood went to make the frame were felled between 1289 and 1311, probably locally. It's curious that we can't be completely certain whether it actually was Richard, or some other monk, who made Mappa Mundi, although we know so much about these stained old planks. Wouldn't men such as monk Richard have thought the knowledge that we nowadays possess to verge on the magical?

The map itself is of vellum from a single calfskin. Richard of Haldingham probably created it at Lincoln's monastery. The Bishop of Hereford, Richard de Swinfield, invited him to join Hereford's Chapter in 1305, and it's reasonable to assume that he brought his great map south with him, subsequently incorporating a bit of local detail – Hereford, the River Wye, the Clee Hills – to suit his new location and employer.

Mappa Mundi is the oldest complete example of its particular type of map, a compendium of collected knowledge and speculation about the Christian world of the northern hemisphere, allied to a fair guess as to its geographical dimensions. In the protective half-light I peer at the vellum, once white and now a caramel brown, at the faded red and tarnished gold lettering of the labels that explain in Latin the many detailed line drawings around the map. Gradually, with the help of an English-language, colour-enhanced reproduction, things become clearer.

Mappa Mundi is a vision of the past, present and future of humanity. The world is tilted ninety degrees anticlockwise, so that east is at the top, west at the bottom; Europe on the left, Africa on the right. The biblical world of Asia occupies all the top half of the map. The twelve winds blow around the edge of the circle, winter gales bringing hardship and hunger, soft summer zephyrs spreading fruitfulness. The earthly plain teems with life, with real animals and mythic ones, Bible stories and Greek legends. Towns and cities, trade routes and pilgrim paths bring a bracing dose of reality to the remarkable scene.

Christianity is in control of all. Christ sits in majesty at the apex of the world. On his right hand the resurrected righteous are ejected in a whirl of limbs from their coffins and up to Heaven; on his left the damned are stripped naked, roped together and dragged off to the mouth of Hell by a noticeably priapic devil. All across the map the spiritual journey of humanity is traced. We see Adam and Eve expelled from their paradise garden in the east, their Heaven on Earth, a biblical Fiddler's Green. Eden's impregnable gate is closed to humankind. Noah's Ark rests on the 'mountains of Armenia'. Near the centre of the map looms a massively fortified Babylon, topped with a Tower of Babel. Lot's wife, naked and regretful, contemplates the wreck of Sodom and Gomorrah as they capsize like two ships into the Red Sea. The Children of Israel attain the Promised Land. At the centre lies the fortified wheel of the walls of Jerusalem, with Christ crucified on 'Mont Calvarie'.

The shape of Jerusalem is mirrored by the circular maze of the Labyrinth in a tongue-shaped Crete just below, the exit point from biblical journeying into the wild world of medieval imaginings. This is tremendous fun. Scattered about are salamanders and unicorns, mermaids and mandrakes. 'Enormous ants hoarding golden sands' are labelled in Africa. A curly-horned bonnacon, a heraldic beast with twisted horns and a nasty habit of 'spraying scalding excrement the length of three acres', aims a volley of turds in the direction of Mount Libanus, source of the River Jordan. Here is a naked Albanian with an enormous penis, there a woolly-hatted Scandinavian on skis. I spot an African man with an outsize nether lip, an Indian man with a single, gigantic, nine-toed foot, both appendages sheltering their owners from the sun.

At bottom left Emperor Caesar Augustus in a papal crown disperses his surveyors to take a census of the world. And in the bottom right corner, beyond the Upper Nile, a magnificent horseman rides a finely caparisoned steed out of the round world and away. He turns in the saddle to wave goodbye to a huntsman afoot, who restrains a pair of greyhounds on a tight leash. 'Passe avant,' says the huntsman. 'Go forward.' Out beyond the rim of the world, beyond the Blemmyes with eyes in their chests and the headless Epiphagi with eyes on their shoulders, the Ethiopians 'in whom there is no friendship' and the Troglodytes who 'catch wild animals by dancing on them'.

Before setting sail for the unimaginable unknown with this envoy into space, what of these British Isles of ours? Here they are, ragged with estuaries, crammed into the bottom left corner. I can make out the trio of Three Choirs cathedrals; Ely and Lincoln, too, York and Durham. Beyond a narrow neck of land Scotland bulges out northwards by way of Berwick and Edinburgh, and on past a porridgy lump that represents the Grampian Mountains.

And what's this out here in the cold blue sea, way north of Scotland? A disc surrounded by twenty tiny blobs, like a tambourine with its jingling zils. There's a red and black label across it. I push my nose as close to the vellum as I can.

'Orcades Insulee XXXI.'

The thirty-one islands of Orkney. My next port of call, and my very own Fiddler's Green.

10

Kirkwall

The Orkney Boat

It's six o'clock on a may morning in 1988, and I am reeling to bed with the dawn chorus after a riotous time at the Orkney Folk Festival. I'm in a farmhouse on the island of Shapinsay, not quite certain how I've fetched up here. The week-long jig around the Orkney archipelago has just ended in a ceilidh down below, packed with kilted youths and sticky-haired girls, all alight with beer and joie de vivre, flinging themselves and each other around as their grandparents waltzed two by two between the flying bodies. I'm too exhausted to sleep, high as a kite on pure elation, and already dimly aware that I may never again drink, dance, laugh and roister quite as recklessly as I have done in this Fiddler's Green of the northern seas.

Orkney's scattered isles lie among rough tide races off the northern coast of mainland Scotland. When you discover that the islands were under Norwegian rule for six hundred years until as late as 1472, a lot of things about Orkney become clearer, particularly the preponderance of Norse place names (Knowe of Grugar, Grimbister, Yettna Geo) and personal names (Hakon, Rognvald, Freya, Solveig, Ola). Through many islands over the course of that famous Folk Festival I danced with young Freya, bought a beautiful silver necklace from Ola, clinked beer cans with middle-aged Hakon and slapped old Rognvald on the back. I scraped away at a Hardanger fiddle under the sceptical eyes of Norwegian musicians, and cycled out to explore the Neolithic village of Skara Brae in a mixed company of hilarious Orcadians and Vikings whose broad faces, heavy beards and singsong, epiglottal modes of speech seemed, to these southern ears, indistinguishable.

As for Magnus . . . I encountered Magnus Magnusson and his son Magnus, Magnus the bull, Magnus the sheepdog, *Magnus* the sailing boat. I found I couldn't walk far in these islands without stubbing my toe on the name of Orkney's favourite martyr. From their conversations to their naming of household pets Orcadians demonstrated a real and deep affection for their patron saint, and a proprietary love for the great sandstone cathedral that has stood in his name over their capital town of Kirkwall for the past nine hundred years.

The image of that big red church sailing among the grey roofs of the northern harbour town has come often to mind over the ensuing years, and I know it has to be one of my chosen Ships of Heaven. I catch a plane from Inverness to Kirkwall, and on a bright windy morning I go to seek out St Magnus.

From the aptly named Broad Street to the west, St Magnus Cathedral looks like a holy crag, a great block of a building every bit as formidable as any Norman cathedral further south. The effect is massive, enclosed and forbidding, the tiny windows like slit eyes in walls patched haphazardly with blocks of sandstone in red and white. The prevailing west wind has blurred and softened all sculptural details. I glance up past the interlacing of foliage and tendrils to a pair of monsters, hollow-faced hags with Gollum fangs who flank the central gable, one shouting silently from behind its gnarly hands, the other cupping a fungus-like ear to listen.

In the west front, three narrow arched doorways under three recessed hoods offer admittance. Inside there's an uninterrupted view from the west through to the rose window at the east end. The impression is of a big oblong stone box, very tall and slim, admitting a dusky twilight through small narrow windows. Jointed ribs of vaulting crisscross the ceiling, their pink and yellow strips giving the disconcerting image of a line of spider crabs holding the place together. Round tub pillars rise to round arcading, calling to mind Durham Cathedral's plain Norman solidity without its militaristic feel. These soft sandstone pillars of St Magnus are scratched and incised with the graffiti of a sea-faring community: a little boat, a harpoon, a fish hook, waves in rippling lines. The pillars, like the transept arcades, show signs of weathering, an odd phenomenon in a church interior until you learn that the transepts, and the first part of the nave to be built, had no roof in the early days of their existence.

In the early years of St Magnus Cathedral, the crews of Scandina-vian trading ships that were due to spend any time in Kirkwall harbour would bring their large square sails into the cathedral and hang them up to dry between the pillars. Today I find banners hanging from poles in the arcades, forming an Orcadian Stations of the Cross, each banner braced like a longboat sail, furnished with a one-line poem by Orkney's national poet, George Mackay Brown, and wonderfully painted with a bold design, some of these by Erlend Brown, nephew of the poet. They tell of the pilgrimage of Earl Rognvald and Bishop William the Old in 1151 to the Holy Land in 'Fifteen keels laid in Norway for Jerusalem-farers'. Here is 'The bishop's ship, a small storm-tossed kirk'. The pilgrims find 'Palm branches in Jerusalem – The "Via Crucis"', and then shape course for 'Byzantium, golden city: the ships and the domes'. And then home to 'Drying sails in the lofts of St Magnus', a homely touch that links back to the cathedral.

I imagine the sails of Norse longships hung up there, the dripping and creaking, the tarry smell and dribbles of dried salt and sand. These modern sail banners are so large and colourful, so overwhelming in their effect, that I feel an impulse to share my delight in them. 'Don't you love these?' I ask a passing cleric. 'No,' she crisply replies, 'I don't. They block the light.'

In the southeast corner of the cathedral lies the effigy of 'John Rae. M.D., L.L.D., F.R.S., F.R.C.S., Arctic Explorer. Intrepid Discoverer of the fate of Sir John Franklin's last Expedition. Born – 1813. Died – 1893. Expeditions: – 1846–7: 1848–9: 1851–2: 1853–4.' Orkney-born John Rae, surgeon and Hudson's Bay Company employee, one of the greatest and most self-reliant Arctic explorers, found fame a double-edged sword when in 1854 he brought news of Sir John Franklin back to England. Franklin's 1845 expedition to find the Northwest Passage had not been heard of since shortly after it set out, but Rae had collected Inuit reports of white men dragging a boat across the ice and of thirty corpses subsequently found. He returned with hard evidence, including a silver plate inscribed 'Sir John Franklin, K.C.H.' He had more unwelcome news, too. The Inuit told him that the human bones they had found showed knife cuts – evidence that Franklin's starving men had resorted to cannibalism.

No one in Victorian Britain wanted to hear that sort of thing about lost heroes. Rae had a long struggle to receive the £10,000 offered as a reward for finding evidence of Franklin. His name was blackened, many called him a coarse liar, and he was never honoured with a knighthood for his Arctic expeditions, his mapping and his role in finding the Northwest Passage. Rae is buried in St Magnus kirkyard, name and fame now properly restored, and his marble effigy is certainly of a splendour fit for a hero. He is shown with kiss curls and ox-horn moustaches, recumbent and smiling in his sleep, hands folded casually behind his head, cap falling off, his shotgun and journal by his side. A fine fur covers him; his feet are in moccasins, his buckskin leggings well laced.

Rae is in good company, for this is St Magnus's 'corner of honour'. Here are plaques to poets George Mackay Brown and Edwin Muir, author Eric Linklater, 'scholar and philologist' Hugh Marwick, Her Majesty's Painter and Limner Stanley Cursiter, antiquary J. Storer Clouston, and Robert Rendall, 'poet and conchologist'. It is a healthy society that honours its poets, writers, painters, artists and shell collectors.

By the west door I meet Fran Flett Hollinrake, Custodian of St Magnus Cathedral. 'What does the job of custodian entail? Oh well, let me see. My main job is actually visitor services, and I do a lot of historical research, but in my seven years working here I've also done mainten-ance and lighting. The cathedral's an art gallery and a performance space, so my task is to interpret it, too. Also, let's think: clerk, tourist guide – on a busy day we can get three thousand five hundred visitors, especially if there's a cruise ship in . . . clock winder, amateur plumber, floor polisher . . .'

St Magnus Cathedral is not owned by the Church of Scotland, and it's not owned by the state. Instead, Orkney's cathedral is owned by the people.

When twelve-year-old Margaret, daughter of King Christian I of Denmark, Norway and Sweden, was betrothed in 1468 to King James III of Scotland, her cash-strapped father pledged his holdings in the Isles of Orkney and Shetland to James in return for a loan – 50,000 Rhenish guilders for Orkney, 8,000 for Shetland. The Scottish Crown from then onwards refused to let the Scandinavian Crown redeem the pledged islands, and in 1472 Scotland annexed them. Norway had lost the Northern Isles, and would never regain them. King James gave St Magnus Cathedral to the newly created Royal Burgh of Kirkwall in 1486, and although run by Orkney Island Council these days, it is still the proud possession of the people of Orkney. This goes a long way to explaining the affection for the building that I had remarked the first time I came to Orkney.

'The people of Orkney are very protective of their cathedral,' says Fran. 'People here have a sense of place that I never see anywhere else. They have a very strong connection to *their* place, *their* land, *their* cath-edral. The congregation on a Sunday is somewhere between fifty and two hundred – a tremendous number, when you consider the size of the place. Back in 1929 it was decided that whichever was the majority religious denomination in Scotland should use the cathedral as their parish church. Nowadays the Presbyterian Church of Scotland have it on a Sunday morning, complete with their minister, elders and beadles. Then at one p.m. they leave, and it's open to all.'

Fran Hollinrake can only dream of the sort of resources that, say,

Canterbury and Durham have to draw on. St Magnus is well loved and well looked after, but it's far from any mainstream centre. The pink cathedral with its eerie half-light and photogenically eroded stone would be ideal for a film set, but it is hard to sell the idea to a film company – Orkney is just too remote, too expensive, too difficult. When the BBC presented live coverage of the centenary of the Battle of Jutland in 2016, they had spent the previous three and a half years setting up the programme, which ran for under two hours.

'It's not easy and not cheap to get here,' Fran says. 'And it's not necessarily easy to live here. Often incomers find they can make it through the first winter. In fact it's not the winter, but the lack of spring that gets you. There's an expression here, "da Gab o' May", meaning the few days in May when winter seems to return just to depress you. You can come through that, but the second winter will get you. Yet . . . in the wildest winter storm you get a sense of the strength, the beauty of the land. Orkney is one of those "thin" places, one of the most liminal places in the world. Not really *in* the world, perhaps – more like a place on the boundary between two worlds.

'People who come to Orkney to escape everything have got it badly wrong. Orkney is not like that. There's no hippy or New Age culture here. It's too real. There's pragmatism in the Orkney character. What you get is the space to loosen up a bit, to think more clearly, and to gain a sense of community. That's what works here.'

I am intrigued to know when to see St Magnus Cathedral at its best, when to visit in order to find the community of Orkney most closely invested in their cathedral.

'Ah! The tree-lighting ceremony and St Lucy's Day – that's the one, early in December. That's our great day. To me it seems a combination of Christian and pagan Norwegian traditions. The people of Norway give us two trees, one from Grimstad where St Rognvald was from, and one from Hordaland, the county we're twinned with. All sorts of musicians and dignitaries come over from Norway. St Lucy is the patron saint of light, you know, all-important in a northern winter. The cathedral is absolutely full, there's a wonderful carnival atmosphere – a winter carnival, always best when it's snowing! A local girl from the primary school is chosen as St Lucy, and she processes into the darkened cathedral in a crown of candles to the sound of a children's choir singing the Hymn to St Lucy, with the light following her. Bringing the light into the northern winter: it's a piece of magic. Then we light one of the trees outside, and the light shoots out and up.'

The image is tremendously striking, and I file it away to mull over later.

When Vikings arrived in Orkney early in the ninth century, raiding, they found good soil and a climate that suited animal husbandry. They also found pockets of Christian hermits and monks of the Celtic Church, living as close to nature as they were to God. The Vikings probably wiped some out, and they settled in the islands themselves. Orkney reverted largely to paganism, not to return to Christianity till AD 995 when Olaf Tryggvason of Norway, a Christian Viking, stopped by and 'persuaded' pagan Earl Sigurd and his people to undergo baptism.

Early in the twelfth century, ownership of the earldom of Orkney was divided between Magnus Erlendsson and his cousin Hakon. This sharing of leadership led to squabbles, bloodshed and confusion. Shortly after Easter one year, probably 1117, a peace parley was arranged on the island of Egilsay. Each earl agreed to bring with him two ships full of men. Magnus stuck to his side of the bargain, but Hakon turned up with eight ships. Advantage Hakon. After a night of prayer in Egilsay church, Magnus was captured, tied up and axed to death. According to the admittedly hagiographical *Orkneyinga Saga*, no one would volunteer to strike the fatal blow against gentle, handsome, decent and pious Magnus, so horrid Hakon ordered his butcher Lifolf to end matters, which he did as Magnus stood before him. Magnus's body was then buried in a hastily dug grave with no Christian ceremonies.

When Magnus's relics were discovered eight hundred years later, concealed in a pillar in St Magnus Cathedral, the martyr's skull was found to have a gaping rent on the left side, exactly where Lifolf (if a right-hander) would have landed his axe blow.

Magnus Erlendsson's mother Thora had prepared a feast to welcome home her son and nephew in peace and reconciliation. When Hakon returned alone, flushed with pride, Thora plied him with food and ale, then begged him to return her son's body to the main island for a decent Christian burial. The bereaved mother pleaded, Hakon relented, and Magnus's body was brought from Egilsay. It was carried ceremoniously to Birsay at the northwest tip of the main island, and buried in the cathedral that had been raised there by Magnus's grandfather Thorfinn.

Heavenly lights were soon seen and heavenly odours smelt around Magnus's grave. Prayers to his spirit were answered, and sick folk healed. The halt, blind and leprous flocked to Birsay. Earl Hakon and Orkney's Bishop William the Old tried to suppress the cult, until William himself experienced a Pauline moment after being struck blind in the cathedral. The bishop stumbled over Magnus's grave, and in return for vowing to translate Magnus's body to a shrine, the scales literally fell from his eyes.

A farmer from the Isle of Westray, Gunni by name, reported a dream in which Magnus had demanded to be moved from Birsay to the little harbour town of Kirkjuvagr, the 'church in the bay', twenty miles to the east. A procession carried out the task, bearing the relics ceremonially to their place of interment in a reliquary above the altar of St Olaf's Church in Kirkjuvagr – a.k.a. Kirkwall.

Magnus's nephew Earl Rognvald arrived from Norway in 1136 to claim his uncle's half of the earldom from unpopular Paul the Silent, who had found his tongue for long enough to declare himself Earl of All Orkney. In the event Paul the Silent was 'disappeared', and Rognvald ended up Earl of Everything. The following year it was he who, in grateful fulfilment of a vow, laid the foundation stone of the cathedral that would house St Magnus's bones in a splendid shrine.

St Magnus Cathedral was located on the foreshore of the bay, a sloping sheet of rock that contained an east–west flowing stream. It was far from an ideal site. Courses of stone laid straight simply sank, so more stone was piled on top until the foundations stabilized. The cathedral was built east to west, with a tall and spacious nave for the storage of sails. An apse at the east end accommodated pilgrims to St Magnus's shrine, a reliquary above the high altar. The whole church was ready to be consecrated to St Magnus by 1146, when the saint's relics were brought with much ceremony from St Olaf's Church.

Rognvald met his end in a fight in 1158 and, on the principle that one can't have too much of a good thing, was himself canonized by Bishop Bjarni Kolbeinsson a few years later and installed in his own shrine alongside that of Magnus.

Cathedral guide Ross Flett, with white ponytail and impressive moustache, leads a small party up along the triforium into the seldom-seen upper levels of St Magnus. The red and yellow stone that built the cathedral came from local quarries near Kirkwall and on the island of Eday. I picture the effort it must have taken to transport those big stones, heavy and unwieldy, across the turbulent sound in small, unsteady craft. Hundreds of oyster shells have been discovered throughout the building: the masons used them, Ross tells us, as spacers between the stones. While renovating the building across the road that's now the Orkney Museum, excavators found the remains of a stone jetty that would have gone down into the sea, flanked by discarded lumps of red and yellow sandstone. That was the old shoreline, and showed clearly where the stone for the cathedral was brought ashore.

Some of the masons' marks are identical to those in Durham Cathedral; those men were an élite force, in demand all over Europe in the great age of cathedral and monastery building. The earldom of Orkney was an important place in the northern world, a Norwegian colony, prosperous and relatively stable, and St Magnus Cathedral was planned to reflect that. As luck would have it, the classic Norman cathedral at Durham had been completed in 1133, and the stonemasons – the best in the business – had moved north to work on Dunfermline Abbey. Earl Rognvald and Bishop William brought them further north to Orkney in time to start construction in 1137.

As in the Stone Store at Ely Cathedral, the triforium in St Magnus is a repository for all manner of odds and ends. Here is a seventeenth-century gravestone with what to modern sensibilities seems a thoroughly morbid motif, a face looking out with a blank expression, the mouth wide open. 'The last gasp of life,' says Ross Flett. Nearby a ladder lies on its side – a curious ladder, extra wide, divided in two longitudinally by a central rail. 'Guess what?' Ross invites his audience. We can't. 'It's the Kirkwall hangman's ladder. Two went up, one either side, but only one came down.' At one side is a little portable harmonium: 'They used to take it round to folk who couldn't get to church, so they could enjoy a hymn. Nowadays? Oh, they use an iPad.'

We follow our guide up a spiral wooden stair to a landing below the spire, and out through a door on to a walkway round the parapet. A soft rain freckles in, blurring the roofs of Kirkwall and the outline of a vast cruise liner entering the harbour. The isles of Shapinsay and Rousay lie low and grey beyond, and the great shapely lump of Ward Hill in the distant Isle of Hoy moves like a whale out of the raincloud to the west.

By the time of the Scottish Reformation in the 1560s there were thirty-six parishes in Orkney. Few had their own priest, and most churches were in bad condition. Priests had to travel in small open boats between several parishes on far-flung islands, necessitating sea crossings that in winter ranged from uncomfortable to very dangerous. In an echo of today's situation nationwide vis-à-vis the relative prosperity of cathedrals and parish churches, most tithes raised around the island parishes found their way to Kirkwall for the upkeep of St Magnus

Cathedral and the maintenance of its clergy – and especially the bishop, who dwelt in fine style in his own handsome palace opposite the cathedral. Incentives for Kirkwall residents to attend service in St Magnus Cathedral were strong; anyone failing to show up three Sundays in a row was obliged to spend three days and nights as a 'guest of the bishop' in his palace, in a bottle-shaped dungeon just big enough to contain a person.

In 1560 the Scottish Parliament adopted a Protestant Profession of Faith, outlawed Mass and rejected papal authority. But it took decades more for the Reformation to take proper hold of Scots hearts and minds. John Knox's original proposals were for a kind of Christian democratic socialism in which the state would fund a Kirk whose ministers would be chosen by the people, and whose previous wealth would be redistributed to pay for schools and social welfare in every parish.

The only cathedrals to survive the Reformation intact were St Mungo's in Glasgow, and St Magnus. The shrines of St Magnus and St Rognvald were broken up, but the bones of the saints were reinterred within the pillars of the church. In Scotland, the majority of monastic abbeys were not torn down. The rich and powerful grabbed their buildings, lands and wealth, and responsibility for finding funds for parish churches and ministers devolved on the 'heritors' or owners of land and property. The Orcadian heritors in particular were reluctant to foot the bills, and the situation became dire. Two hundred years after the Reformation, every single kirk in Orkney was either in the process of falling down, or had actually done so – an extraordinary thought.

In the seventeenth century, the Church in Orkney was in a bad way. Witch-burning was commonplace. St Magnus Cathedral was impoverished. The spire, struck by lightning, burned down in 1671. The roof was in holes. By the early eighteenth century St Magnus was dark, with most of the windows boarded up, a dirty semi-ruin with parts used as a cattle stall and a hitching post for the minister's horse while he preached. The graveyard became a grass meadow and cornfield, reaped by a local farmer. During Lammas Fair in August – essentially a rerun of Lughnasa, the Celtic druidical harvest festival – the Town Guard would base themselves in St Magnus, where they scandalized the Kirkwall Presbytery with 'shooting of guns, burning great fires on the graves of the dead, drinking, fiddling, piping, swearing and cursing night and day within the Church'.*

In the 1840s there was a movement to abandon the semi-derelict cathedral. In 1845 the Crown's Office of Woods and Forests, having taken on the bishopric estates in Orkney and believing it owned the cathedral too, expelled the congregation and initiated a grand clean-up. In riposte, the Royal Burgh of Kirkwall pointed to the charter of 1486 by which King James III had gifted the cathedral to the town. That ancient document prevailed; back came the congregation, and on went the gradual dilapidation of St Magnus. Then in 1903 an eccentric and generous sheriff, George Hunter Thoms, left nearly £60,000 – several millions at today's value – for the repair of the cathedral. George Mackie Watson, an Edinburgh architect, did it up in a very Victorian style. A new taller spire was added, the roofs were reslated, stained glass enhanced the windows, and the pillars were cleaned to reveal the lovely rose sandstone beneath the whitewash.

But things never stay stable for long in the massive structure of a cathedral. In the 1970s the Custodian, Albert Thomson, noticed that the building seemed be moving. Investigation showed that the weight of the tower was pushing the west end outwards, thanks to a poor piece of work in the fifteenth century. More repairs, more expenditure, another reprieve for St Magnus.

'What's special about St Magnus Cathedral,' says its minister, Fraser Macnaughton, 'is that it's owned by the people of Orkney. The island community has a long-standing relationship with St Magnus that actually works very well. There's a very strong sense here among Orcadians

* Kirkwall Parish Records.

that they own the building. In fact, some think they can do what they like in it. People who want to hold a humanist wedding in the cathedral, or those at a ticketed event who'll say, "Why can I not come in here for free? I own this building!" Those attitudes have to be managed quite carefully.'

It's a delicate balance to be struck for a minister who, true to the best Presbyterian traditions, believes strongly in not telling people what to think, or how to pray, yet is keen to reinforce the fact that St Magnus Cathedral is a living, working religious building. 'The role of the cathedral, I think, is vital in giving people access to a spiritual experience that has some meaning for modern minds. That's the way the Church has to go if it's to mean anything to people living in a twenty-first-century technological world. The Church still uses medieval metaphors in its hymns, medieval symbols, medieval language and parables, yet we've entered a post-colonial world – a post-Christendom world, in a political sense. That old version, the Christianity of Empire – that's outmoded, I feel. We're feeling the birth pangs of a new spirituality, a new Christianity to engage with modern living.'

But how can a Church still strapped to medieval metaphors and buildings tap into the modern experience? Fraser Macnaughton cites the funerals that are still so well attended in the islands. 'Almost all funerals in Orkney still take place in churches, for example, so there is your opportunity to engage in discussion. Life after death – how to envisage that? What does it mean? You live on in your DNA, in your genes, in other people's memories. The cosmic aspect, in other words. People learn that at school, they know it already, and they're not satisfied with the old stuff. The Church risks becoming irrelevant if it doesn't engage with modern scientific understanding.

'We operate in a spiritual marketplace – yoga, crystals, New Age dabbling – but the Church so often still presents a medieval mindset. Yes, we mustn't throw the baby out with the bathwater, but at the same time we mustn't be afraid to see what the new bathwater looks like. The Christian "in" club is an outmoded model. It can't any longer be a question of being either in or out. We need to be open-armed and bigger-hearted, to start conversations. Sometimes my role is just to be a spokesman, deflecting people's stances back to them. "Tell me about this God that you don't believe in! Tell me what you do believe in!" We all have a life journey, and we're all open to faith; I believe that.'

What's remarkable is that St Magnus Cathedral, as characterized by Minister Macnaughton, has more secularity, more forward thinking and sense of engagement with the real world, than I'd ever imagined. What did I think I'd find? A dour, narrow, Presbyterian blinkeredness, exacerbated by the cathedral's remoteness?

Yes, I did anticipate just that. Well, that's my bad.

I mention my visit to Orkney thirty years ago, the hospitality and the wild celebrations, the sense of strong Norse roots and of a community tightly knit in the face of wind and weather.

'Well, yes.' Fraser nods. 'People here are close to the land and what's going on in the environment round about them. Fishing, farming, the sea – you're close to life and death on a daily basis. It's a sort of pre-Industrial Revolution feeling, and one gets a sense of what's been lost by urbanization in other places. And yes, it's not a Gaelic culture here, it's a Norse one. We're twinned with the Norwegian region of Horda-land, whose capital is Bergen; we celebrate Norwegian Constitution Day on the seventeenth of May, and there's a constant traffic of yachts between Orkney and Norway.

'There's a romantic element to this Norse connection, of course. But life in Orkney is not just a romantic dream. It's a socially conservative society here. It's not an idyll. We've a food bank in Kirkwall, a Women's Aid refuge. That might surprise some people who see island life in ro-mantic terms. Domestic violence is a problem. We're in great need of care assistants. There's no racism in Orkney, people say proudly – but there's very little ethnic diversity, either.'

As Kirkwall rapidly expands, Orkney's small islands are emptying. But unlike the common experience all over Britain of parish churches waning as the cathedral congregations wax, Fraser Macnaughton points to a strengthening bond between the island churches and their communities.

'The Church in Orkney is nearer the centre of the community, less pushed to the margins, than in urban Britain. And over the fifteen years I've been minister at St Magnus, I have seen the churches in Orkney respond to that sense of being a valued part of the community – they've refurbished their sanctuaries, upgraded their facilities and provided a space for community activities. They benefit the community, so there's an affection for the Church, quid pro quo.

'Part of my job, as I see it, is to warn that our community spirit isn't a given – it has to be worked for. Youngsters are vital to that. Of course some are bound to leave, to go off to university or just to see the wider world, but they don't necessarily find good jobs or happy lives elsewhere. There's a strand of young people that come back to the islands to start families, because they come to realize the benefit of their own childhoods in Orkney and they want it for their own children. There's Orkney's future, right there.'

Orkney is the land of stones, the ones that men raise to honour their gods and mythologize their dead. The islands are littered with standing stones, phallic monoliths two or three times the height of a man, erected four or five thousand years ago, solo or in circles. Orkney is dotted with magnificent passage graves, with round tombs, with ancient furnished houses from the dawn of such structures. Modern houses overlie medieval farms, footed on Norse longhouses that stand on the remnants of Pictish dwellings, themselves founded on round brochs or defensive towers two thousand years old. All is a tangle and a jumble of significant stones, stones mythologized and freighted with meaning, of which St Magnus Cathedral is only the most artfully ordered and magnificent example.

St Margaret's Church, South Ronaldsay, holds a treasure perhaps historical, perhaps mythological: the Ladykirk Stone, a whinstone with two footprints shallowly incised. Possibly it is a Pictish coronation stone, on which a new monarch stood to be inaugurated. Or perhaps it is a sea monster turned to stone by a priest. You can take your pick. Locally it is known as St Magnus's Boat. When St Magnus Erlendsson wished to cross the firth but had no means of doing so, he placed his feet upon the Ladykirk Stone, which instantly transformed itself into a boat and carried him across. This footprint stone inspired Beatrice Searle, artist and stonemason, to an expedition where art, spirit and physical endeavour came together on pilgrimage.

I meet Beatrice by chance the day before St Magnus Way finally comes to fruition. This pilgrim trail of fifty-five miles traverses the coasts and moors of southern Orkney as it follows the route of Magnus's restless bones from the murder island of Egilsay to his shrine in Kirkwall's great cathedral. It has been a long time in the planning and more than a year in the walking. Four of the five stages have already been opened, and tomorrow a crowd of pilgrims will inaugurate St Magnus Way by walking the eleven miles of its final stage from Orphir to Kirkwall.

'Talking of movements,' Beatrice says, 'we're all witnessing one around the Mediterranean at the moment, an epic one, the greatest mass human migration the world has ever seen.' Her words switch the focus worldwide. 'People have a feel for the land and stones they belong to. Aboriginal people's feeling for their land is also their law and their ethics, a person's reason for existing. Without land they become ghost people.'

Stone is ancient, strong and wise, she says. 'Thinking of footprint stones, I was struck by how they harness strength, wisdom and resilience through the rock. I wondered whether I could raise an anchoring stone in the landscape, a stone through which I could be constantly in contact with a piece of Orkney. Then I thought: But could I also carry my anchor with me? I thought of St Magnus's Boat, and I knew that my stone could be an Orkney Boat that people could stand in and feel connected to.'

Beatrice pauses to put her thoughts in order. 'It couldn't be too big, heavy and awkward to drag along with me. But it had to be typical of Orkney in its strength, and big enough to accommodate a wide stance, so people could feel stable as they stood in it. I found what I was looking for in Marwick Bay, a piece of Devonian siltstone nearly four hundred million years old, with a diagonal break that produced a diamond shape. It turned out to weigh about forty kilos and measured about ninety by sixty centimetres. I chose it from the beach on the day Storm Doris swept through Orkney – a very suitable stormy and elemental beginning.

'I carved the two footmarks in the stone. And I decided to walk with it on Norway's longest pilgrim path between Oslo and Trondheim, a journey of four hundred and fifty miles over fifty days. To move through that landscape with a very defined role, to encounter fellow pilgrims and offer them to stand in my stone, this means of contact with Orkney.

'Along my journey I discovered the need for four things. Optimism. Preparation. Tenacity. Grit. I imagined that we are all capable of so much more than we think we are; we just need the incentive . . . Oh, practical details!' Beatrice claps her hands together and grins. 'Well, yes. Of course, I needed a wheeled trailer to pull the Orkney Boat along. Once I had that, she weighed fifty-seven kilos. And off we set from Stromness for Norway in a wooden Shetland boat.'

Artist and artefact slogged across moors and mountainsides, through forests, rivers and gorges. 'The trailer broke down, the wheels sheared off, the bearings broke. Sometimes I hated that trailer! Carrying the Orkney Boat led me to fear and discomfort, but it – I came to feel – was ever solid, ever patient, ever anchoring. I thought of stones of myth – the stone on the Hill of Tara that cries out when it recognizes the rightful King of Ireland. I came to think of the stone as essential. This piece of Orkney forced me to be involved with and feel part of the Norwegian landscape. When it capsized and rolled to the bottom of a bank with the trailer on top of it, in a really inaccessible and difficult part of the route, I just had to rescue it. We all carry our pilgrim burdens with us, and this was mine. Strangely enough, I never once resented it – though I resented the weight of the food, and I raged at the trailer and its clumsy weakness. There were times I thought that only a retreating glacier would get the stone to Trondheim. But it did get there, and so did I.'

At the end of the pilgrim path, why not just erect the Orkney Boat or set it in the ground as an inspiration to other pilgrims?

'As a stonemason,' Beatrice tells me, 'I've worked in cathedrals and seen monuments to God and man, but this stone is not a monument. I don't want to see it erected anywhere. It has created a community wherever it's been. People have stood in it, spoken from it, sung to it. I met Jürgen, a German, also walking to Trondheim, who told me about a shaman who'd given him a piece of driftwood into which he'd poured three gifts: speak the truth, find the words to speak the truth, find the time to speak the truth. Early one morning, before I woke up, Jürgen went to stand in the Orkney Boat, and he told me later that he'd begun to laugh and laugh, he couldn't stop laughing, but gladly, and then he had felt himself rising up over the whole world which was laid out below him like a map.'

She ponders. 'Did the stone accumulate more power or take on a greater function because of my myth-making, because of many people's myth-making, around it? Or was it just a stone?'

It's a spitting, dour morning out at Orphir, the day we launch the final leg of St Magnus Way. But Minister David McNeish is in no way daunted. In fact you couldn't think of a less dauntable person than this man of God who has made the completion of St Magnus Way his personal mission. If ever there was a saint who found his advocate, it is Magnus and his David.

The minister holds a rhombus-shaped stone, far smaller than the Orkney Boat, incised with the sign of the Way, a wavy line that is both an M and a sea billow from which rises a simple cross. This stone has gone the distance along St Magnus Way, and today will complete its own pilgrimage, hand to hand and pilgrim to pilgrim, till it reaches journey's end in St Magnus Cathedral.

Here are the brave pilgrims gathered for the final leg in their anoraks and rain trousers, gleaming like a set of selkies. On the wall in the road perch the kids from Orphir School, their hoods up, shrilly cheering and waving as we set out in steady chill rain. As we walk along the road an equipage dashes past us in a flash of stone and a bounce of wheels, momentarily seen through steamed-up and spattered glasses – Beatrice Searle and her trailer, haring down the Way, bearing the Orkney Boat to greet us in Kirkwall.

Down the track towards the sea. Scapa Flow stretches away south in shades of grey. There's the low smear of South Ronaldsay on the skyline, the pale shoulder of Hoy. A rushy burn winds down and snakes into the mud flats of Skaill Bay. Beside the Way, clumps of monbretia stab the dreich day with brilliant orange flames of colour. Down on the coast we collect and bag up the tide-strewn rubbish, three bits apiece, in lonely bays of red seaweed and green rocks, the sandstone cliffs jointed and squared. St Magnus's stone is carried forward, passed from pilgrim to pilgrim.

We hunch into the rain through Hobbister Hill bird reserve, pinching green leaves of wild borage for the citrus savour they leave on the fingers. This section of St Magnus Way has not yet been trodden into reality by the passing of pilgrim feet, and we stumble and lurch through trackless moorland, into holes and hollows, looking for the waymarks among the sphagnum and heather. Bog asphodel, lousewort, milkwort and meadowsweet. The steaming sands of Scapa, smoking with hot water run-off from the distillery on the cliffs, a spiral of ecstatic tipsy gulls over the chimneys, a sweet peaty tang on the damp air.

A curve of sand on Scapa Bay. A frisson of remembrance at the war memorial that faces the cold, rain-deadened waters of Scapa Flow. On 14 October 1939, 834 men died there when Kapitänleutnant Günther

Prien in submarine U-47 torpedoed their battleship HMS *Royal Oak*. We bow our heads, then trudge through the streets towards our aiming point ahead, the squat tower and spire of the cathedral rising from the glistening roofs of Kirkwall.

St Magnus's stone has reached its long home. But the Orkney Boat has no such ordered destination. Soon its creator will lay it to rest back on the shore at Marwick Bay, face down, indistinguishable once more, one stone among ten thousand.

We gather in the nave. David McNeish says a short prayer, a little word of Nunc Dimittis. On the floor lies the Orkney Boat, its twin foot-mark recesses inviting all comers. I ease off my boots and socks. The footmarks are cool and rough on my sore soles. I stand on, or in, the Orkney Boat and make my vow: that I'll come back in the depths of winter for St Lucy's Day, one witness among many, as a small child banishes the darkness with her crown of lights.

11

St Davids

The Ship in the Hollow

ARRIVING IN ST DAVIDS (Britain's smallest city, they gleefully and incessantly inform you), one's first thought is: But where is the cathedral? Behind the closely massed grey houses, a sizeable tower top with pinnacles at its four corners is visible. But it seems so close to the ground, quite insignificant among the neighbouring buildings. That can't be it, can it?

It's not until you have stepped through the archway of Porth-y-Twr gatehouse that you get the Big Reveal. And it's a breathtaking one, completely unexpected: a great building stretched out far below along the bottom of a green valley, all but the upper works of its tower invisible from the city that flanks it. The cathedral and its enormous ruined Bishop's Palace beyond fill the hollow. A Welsh dragon flag flies proudly from the tower, but in truth the cathedral's aspect is modest, even self-effacing as it crouches there. There's a bird-like sensation of being poised to fly down to it. Rugged outcrops like crumpled mini-mountains embellish the unseen coast beyond, where a flare of light leaks up into the grey wintry sky and hints at the presence of the sea a mile or so away. You'd imagine that the site might have been deliberately chosen to shield the presence of holy men and their valuables from the notice of sea-borne rogues, pirates or Vikings. Locals like to tell you that that's the case.

If so, the stratagem didn't work. The monastery of Menevia that St David established here in the mid-sixth century was attacked again and again. Bishops and monks were murdered, buildings sacked, treasures looted. But the sea also proved saviour. It provided fish, shellfish, seabirds and their eggs for the monastery. Pious (and rich) notables and ragged pilgrims, good news and dire warnings arrived by way of the rocky coves that lie just out of sight. And the cliff quarries yielded the hard purple sandstone that built the great cathedral towards the end of the twelfth century.

Acres of lead roof gleam in the weak November sun as I descend the thirty-nine steps (yes, I count them all) to the lower part of the valley. The south wall of the church begins to loom higher, glowing rich gold and purple against the sunlit green of the grass. So do those of the palace beyond, roofless but magnificent with its runs of Romanesque arches, tall lancet windows and tower-like chimneys. The pale tracery of a rose window floats in mid-air there, a delicate confection in the midst of so much sternly masculine stone.

Round on the north side, darkly shaded by a bank that rises right from the walls, the cathedral's aspect is plain and unadorned, the sandstone mossy and shaggy with usnea and white crustose lichen. The eastern prow of this great purple ship has a blunt and snout-like look, square-rigged and geometrical with its three flanking chapels and the big ambulatory built in the thirteenth century to give the crowds of pilgrims to the shrine of St David a freer flow. Hidden in the steep bank beyond is St David's Well, a mysterious subterranean fount that still whelms after heavy rain. As for David, catalyst for all this magnificent construction and these undying devotions, he himself is a mysterious and well-hidden figure. Hermit of extreme asceticism, rank misogynist, charismatic leader whose monks were bidden to pull their ploughs themselves without benefit of horses, eat only bread (they were permitted salt and herbs to go with it), drink only water and possess absolutely nothing whatsoever; a man whose myth has him dying on the lonely island of Bardsey at the age of 146: what is the modern mind to make of such a soul?

'David?' says Bishop Wyn Evans. 'You didn't want to cross him, I'll say that!' We are talking in the library of St Davids Cathedral, where the now-retired Bishop of St Davids holds court daily to answer any and every query about his beloved cathedral. 'He may be the national saint of our whole country, but he's actually very much a saint of South Wales – there are no dedications to St David at all in North Wales. A difficult man to warm to, David, but what he did do was to spread the word of God very vigorously all across what's now South Wales, the West Country and into Brittany.'

Bishop Wyn pauses to consider the character of this awkward holy man. 'I look at him this way: extremely austere, fiercely vegetarian, fiercely ascetic, very much not in favour of women. He wasn't a comfortable or a kindly man. Not a man for today's tastes, but actually a heroic figure from an age of heroes. His followers practised vegetarianism until the nine hundreds, so his personal influence lasted four hundred years at least after his death, which tells you something about the long shadow he cast. And the first bishop to reject his vegetarianism was killed – by Vikings! – for betraying David's teachings, so that lent a certain force to his tenets.'

I rummage about to find a picture of David, an icon of a bald, heavily bearded, sour-faced man with sunken cheeks and hooded eyes, and I'm aware, as so often among the frescoes and memorials of the Ships of Heaven, of how one's imagination works on these unfathomable characters from the deep past, spinning yarns, drawing deductions quite unsupported by fact from what's depicted in paint and alabaster.

Down in the cathedral treasury lies a purple sandstone tomb monument to an unknown priest of the early fourteenth century. He wears high-collared Mass vestments. His hands in long sleeves are crossed on his breast. His pillowed head is in high relief, his body incised in flat lines into the slab. He has a flattened nose and a wryly down-turned mouth, his jug ears fanning out the sides of his tonsure – very much the portrait of an actual man, although seven hundred years and unfathomable gulfs of culture lie between him and me. I stand and watch this priest, the self-deprecation and quirky humour that speak directly to me through the sculptor's skill, and I feel the imaginary past blow through me like a breath.

There's a dusky grey light inside St Davids Cathedral, a product of the winter afternoon and the faded purple of the sandstone. But I can easily make out the slope of the floor – a remarkable fourteen feet from the east end downwards towards the west. I imagine a naughty choirboy letting a marble drop from his choir stall and watching it roll down the nave and all the way to the west end. There is a definite sense of proceeding uphill as I walk under the wooden ceiling, a subtle ashy-brown, fretted with sixteenth-century oak carving.

Specialist craftsmen from Flanders or Germany must have been called over to carry out such intricate work. It's a beautiful jigsaw. This snugly fitted ceiling seems in some ways the most solid part of St Davids Cathedral. From the nave I can see multiple clues that the old building is wobbly on its pins and in need of a little TLC. Several chunks are missing from the lower arcade mouldings. In the clerestory arcade above, one of the keystones has slipped. The arcades themselves are not only irregular in style, they are uneven in height, their arches and piers growing perceptibly taller as they march towards the west, in order to counter the east–west slope of the site. They lean very visibly outwards, too, a result of the stresses and strains imposed on them eight hundred years ago by a roof whose original design was too steeply pitched.

Parts of the fabric are in a parlous condition. In the south aisle I stop to admire the effigy of an unknown priest which lies in a recess under a beautiful ogee arch that curls like a stone flame. I run my fingers lightly along the curve of the arch, and a chunk of pale grey stone three inches long breaks off and drops into my palm. It's weightless, as dry and flaky as tinder. Another splinter of stone hangs, ready to fall away. I glance guiltily round, but no one has noticed. The fragment goes into my pocket, where I'll find it that evening reduced to a mess of grey powder.

The tower of St Davids has its own sorry tale. The original, built late in the twelfth century with the rest of that first cathedral, lasted less than forty years before collapsing. Its successor had hardly been put in place when in 1247 an earthquake rocked it and the rest of the recently completed cathedral to their inadequate foundations. In the fourteenth century Bishop Henry Gower added a second storey to the tower; in the sixteenth century Bishop Edward Vaughan piled yet another stage on top, making the structure top-heavy. A hundred years later, Roundhead troops smashed a great hole in the southern face of the tower as a prelude to stealing the bells. George Gilbert Scott braced the whole thing with tie rods during his great renovation of the 1860s. But it was still basically unstable, and so it remains – some five thousand tons of stonework, whose weight has overwhelmed the stability of its foundations. In fact the whole tower has been on the move for several centuries now, inching itself down the slope, shoving everything west of it out of alignment with the force and deliberation of a glacier. By the 1790s it had pushed the top of the west wall three feet out of true. Fashionable architect John Nash was brought in to rebuild it, but his eclectic mix of Gothic and elaborate Perpendicular styles proved more pretty than practical, and by the time Scott arrived on his rescue mission of the 1860s the west front was again in danger of tottering over. Scott stabilized things. But for how long?

'Oh,' says the steward who saunters up to see if she can help the stranger who is scratching his head at these signs and wonders. 'The real problem won't go away. It's right under our feet.' She taps the flagstones. 'We're founded on gravel, an old riverbed down there. So what with our famous slope, and the earthquake shaking the whole cathedral up when it was brand new . . . well, it's not surprising we've got a few rheumatics nowadays, poor old thing.'

Des Harries, master mason at St Davids, conducts me on a walkabout of the cathedral's exterior. There's been a cloudburst, and the paving shines with rain. The stones of the building are dulled by the heavy cloud overhead, but they, too, take on a rainy sheen. Des points out the three main types of stone: local purple sandstone, dense-grained and hard; Clipsham limestone from Rutland, a beautiful colour between honey and cream; and Forest of Dean sandstone, replacing rotten sections in the projecting hood mould strips above the windows, where its lighter hue makes a pleasing patchwork contrast with the darker local stone.

'Well,' says Des, 'you might not believe it, but a stonemason can tell the difference between various sorts of stone just by the taste of them. Sandstone like the Forest of Dean has a dry taste that burns the back of your throat. You can get silicosis from it – the tiny flakes of silica cut your throat and scar your lungs. But Clipsham – it's like food, odd though that might sound. At the end of the day you'll have your lips caked with it, your nose will be full of it. But the taste in your mouth . . . it's a smooth, limey sort of taste that'll set your saliva flowing. A lovely taste, I have to admit.'

A man who can not only see and feel, but also taste the difference between one stone and another must surely have had 'stonemason' written in his stars. 'It looks that way, doesn't it? I'm born and bred Pembrokeshire, with a father who was a fisherman. He didn't want me to follow him to sea. I wasn't much good at school, and when I left at fifteen without proper qualifications his advice was, "Get a trade." So I got qualifications in carpentry, bricklaying and technical drawing. Caroe's, the cathedral architects, were looking for a long-term commitment from a mason, and they were prepared to invest in young blood. I was very lucky to be in the right place at the right time.

'I was sent off – probably the Dean and Chapter paid for it – to Chichester Cathedral to learn my trade in the masons' workshop there. This would be forty years ago; they had a dozen masons working there back then. A mason could turn up on a pushbike. "Anything on?" "OK, work on this bit, and we'll see how you go." They'd give him a two-day trial, and if he was all right they'd keep him on. All informal, and all to do with practical skills. I worked there, then on Wells Cathedral at the time they were restoring the west front. The quality of the stone they were using, Doulting stone, well, it wasn't too good. Bits were forever dropping off. The masons would just stick them back with Akemi glue. I'd say, "Hold on, you can't do that!" and they'd say, "Oh, there's no other way. We've got to!"

'When I came back here to work for the Dean and Chapter I was about twenty-two, and I'd learned on the job. There was no workshop here, no mason's yard, no circular saw even. I used the old-fashioned method for splitting stone, with plug and feathers. Mark your line on the stone, drill some holes along it, stick a set of plug and feathers – they're wedges, basically – into each hole, and keep tapping 'em in turn till the stone splits along the line. It was a real struggle, with so few tools for the work. But I've grown to love it. When I first began, the cathedral didn't really mean a lot to me. But now it's got a proper grip on me.

'The stone is the thing, the basis of it all, where the proper craft lies. The methods are the same the world over – only the stone is different. Here at St Davids the Dean and Chapter have quarrying rights at Caer Bwdy, that's a little cove down on the coast a couple of miles from here, and that's where most of our stone comes from. It's sandstone, in three layers of different quality. The top layer has been exposed to frost and weathering, so it tends to break and split – it's not really any good. The next layer down is good workable stone, not too dense, so quite easy to carve. And the lower layer has been compressed by the weight of several feet of stone above it, so it's dense and difficult to work, a darker purple, very strong stone. It has to be bed-laid – that is, laid with the strata going the same way they did in the ground. Otherwise bits split and break away. Really it's a dreadfully difficult stone to deal with – I've always been amazed at how the medieval masons managed to work with it.'

Caer Bwdy lies at the end of a muddy track. It's a tiny inlet fifty yards wide between dark cliffs a hundred feet tall, its snippet of sand overwhelmed by large, ovaloid boulders of a dusky purple, a few pale green rocks scattered among them. These boulders are slippery with weed and algae, and it's only with difficulty that I skid and teeter my way out to the tideline at low water to peer round the corner of the western cliffs.

It's hard to distinguish the cathedral quarry at first. The default aspect of these cliffs is of steep angles and smoothly sloped faces. But recalling Des Harries's description I soon zoom in on the three layers of sandstone, which are bent in a gentle convex arc towards the sea – the upper layer of rough, fragmented rubble sitting on top of a thick band of milky mauve rock of the same hue as the beach boulders, and down near the shore, fifty feet or so below clifftop level, a bed of much harder, darker rock, closer-grained, heavier-looking and of a far more intense purple. The lower cliffs are banded with a belt of yellow lichen, above which the storm waves of millennia have reached halfway up the cliffs to paint them pale with salt. I find a none-too-comfortable seat among the mussels and barnacles, and sit staring and picturing the masons of 1180, thumbing and reading the rocks, teasing these blank-faced cliffs to bring forth the corner stones and arches, the walls and towers of the great chimerical cathedral in the hollow.

'Glad you found it,' says Des Harries when I get back to the cathedral. 'As I said, I'm in awe of those old masons and how they managed. Things have changed such a long way since then. But actually it's hard to see how the craft will survive, because nowadays the masons are all threatened by the march of technology.'

What does he mean by that? 'Well, I'll tell you. I went to a stonemasonry exhibition at Olympia recently, and they had a machine there with computer-driven mechanical arms cutting a block of marble, reaching for a tool from the workbox, using it, replacing it and picking out another. A tireless machine that can cut perfectly each time, twenty-four/seven, night and day, doing the work at a quarter of the cost of a mason, and more accurately. Human masons can't do that. Organizations like English Heritage say, "Oh, we like the human element, the imperfect effect. We need to retain that." Yes, but will they pay to retain it? Will Pembrokeshire National Park allow us nowadays to cut the piece of stone we actually want, after we've "read" it in the face of our quarry at Caer Bwdy, without complaining about the visual effect of the quarrying?'

What of the future for stonemasons at St Davids Cathedral? 'I've no apprentice,' says Des matter-of-factly, 'no one to follow me after my forty years. I've tried, believe me. I've trained up some youngsters, but they are not in it for the long haul or the love of it.

'I understand their attitude, if I'm honest. It's partly to do with our location, down here in southwest Pembrokeshire, in tourist country. Tourism accounts for ninety per cent or more of the economy here- abouts. And the tourism has shifted from being a short summer holiday season to being most of the year round. Youngsters can be warm and dry behind a bar or in a restaurant, or they can be doing some- thing glamorous like driving a boat full of tourists out round Ramsey Island. No one would rather do this work. Would you? It's wet, it's dirty, it's hard and heavy labour, and it's not all-year-round employment, either.'

Des rasps his hand along the parapet of the cloisters where we're chatting, and inspects the pale stone dust on his hard palm. 'I'm of the last generation of masons who'll work for nothing, who love their work, who get totally engrossed in it.' He sighs, half rueful and half humor- ous. He's a realist, rather than a nostalgist. 'Masons are independent people, insular, bloody-minded if you like. We're like old-fashioned blacksmiths; we like to be told what the job is and then get on with it, with no interference. As for health and safety – well, I'll turn up for work dressed like I am now, old sweater and trousers, old shoes, and the first thing they'll say is, "Where's your hard hat?"

'I can't be bothered with all that. I love the job, and I do it for the love of it and for this cathedral. That's the truth of it, and most masons would say the same, I think.'

*

In the quire the ornate pinnacles of the cathedra or bishop's ceremonial chair rise halfway to the ceiling. Little sharp faces look out of the backs of the stalls, two by two. The bench arms terminate in carvings of faces in hoods and caps, all shiny with centuries of idle fondling by clerical fingers. The seats are all tipped up to display the misericord carvings. A fierce and handsome Green Man. Two spiny creatures, eels or dragons with pointed ears, writhing together in curlicues. Five pigs eating a screaming dog. A pair of shipwrights enjoying their lunch break. Two capering clowns playing bump-arse. A boat full of storm-tossed travellers, one puking over the side as her husband pulls her long hair back out of the way.

To one side stands the most venerated object of pilgrimage in Wales. The shrine of St David was restored and rededicated in 2012, another example of the trend that saw a spanking new top added to the shrine of St Thomas of Cantilupe at Hereford. The overhanging top of St David's shrine is brightly coloured, royal blue with gold stars, its ribs candy-striped in scarlet and white. Large colourful icons of St David, St Patrick and St Andrew adorn the niches. Three arched recesses pierce the lower front of the shrine; they hold a great iron Bangu bell, a replica of St David's own 'dear one', and two reliquaries for ancient bones.

'Of late,' Bishop Wyn tells me, 'we've seen a big rise in the number of pilgrims to St Davids. It probably started back in the 1960s when we first televised services. In the 1970s there was one visitor season a year, the summer, when everyone came. Now it's all the year round. And with Brexit we can only expect the numbers to grow – like with the Napoleonic wars, when people felt a lack of desire for foreign travel. Organized groups come, school groups getting "the Experience", and also individuals. We restored St David's shrine, and we opened Tŷ'r Pererin – the House of Pilgrims – to cater for them.

'Cathedrals look monolithic and unchanging, but that's the last thing they are. We need to build bits on. In my time we built a north porch, and to do that we had to scramble and scrape together money from the Lottery, from the Arts Council, from the EU. It costs two thousand five hundred pounds a day to keep the cathedral running, and this diocese has always been poor. We have a clicker on the door, and it tells us that we get about three hundred thousand visitors a year. When you consider that the peninsula as a whole gets five hundred thousand, you can see what a draw the cathedral is. It's a holiday area, and people come back year after year, generation after generation. The old saying has it that if you come to St Davids you're bound to return, and that seems to be borne out.

'We hope to turn visitors into pilgrims – that's the strapline!'

Around AD 1089 the reliquary that contained the relics of St David was stolen from the monastery by Viking raiders, carried outside the town, broken open and plundered of its jewels and contents. So whose bones were they that lay within the reliquary that stood in the cathedral sanctuary behind the high altar all through medieval times, the object of veneration to millions of pilgrims?

I walk round from the sanctuary through the north quire aisle, and turn right into the tall and spacious Holy Trinity Chapel that stands directly east of the high altar. From this chapel you can glance back into the sanctuary through a tiny stone window, a hagioscope, built in the form of a Maltese cross with hollow spaces between the four arms. These four peepholes offer a clear view of the back of the high altar, and of any reliquary kept in the 'aumbry recess' or little compartment between hagioscope and altar.

No wonder that Edward Vaughan, Bishop of St Davids from 1509 to 1522, wanted to be buried in the Trinity Chapel, and had the ceiling done up with fabulous fan vaulting to make sure that he lay in the style to which he was accustomed. If the contents of the aumbry recess were truly what they were said to be, the bones of St David and his friend and fellow misogynist St Justinian, the bishop would have lain in state within touching distance of the corporal remains of Wales's two most prestigious saints.

But were those really the bones they were cracked up to be? Bishop Wyn Evans is sceptical when I ask him for his opinion.

'Was David even buried at St Davids? That's an interesting point. The fact is that he'd been attracting pilgrims for centuries before he was canonized in 1120. And it was here that the cult of David really caught on. By the eleventh century, well before his canonization, we have a description of someone wanting to visit David's tomb and having to cut his way through a thicket of thorns. That suggests that the relics were thought to be here. And in the ninth, tenth and eleventh centuries there were Viking raids here – and Vikings were no fools. They wouldn't have wasted time and energy on an insignificant place with no treasures.'

Come the Reformation, sacred shrines that had been venerated for hundreds of years suddenly became no more than heaps of old bones in fancy boxes. In 1538 Bishop William Barlow, the first Protestant Bishop of St Davids, opened the tomb of the saint. 'Barlow reported to Thomas Cromwell', says Bishop Wyn, 'that he'd found two rotten skulls stuffed with rags and enclosed in silver, an arm bone and a book. More or less saying to Cromwell, What shall I do with these? Destroy them here, or would you like to? We don't know what happened to the relics after that, or if they really were the skulls of David and Justinian, but it's a good bet they were sent up to Cromwell to be ceremonially burned.'

In the 1860s, during George Gilbert Scott's renovation of the cathedral, Scott's 'very excellent Clerk of Works Mr Clear'* discovered some bones walled up in the aumbry recess behind the high altar. They were reinterred under the pavement in front of the niche. When Dean William Williams wanted to re-establish enthusiasm for pilgrimage to the cathedral in the 1920s, he dug the bones out again and proclaimed them to be those of St David. 'In fact,' says Bishop Wyn, 'they were the bones of three separate people mixed up together, one of them probably female – which would have been a big problem for David and Justinian,

---

* Described thus by Scott in his *Report on St David's Cathedral* (1873).

with their well-known views on women! But one of the sets of bones was of a tall man, and David was said to be tall. That was good enough for Dean Williams. He *wanted* the bones to be those of David and Justinian – so they had to be!'

There was a political and economic backdrop to this push to have the bones authenticated as those of the saint. Dean Williams had been appointed just before the Church in Wales was disestablished, i.e. cut its links with the state, in June 1920. The Anglican Church in Wales had come to be seen as a Church of England set-up, and there were more Welsh men and women worshipping in Nonconformist chapels than in Anglican churches.

This was not a rerun of the Reformation. The newly created Church in Wales kept all its church buildings and properties. But it did lose its tithes, and also all the endowments or donations that pre-dated 1662, the year that an Act of Uniformity standardized the prayers and rites of the Established Church of England. Loss of tithes and endowments was a big financial blow to the Church in Wales, and there were serious fears about how St Davids Cathedral would pay for itself. Also there was a desire to prove that the Church in Wales was an authentic entity with long roots back to the Age of Saints, way before the Church of England was ever a twinkle in the eye of King Henry VIII.

A revival in the lucrative and venerable tradition of pilgrimage seemed just what the doctor ordered for the ailing patient. The bones discovered by the 'excellent Mr Clear' were housed in a new reliquary and returned to the aumbry recess, and formal pilgrimages to 'the relics of St David' resumed. A major controversy over the matter blew up and raged throughout the inter-war years. In 1929 Canon W. G. Spurrell, a member of Chapter, was forced to withdraw his pamphlet *Re. The Bone Relics*, which rejected their authenticity. Debate got so heated that Dean Watkyn Morgan forbade any mention of the subject during Chapter meetings.

'There was a stalemate for decades,' affirms Bishop Wyn. 'Now, I became dean in 1994, and I realized it needed to be settled once and for all. I called a Chapter meeting to discuss it, and we decided to have the bones examined at the Royal Infirmary, Cardiff, and at the Radiocarbon Accelerator Unit at Oxford. The results of the radiocarbon dating came back – and sadly, the bones dated to the twelfth or thirteenth centuries. So they were definitely not David's relics, as Dean Williams had claimed. In fact,' Bishop Wyn adds, 'Williams himself hadn't really helped the cause of truth – he'd stored the bones with others from St Justinian's Chapel, and he'd kept the lot all mixed up in a box under his bed!'

West of St Davids Cathedral lies the massive, roofless shell of the Bishop's Palace. As extensive as a monastery or a castle, arcaded and crenellated, turreted and many-windowed, almost as big as the cathedral it lies alongside, the palace grew over the course of two centuries to reflect the power and prestige of the Bishop of St Davids. By the end of the fourteenth century it was pretty much complete, with a huge hall, private apartments, a chapel and a vast vaulted undercroft.

The elaborate cast-iron gates under the gatehouse are closed, but I manage to negotiate a passage. Steps rise into the great hall, spiral stairs mount into chambers darkening in the evening light. Eroded stone faces watch me as I walk the walls. Rooks produce their sore-throat complaints from the trees beyond, and jackdaws hop in and out of the window holes with a cheerful, musical *chak-chak!* It's a strange little stroll among the massive ruins, chilled by the cold graveyard breath of the undercroft chambers, and I'm glad to squeeze back through the gates and see the diffuse yellow lights of the cathedral blurring the rainy air of the hollow.

Bishop Wyn: 'I always think that the spectacle of a service in St David's Cathedral is a Victorian, or better still an Edwardian, experience. And it never skimps or lets you down. There's full measure, no matter who's present. The test is on a wet Tuesday in November when everything's grey, cold and empty. No one's here. But the boys' choir is singing and the clergy are officiating, doing for a congregation of perhaps one person exactly what they'd be doing for a full house. That's what cathedrals do – they keep up the standard.'

A wet Tuesday in November. Evensong in the dark echoing chamber of the cathedral. Ten or so people in the stalls. The reading is from the Book of Joel. I can't remember ever having heard of it before, but I won't forget it in a hurry. A dark army with the cheek teeth of a great lion, an enemy host strong and without number, is at the gates, and the harvest has been eaten by palmerworms and cankerworms and locusts.

My God. What can the little choristers be making of this apocalyptic stuff, threats and warnings I can imagine issuing from the disapproving and humourless David himself? I glance across. The children sit and stare. Two of the lads, one ginger, one dark, fidget and poke each other. Someone yawns – it's pretty late at the end of a school day. The choirmaster, with a lean and hungry look, waves them to their feet. Psalm 63 now. He gestures to his charges with hands and eyebrows: hold that chin up. Mouth a little wider, please. Wake up, you two! Concentrate! More power there. Down just a notch, thank you.

From the shadows beyond the high altar comes a rustling noise. It's only a stray bat looking for a late midge or two, but just for a moment I imagine the bones of David and Justinian, or whoever now lies in that sacred niche below the little stone cross, sitting up to listen as the wretched Joel is put in his place by these youngsters with their earthly yet heavenly voices.

The children get their chins up. They open their mouths. The dark cathedral fills with celestial images of thirst slaked and lips that praise, of a satisfied soul and a peaceful meditation in the silent watches of the night.

12

St Paul's

Ship of State

IF YOU LOOKED ACROSS THE Thames from Bankside in the 1960s, you saw the London waterfront of Bill Sikes and Sherlock Holmes: wooden wharves where the dirty old river slopped and slapped, slimy loops of chain, flights of steps leading to alleys where the sun never shone, and dingy warehouses eight storeys high framing the grimy dome of St Paul's Cathedral far beyond. Today you cross the Millennium Bridge and it is all change, with skyscrapers so tall you question how they stay upright, and so Polaroid of window glass you wonder what the occupants have to hide. The warehouses might still be there under the balconies and sundecks that have been stuck all over them. The river wall is still as slimy and sloppy as ever, though, and somehow, miraculously, the view of St Paul's is better than it was, a Taj Mahal prospect, the eyes and the feet led forward by converging lines above the water to the newly scrubbed dome gleaming like a lighthouse over the city.

Walking through the cathedral's churchyard I come upon St Paul's Cross, a statue of the saint hoisted high in gilt and stone. This was the spot where Londoners traditionally assembled in times of crisis. Folk-moots or common gatherings to sort things out took place at 'Paul's Cross' in early medieval times. Erring churchmen did penance here, their heretical books and writings torched before their eyes. Excommunications and papal bulls were promulgated, royal proclamations made at the foot of the cross, until Puritan fanatics destroyed it in 1643. A generation, a commoners' revolution and a Restoration later, Sir Christopher Wren's new Baroque cathedral began to rise from the ashes of the Great Fire of London of 1666 that had gutted its Gothic predecessor.

St Paul's Cathedral in its splendour lies moored in the heart of London. Its natural role as indomitable Ship of State was sealed in one instant of time by *Daily Mail* photographer Herbert Mason with his remarkable 1940 photograph of the cathedral's dome rising solid and serene above the smoke and flames of the Blitz. When the Duke of Marlborough beat the French at the Battle of Blenheim in 1704, when Britain celebrated the ends of the First and Second World Wars, St Paul's hosted the national services of thanksgiving. Martin Luther King preached to a congregation of four thousand in the cathedral in 1964. Sir Winston Churchill's funeral was held here the following year. Prince Charles and Lady Diana Spencer were married at St Paul's in 1981. It has been the setting for royal jubilee celebrations from Queen Victoria to Queen Elizabeth. Poets, painters and national heroes have come to rest here – Lord Nelson, the Duke of Wellington, J. M. W. Turner, John Donne. Sir Christopher Wren lies in the cathedral he designed and is forever identified with, his epitaph set into the floor under the dome: 'Si monumentum requiris circumspice' – 'If you seek his monument, look around you.' This building is what matters, it seems to say, not all the pomp and ceremony.

Nowadays the twin towers of the cathedral's west end look out over the paved Paternoster Square on to coffee shops, a Pizza Express, a French restaurant, a Marks & Spencer store, the Tokyo Stock Exchange. There's no grand isolation for St Paul's, no cathedral green or hushed close. It breasts the tides of London life, surrounded by modern temples of commerce, with the Shard peeping over their shoulders from the south bank of the Thames – a grand establishment church at the heart of things.

The west front steps of St Paul's are thronged with tourists on this spring day. But a recent image of a different kind nags at my memory: small tents and makeshift shelters on the flagstones, indignant placards waving from the steps, a phalanx of helmeted riot police somewhere in the background – another era of Londoners gathered at St Paul's to protest in a time of crisis, and non-Londoners, too, lots of them. For a few months over the winter of 2011–12 the media gaze came to rest, briefly, on what were portrayed as little rafts of righteous protest, cheekily bobbing round the British establishment's haughty Ship of State.

Occupy London was a movement, organized on Facebook, of people looking for social justice and 'real democracy', part of an international surge of youth and left-wing indignation. OL's 'Initial Statement' declared it to be against capitalism, austerity cuts, bank bail-outs, wars, arms dealing, pollution, global inequality and oppression. No one could really argue with that, even though a more shadowy undercurrent showed itself when the self-styled 'Anonymous' group, with its sinisterly grinning Guy Fawkes masks and inchoate philosophy as 'an Internet-based, non-extremist, socialist community movement that looks for answers to questions that are unanswered', hitched its wagon to OL's star.

On 15 October 2011 about three thousand people gathered at St Paul's under the auspices of Occupy London, of whom two hundred or so camped overnight on or around the steps. By next day, about 150 tents had been pitched there. It was the start of a four-month occupation of the churchyard, a natural, media-friendly stage where the police and bailiffs might hesitate to act too briskly in front of the cameras – and also an institution whose staff were likely to be more sympathetic to those encamped on their doorstep than, say, the institutions of the Square Mile that were OL's actual target. 'Global Democracy Now!' demanded the placards and banners. 'Capitalism Isn't Working! The Banks OWN You – And YOU are their Collateral!' There was a smugness about some of the slogans – 'We are the Good Guys! We are the 99%!' – but it was the rather more situation-conscious 'What Would Jesus Do?' that posed a question with which St Paul's Cathedral was seen to struggle, to its own acute embarrassment.

Initially there was goodwill and tacit backing for the protesters. The Canon Chancellor of St Paul's, Giles Fraser, asked the police to leave the steps of the cathedral and let the people exercise their right to protest peacefully. A week later, with the steps still cluttered and the public deterred from visiting, the Dean of St Paul's, the Right Revd Graeme Knowles, announced that the cathedral would be closed until further notice, and asked the protesters to go. They didn't. It was implied that the Dean and Chapter were sympathetic to forcible removal of the encampment. Canon Fraser resigned in protest, and after a fortnight of unfavourable publicity, and having climbed down and reopened the cathedral, the dean, too, resigned his post.

The impasse lasted till the end of February 2012, when an injunction was activated and bailiffs moved in to clear the tents and remaining protesters with minimal resistance. The occupation was over. But the cathedral authorities had been badly wrong-footed, and made to appear clumsy, uncertain and arrogant – un-Christian, even. This perception wasn't ameliorated by an article in the *Guardian* of 24 May 2015 by Giles Fraser, looking back at how St Paul's had dealt with the OL affair, in which he questioned . . .

> . . . if it was possible for such a fabulous building to speak about the life of a man born in a shed and who lived in solidarity with the down-and-outs of society. St Paul's, designed by a scientist, speaks vividly of the cosmological God, the omnipotent God of the stars and the heavens. But it finds it much harder to speak convincingly of the poor, incarnate, vulnerable God of Bethlehem. That God was, to my mind at least, much more clearly articulated within the camp itself.

Giles Fraser was scarred by the whole experience. Depression and divorce followed his resignation, as he struggled to come to terms with having put himself outside the charmed circle of the cathedral. 'Being a canon of St Paul's was good for the ego,' he confesses in his article. 'It made you feel important just to be there, among important people, always at the centre of things. But precisely because of this insidious temptation to self-importance, it's also a place that contains a great many dangers for the soul, as it certainly did for me.'

Four canons of St Paul's are whispering together at the west end – a Dutch Old Master grouping in their black cassocks, confidential, powerful and self-contained. Another canon hurries to join them, striding past a Japanese visitor whose body language suggests she'd like to ask him something. The cathedral is packed with tourists. From the little coterie of canons comes a burst of theatrical laughter. A hand in a wide black sleeve waves around in a gesture both camp and self-conscious. Meeters and greeters scurry by, self-absorbed and distant. I want to find out the times of the cathedral tours, but it's hard to attract anyone's attention. It must be a London 'no-time-to-spare' thing. Oh well, just follow the advice of Wren's epitaph, why don't you?

The first impression is of high, rounded arcades, of ceiling roundels ablaze with colour, and of the bulk and power of stone. The nave cross-ing is a circus of semi-circular arches. This is a *Grand Designs* kind of building, planned for a new age of Protestant worship, the first in Britain to be built in a post-Reformation world. Wren needed to create something fresh to reflect the new form of faith, yet with a nod to trad-ition and the restored monarchy; something that contrasted with the old Gothic cathedral, built in the Roman Catholic era, that stood here until 1666 and the Great Fire of London. Yet his inspiration seems very much Old European, the Romanesque arches, great dome and Byzantine-looking mosaics creating a splendid basilica that would not look out of place in Rome itself.

Under the dome I look up to see the massive railed circle of the Whispering Gallery a hundred feet above, dotted with heads and hands, with faces staring down. A flight of wooden steps leads me to the upper realm and a long corridor within the walls, running west from near the altar to the Whispering Gallery. Wall grilles allow glimpses into an elongated loft, thick with dust, from whose floor rises a line of shallow brick domes, like kilns in shape. These are the upper works of the saucer domes above the quire and high altar, functional, plain and workmanlike, in contrast to the glittering mosaics that decorate the lower concavities of the domes: angels beautiful and angels sternly terrifying, Christ figures, lions, palm trees, birds, fishes.

Schoolkids are sitting sideways on the benches round the Whispering Gallery, their mouths against the walls, whispering rude words to their sniggering mates opposite. I join the circle leaning on the rail and look across the great empty pool of space to other galleries under the arches, one filled with a pile of spare organ pipes, others with stepladders, theatrical flats and floodlights. Down below, foreshortened people stroll the chequerboard floor of the crossing. Up above . . . I tip my head back to see chinks of greasy light shining through the arched windows of the Golden Gallery, nearly two hundred feet overhead.

Another hundred steps up to the Stone Gallery, open to the wind, with a superb view over London. Not as superb, though, as the one of which I am lord and master after I've climbed yet another hundred steps to the little railed crow's nest of the Golden Gallery, 280 feet up, dizzyingly high above the tops of the west towers, the streets and the river. A prospect overtopped by any grand glass tower erected in this millennium, but what a mind-blower it must have been when opened three centuries ago.

Down again on the floor of St Paul's, I notice for the first time the plethora of memorials, of horses and cannon, of gallant soldiers and weeping widows. Once they've claimed my attention, I can't get over them. Suddenly this whole aspect of the cathedral opens out like a casement. These splendid martyrs are all storybook heroes. St Paul's is a timeline of Empire, a compendium of tastes in mourning, a monument to honour and self-sacrifice in both history-making battles and forgotten skirmishes on the other side of the world. It's a love letter by the British establishment to itself. The realization is nothing earth-shaking, I suppose, but it's more pronounced here than in any other cathedral. Once I've caught on, I'm completely absorbed in drooping drapery and downturned torches of life, in little battle scenes in marble, in jackboots and frogging and cavalry sabres. If you're going to die at the moment of victory, cut in half by a cannon ball or dashed from your saddle by a volley of grapeshot, then do it like this, one arm aloft, eyes fixed on a far horizon, with a scantily draped angel gliding forward to bear you up as your charger plunges his nose into the ground.

When Nick Jenkins, self-effacing 'narrator' of Anthony Powell's epic sequence of novels *A Dance to the Music of Time*, attends a service of thanksgiving in St Paul's Cathedral at the end of the Second World War, he finds himself distractedly looking round for familiar monuments. Now I'm determined to seek them out too, the extravagant memorials that feature so seductively in R. H. Barham's comic compendium of 1837, *The Ingoldsby Legends*. Like the fictional Jenkins, as a child I loved Barham's humorous verses, especially 'The Cynotaph' in which he ponders where to bury his 'poor dog Tray'. Back then I'd never been to St Paul's, or central London for that matter, and had only the vaguest notion of what Barham was on about, but the breezy wit and awful rhymes of his nineteenth-century doggerel tickled my funny bone.

I've had Barham's big, shadowy shapes in my head ever since. Now here they are, made marble if not flesh, these tremendous martial heroes of Empire who died fighting the French.

> *Oh! Where shall I bury my poor dog Tray . . .*
> *I would not place him beneath thy walls,*
> *And proud o'ershadowing dome, St. Paul's!*
> *Though I've always consider'd Sir Christopher Wren,*
> *As an architect, one of the greatest of men;*
> *And,—talking of Epitaphs,—much I admire his,*
> *'Circumspice, si Monumentum requiris;'*
> *Which an erudite Verger translated to me,*
> *'If you ask for his Monument, Sir-come-spy-see!—'*

No!—I should not know where
To place him there;
I would not have him by surly Johnson be;—
Or that Queer-looking horse that is rolling on Ponsonby . . .

Down at the west end of the great crypt of St Paul's I find this Ingoldsby monument. Sir William Ponsonby (1772–1815), a veteran of the Peninsular War battles at Salamanca and Vitoria and the siege of Burgos, was killed on 18 June 1815 at the Battle of Waterloo, in command of the Union Brigade which included English, Scottish and Irish regiments. A counter-attack went wrong when the enthusiasm of the Scots Greys overcame their discipline and took them into a danger zone too near the French guns. Half the force became casualties, and the dashing Ponsonby was killed by French lancers after he misunderstood an invitation to surrender. He was a mature man of over forty, but the memorial depicts him as an all-but-naked youth of lithe musculature. He grasps at a laurel wreath being offered by an angel, herself very lightly draped, while his horse sinks fetlock-deep into the marble plinth. Queer-looking, indeed.

Poor dog Tray is not destined for a niche down in the crypt; neither does Barham care for what's going on up in the south transept.

No! I'd not have him there,—nor nearer the door,
Where the Man and the Angel have got Sir John Moore,
And are quietly letting him down through the floor,
By Gillespie, the one who escaped, at Vellore,
Alone from the row;—
Neither he, nor Lord Howe
Would like to be plagued with a little Bow-wow.

Sir Rollo Gillespie hanged, shot and blew to pieces dozens of Indian sepoy rebels after crushing their uprising at Vellore in 1806, and Admiral Lord Howe, victor of the sea battle of the Glorious First of

June, 1794, has a sneer on his lips and a lion in tow, so both of those big shots could well object to that little Bow-wow. But Sir John Moore (1761–1809) might be more accommodating. Moore was one of the quintessential military heroes of Empire. He fought the Americans in America, the French in the Mediterranean, the Irish in Ireland, the Dutch in Holland. Eventually his luck ran out in the Spanish port of Corunna during the Peninsular War, when on 16 January 1809 a cannon shot smashed his ribs, arm, shoulder and left side. Moore died shortly afterwards and was buried on the ramparts of Corunna, wrapped in a cloak.

Charles Wolfe's poem 'The Burial of Sir John Moore after Corunna', encapsulated the modest, downbeat nature of the ideal heroic end:

> Not a drum was heard, not a funeral note,
> As his corse to the rampart we hurried;
> Not a soldier discharged his farewell shot
> O'er the grave where our hero we buried.

And the memorial in the south transept of St Paul's offers this same quiet model of restraint, as a half-naked young god and a lightly clad angel lower the limp body of the 'sleeping' hero into a sarcophagus, while a cherub solemnly spreads a tactful cloak over the whole scene.

The Ingoldsby monuments are a personal fad of mine. But the whole interior of the cathedral is laden with fascinating figures. Here in the north aisle is hook-nosed Frederick, Lord Leighton (1830–96), painter and sculptor. At his head, a bare-breasted young woman, the Spirit of Painting, with a paintbrush; at his feet a girl, the Spirit of Sculpture, holding a clay sculptor's tool, her other hand cupping a model of Leighton's own sculpture *The Sluggard* – a beautiful youth, naked and curly-haired, luxuriously and sensually stretching himself in the act of being awakened. Wow! Such slinky, slithery sexuality, so overtly expressed in black bronze and streaky marble! It's not quite what I've been expecting from a late-Victorian tomb. I'm getting a bit of a wake-up call myself.

Most of the memorials, though, chart the long and amazingly bloody rise of this obscure archipelago, the British Isles, to a position of power and influence – for good and ill – over much of the nineteenth-century world. They reach their apogee in Major General Charles George Gordon, the Boy's Own Hero, whose effigy lies near that of Leighton in the north aisle of St Paul's; incorruptible Gordon, who defended the soldiers and civilians in besieged Khartoum in the classic tradition of the doomed last stand, before striding out to face a rabble of blood-thirsty Sudanese jihadists alone and unarmed except for his rattan cane. Or so the legend said.

Intransigent; upright; judicious; hot-headed; rigid; impulsive; personally modest; tremendously Christian; a gay individualist with a death wish. Who can now unpick the real man from the labels so freely stuck to his image since his death in 1885? Gordon adventured all over the world, fighting and administering, ruling and relieving, playing the Great Game and the stiff-upper-lip card at the best and worst times of the British Empire.

As 'Chinese Gordon' in the 1860s, he commanded the 'Ever Victorious Army' of Chinese soldiers led by Europeans and Americans, who fought for the rather dissolute Tongzhi emperor against the hungry plunderers of the Nian movement (motto: 'Kill the rich and aid the poor'), and the Christian millenarian army of the Taiping Heavenly Kingdom.

As 'Gordon Pasha', he served the Khedive or Viceroy of Egypt, Ismail Pasha, a vassal of the Ottoman Empire and a bon viveur, from 1873 onwards. 'What an extraordinary Englishman,' Ismail Pasha commented. 'He doesn't want money!' During his tenure as Governor-General of Sudan, Gordon suppressed revolts. He tried to repress and abolish the slave trade and the systematic use of cruelty, torture and public floggings. He sought to put the state at the service of the people – a very un-Ottoman concept. But he was swimming against an irresistible tide of corruption. In 1880 he returned to England suffering from a nervous breakdown, having failed in his objectives.

As 'Gordon of Khartoum', General Gordon reached his summit of glory. In 1884 he was sent to Khartoum in Sudan to evacuate loyal soldiers and civilians in the face of a massive jihadist rebellion against Anglo-Egyptian rule led by Muhammad Ahmad bin Abd Allah, the self-declared Mahdi or Islamic Messiah. Gordon's rigid code of honour meant he felt he couldn't leave Khartoum until every person was guaranteed safety from the Mahdists. His delay led to Khartoum being besieged. After almost a year the city fell on 26 January 1885, and Gordon and ten thousand garrison soldiers and civilians were massacred. The relief army under Sir Garnet Wolseley arrived just two days too late.

Gordon's death as depicted by George William Joy in his epic 1893 painting *General Gordon's Last Stand* – the hero staring down with Christ-like calm at the slyly creeping foe – was the pattern of noble self-sacrifice for every Victorian schoolboy. After Gordon was 'slain', his body was never recovered; mutilated with multiple spear-thrusts over several hours, it was probably eventually thrown down a well. Gordon's head was severed and brought to the Mahdi, who had it put on show in a tree to be stoned by every passer-by. That gruesomely ignominious image, of course, is all smoothed away from the Gordon who lies in bronze on a black marble sarcophagus in the second bay of the north aisle, hands composed upon his breast, his mutton-chop whiskers and moustache all neat and tidy. The inscription is lettered in brass as highly polished as the legend:

> *Born at Woolwich, 28 July 1833.*
> *Slain at Khartoum, 26 July 1885.*
> *He saved an Empire by his warlike genius, he ruled vast provinces*
>   *with justice, wisdom and power.*

*And lastly obedient to his sovereign's command, he died in the
heroic attempt to save men, women and children from imminent
and deadly peril.*

Back down in the crypt I walk slowly among the heroes and villains.
Wide and many-chambered, infused with sombre, tawny-coloured
light, the crypt extends under the entire cathedral. Wren intended it to
act as a solid foundation for St Paul's in the London clay, so liable to
cracking and slipping. Here are monuments of Empire and of Rule Bri-
tannia, and of the never-ending cost of maintaining that grip and that
defiance in actions famous or notorious, and in places forgotten or in
many cases come to prominence once again.

I stand and contemplate the mightily bearded Colonel Sir Duncan
MacDougall, KCSF (1787–1862), of Soroba in Argyllshire. Here is the
authentic Empire fighter, the man for this or any other hour. His bust is
backed by a welter of battle standards, spears, cannon, muskets and
swords. And no wonder. With the 53rd and 85th Regiments he fought
around the globe. In 1805, aged eighteen, he took part in the invasion of
the Dutch Cape Colony by amphibious landing at the Cape of Good
Hope. During the Peninsular War he was at the Siege of Badajoz from
March to April 1812, when victorious British troops took revenge for the
enormous casualties (nearly five thousand men) they suffered storming
the defences of Badajoz by raping and massacring about four thousand
of the townsfolk in a drunken, uncontrollable orgy. On 22 July 1812
MacDougall distinguished himself at the Battle of Salamanca by saving
the regimental colours while badly wounded. He was at the unsuccessful Siege of Burgos and miserable retreat later that year, one of the Duke
of Wellington's rare reversals; and at the Siege of San Sebastián (July–
September 1813), another tremendously bloody assault, followed after
the town's surrender by another drunken mayhem of rape and slaugh-
ter, during which San Sebastián was largely burned to the ground.

Next year MacDougall found himself in America, fighting at the

Battle of New Orleans. That ended finally with a British withdrawal in January 1815 – or, as the old American song had it:

> *We fired our guns and the British kept a-comin',*
> *There wasn't nigh as many as there was a while ago;*
> *We fired once more and they began to runnin'*
> *On down the Mississippi to the Gulf of Mexico.*

During that battle, MacDougall acted as senior aide-de-camp to General Edward Pakenham, the officer commanding the British forces. When Pakenham was wounded and his horse killed under him as he led his men to storm a breach, it was MacDougall who vacated his own saddle in favour of the general. Pakenham was immediately, and fatally, hit with a blast of grapeshot. If MacDougall hadn't made the chivalrous gesture, he himself would have been directly in the line of fire.

Duncan MacDougall commanded the 79th Highlanders till he resigned from the British Army in 1835, in order to join the British Auxiliary Legion in Spain. This was an odd footnote to all that fighting of twenty years before: a corps of volunteers tacitly approved by the British government and paid for by the Spanish Crown, which supported forces loyal to the infant Queen Isabella against the Carlists, Bourbon pretenders to her throne. MacDougall acted as quartermaster general and second-in-command to Sir George de Lacy Evans, his friend and fellow veteran of the American War of 1812. There were lots of battles and skirmishes, setbacks and victories. A quarter of the legion died in Spain, half of disease, the other half at the hands of the foe – and not very pleasantly if captured by the Carlists, who would torture and murder them as alien invaders and heretics.

Our Scots-born hero avoided that end. On his return he was knighted, involved himself with domestic military matters, and died on 10 December 1862, 'a chivalrous soldier and a warm hearted friend', having somehow survived seventy-five years' mid shot and shell in the service of Crown and country.

Two more modest memorials draw a poignant contrast with these tallies of honours and achievements. One commemorates the last kick of colonial Britain in the South Atlantic Task Force, dispatched in 1982 to recapture the Falkland Islands from Argentine occupation. A simple slab of Cumbrian slate incorporating a map of the Falklands, it is large enough to contain the names, in six columns, of the 255 British service personnel who died. Its quiet simplicity reflects the taste of more modern times for unfussy, if not anonymous, remembrance.

Another plaque memorial from the high noon of colonial militarism draws attention to a band of men who never made it into the ranks of glorious Victorian heroes: the special correspondents sent by the newspapers to the Sudan to collect first-hand, dramatic and accurate news on the disastrous British response to the Mahdist rebellion. No embedding, or feather-bedding, for these pioneer reporters who had to find their own food, equipment and transport, and glean what information they could from reluctant senior officers who regarded them at best as amateurs and nuisances. I read the names and think of them: Edmund O'Donovan (*Daily News*) and Frank Vizetelly (*The Graphic*), both reporting on the Battle of El Obeid on 3–5 November 1883, a disastrous expedition by a ramshackle army to relieve a town that had already fallen to the Mahdi. Many of the troops deserted; the remainder formed a square which was attacked for two days by the whole Mahdist army before being overwhelmed. All the officers and Europeans were killed, including O'Donovan and Vizetelly. Frank Power (*Pictorial World*), a young and daring journalist, survived that disaster, but was killed the following year after leaving Khartoum, when the party he was with were massacred by Arabs whom they had paid to help them escape. St Leger Herbert (*Morning Post*), decorated Canadian veteran of several battles, and John Alexander Cameron (*The Standard*), another experienced war correspondent, were both killed at the Battle of Metammeh, 19 January 1885, during the advance on Khartoum to relieve General Gordon. *Manchester Guardian* correspondent

William Gordon died of thirst in the desert on the same expedition, having gone missing on 16 January. And lastly there is poor Frank Roberts of Reuters, who died of typhoid fever at Suakim, the port at which he landed, on 15 May 1885, without ever seeing action at all.

The two quintessential British heroes-at-arms occupy tombs that dominate the space around them with their sheer size, although both plain and unadorned: Admiral Nelson and the Duke of Wellington. Other, lesser victors are allowed their pining pets and grieving maidens, their tallies of battlefield triumphs and their thundering encomia. But the two greatest heroes of Great Britain's military glory are shut away from us in their tombs, eulogized with no phrases, merely named, unreachable and immaculate on their lonely pinnacle of fame.

Arthur Wellesley, 1st Duke of Wellington, KG, GCB, GCH, PC, FRS (1769–1852), lies in a giant marble sarcophagus, heavy and dominant, immovably plonked on the floor slabs. 'ARTHUR DUKE OF WELLINGTON' is all it says. Dozy lions guard the Anglo-Irish soldier who saved the world from the invasive ambitions of Napoleon Bonaparte.

Vice Admiral Horatio Nelson, 1st Viscount Nelson, 1st Duke of Bronté, KB (1758–1805), sails to Heaven in a great black ship, or soup tureen, of a tomb (originally intended for the flamboyant Cardinal Wolsey, before his fall led to flight, death in disgrace and a now forgotten grave). Inscribed simply 'HORATIO VISC NELSON', the tomb is flashily topped with a scarlet, gold and white coronet resting on a cushion, an echo of Nelson's child-like touchiness and vanity about his honours. Rather vulgar, don't y'know, the monument to the frail little Norfolk sailor whose Royal Navy ruled the waves and kept his country safe from invasion.

> No, Tray, we must yield,
> And go further a-field;
> To lay you by Nelson were downright effront'ry;—
> —We'll be off from the City, and look at the country.

*

I'm waiting in the nave of St Paul's for evensong to begin. On opposing pillars, twin twenty-first-century ghost-white sculptures by Gerry Judah commemorate the dead of the First World War. They are not exactly crosses. The main shafts have cross-shaped spars, though, like anchor stocks, weighed down with a tangle of spiky pieces reminiscent of a Star Wars space station. These pieces resolve, as you stare, into blasted buildings, blank tiers of windows, satellite dishes, TV aerials – model cities, built in great detail by the artist, then deliberately wrecked. An ashen, parched vision from any conflict of the past hundred years, of cities ruined and reduced to rubble.

In the rich, soft glow of ranks of choir-stall lamps and the soporific wash of a bewitchingly sung evensong anthem, my eyes wander idly upwards and fix on the mosaics in the spandrels of the crossing arches. There sit the Four Evangelists, designed by G. F. Watts. Matthew (the only one of the four that Watts himself was able to complete before his death), Mark and Luke sit benignly at their books, solid middle-aged bearded sages, with angelic helpers close at hand. St John, at the far right, is the odd man out. Watts has shown him as a young man, cringing away from his writing stance, an arm crooked across his eyes to shut out some terrifying sight. 'Must be the Apocalypse,' whispers the person seated next to me, sensitive to my upward gaze. An angel is tugging at a pale length of material stretched across the Evangelist's lap – either a piece of his clothing, or the scroll on which he has been recording the vision that has so appalled him: perhaps the 'great dragon, that old serpent, called the Devil, and Satan, which deceiveth the whole world'.

The contrast is very striking: the calm triumvirate at their holy labours, and the man in abject terror at the end of the line. I can't help thinking of General Gordon and his appalling end, the crumbling of the colonial dream of benevolent Christian rule over the four corners of the world – if it ever could be benevolent while enforced and administered not by storybook heroes, but by real, beef-eating, bloody-handed men.

13

Westminster

Aloft and Below

My first view of westminster cathedral is from the upper deck of a number 36 bus. It's quite a shock. Whatever I've been expecting of the Mother Church of Roman Catholics in England and Wales, it wasn't this gigantic scalloped Byzantine godown of a building, boldly banded in red and white stripes, with a great phallic tower rising from its northwest corner into the brisk grey London sky. I have to swallow and remind myself that Westminster Cathedral was built at the turn of the twentieth century, not much more than a hundred years ago, to designs that were drawn up during the great era of public buildings for Empire and for Great Britain, the Workshop of the World. London's St Pancras Station, Victoria & Albert Museum and Palace Theatre, Glasgow's Kelvingrove Art Gallery, Manchester's Midland Hotel, Liverpool University's Victoria Building . . . all huge, all massively impressive, and all red, red, red.

As soon as I get inside the west door of the cathedral, that tower is a magnet. I squeeze into a lift along with several other riders, and we clank slowly up to the viewing gallery near the top. An enormous view opens from this eyrie over abodes of God and Mammon. Eastward rises the gold stone tower of Westminster Abbey with the ghostly needle of the Shard looking over its shoulder, the MI6 building hunched by the river, Millbank Tower, Tate Britain, and St Paul's Cathedral dome peeping between two giant cranes and two dour black and brown office blocks. Beyond them the City of Oz – Canary Wharf with its pale cluster of monster towers. To the south stand the V&A, Earl's Court, Victoria Station and Chelsea Bridge; just north, and far below, the grey bulk of Buckingham Palace, and beyond that in the murky distance to the northwest the white arches of Wembley Stadium.

Reading the instructions for summoning the lift to return earth-wards, I learn several ways of saying 'Press Button Once':

'Naciśnij raz przycisk!'

'Nazhmite kinopkin tol'ko odin raz!'

'Aghfas il-buttuna darba biss!'

'I have been out to the Holy Land with the Carmelites,' red-robed greeter Mildred Piper confides. 'I've stood on the spot where Elijah watched the cloud! I've seen where Elijah fought the Great Beast of Baal! That's what one can do today. But things were so different for or-dinary people when this cathedral was built. London was full of Irish navvies then, aliens in an alien town, and there were very few Catholic places of worship for them. It was one of the main reasons that Car-dinal Manning decided to build the cathedral, and also why it's of such a huge capacity.'

When the Benedictine monks of Westminster Abbey reclaimed the nearby swamp of Bulinga Fen, it was the start of a remarkable story. 'Tothill Fields' became the site of a market and a fairground. After the Reformation swept away the monks and their works, a maze, a pleasure garden and a bull-baiting ring took their turns here, followed by a suc-cession of more or less miserable prisons. When the last of these, a circular jailhouse for women and boys known as Tothill Fields Bride-well, was demolished in 1885, the land lay empty for ten years, a sad patch of waste. But Cardinal Henry Edward Manning, Archbishop of Westminster, had his eye on it, having bought it for the purpose of erecting a cathedral grand enough to be the symbol of the recently rehabilitated Roman Catholic Church in England and Wales.

Penal laws and vehement popular bigotry had made life extremely difficult for devout British Catholics since the Reformation. But these penalties and prejudices had gradually been relaxing, and public opinion softening, so that by the mid-nineteenth century Catholics enjoyed the basic civil rights of practising their religion freely, voting, holding land and property, and sitting as Members of Parliament. In 1850 Pope Pius IX declared the former Roman Catholic hierarchy – thirteen sees and the Diocese of Westminster – restored in England. A sectarian backlash followed, with effigy-burning and smashing of Roman Catholic church windows. But it passed, and by the late 1880s a Mother Church in London did not seem so scandalous an idea. Apart from anything else, disastrous potato famines and general poverty in rural Ireland had seen an enormous influx of Irish migrants to London and the other major industrial cities of the UK. Nearly a million Roman Catholics of Irish birth were now living in Britain, over a hundred thousand of them in London, and they had few churches and no focal point for their religion.

Cardinal Manning, originally a High Anglican clergyman and widower who had converted to Catholicism in 1851, died before his cathedral could be started, but his remains were reburied there in 1907 after its completion. And what a palace of prayer it turned out to be. Construction was driven by Manning's successor, Cardinal Herbert Vaughan. Cardinal Vaughan was a cradle Catholic, one of thirteen siblings of whom all five daughters became nuns and six of the eight boys priests – three of them bishops. The poor man never had a chance, it seems. He certainly worked tirelessly to raise money for the building of the cathedral in 1895–1903, choosing the very best professionals and materials to create a great Byzantine tanker for the conveyance of souls to a Roman Catholic Heaven.

I stand inside the west door and watch the world pass by me. Westminster Cathedral is free to enter. Camera-wielding tourists bob in, clock the lights and the marble, go click, bob out again. Women in twos and threes stand, sit and kneel together in the side chapels, interspersing their prayers with sibilant gossip. A pair of red-faced street drinkers totter into the seats at the back and stare challengingly around them. A creased middle-aged woman sits alongside, her velvet collar stained dark by lank greasy hair, six large plastic bags piled on the nearby chairs. A quiet solo figure hunches in despair by the north wall, man or woman, it's hard to say.

The cathedral's day-to-day clientele embodies the idea of Roman Catholicism as a form of faith very much rooted in the secular world, as much about socializing as it is about devotion. Yet there's absolutely nothing humdrum about the house that Cardinal Vaughan built. I've never seen, in these islands, such a flamboyant cathedral. The back-to-basics of the 'Great Scrape', the Victorian eye for the good taste of pure bare ecclesiastical stone, meant nothing to anyone who had to do with the building of this cathedral. If Wells, York, Canterbury, Durham had all their medieval frescoes and shrines, their jewels and gold, magically restored, they might give Westminster a run for its money. But it's doubtful. When you can see Heaven reflected in 120 different shades of marble polished to glassy perfection, why settle for anything duller? And yet . . . this cathedral is not even half the building it set out to be.

The architect engaged for the Westminster Cathedral project was John Francis Bentley, a Roman Catholic convert. The foundation stone was laid in 1895, the main fabric completed by 1903. Mosaic and marble, inside and out, were to be the wonder and the crowning glory of Westminster. But Bentley had died in 1902, leaving no finished mosaics, and very few mosaic designs. Archbishop Vaughan died the following year. The incomplete cathedral had lost its two chief helmsmen. So it was others who designed and installed the fittings, the items of detail that dazzle eyes and minds.

Over the decades money has run low, the principals have changed, other priorities have emerged. In a city and a diocese so beset with social and financial problems, would so much money, time and ingenuity be better spent elsewhere than in finishing off the interior decorations of the cathedral? Westminster Cathedral was incomplete when it was officially opened in 1903. It remains in that state. Every now and then there are calls for the diocese to get on with it, to spend the millions and finish what they started. But so far, it's not happened.

Looking round, the eye and mind are in a quandary – is the 'unfinished' cathedral interior light, or dark? It's a building neatly cut into two by a horizontal line about halfway up the walls. Below, all is dazzling marble, lights, colours, inlays, glittering brass, gold and silver, and constant movement from tourists, worshippers, priests and acolytes.

Above the line, the upper half of the building is a monochrome vault, a soft, sooty grey-black, and utterly still. Millions of dark, unadorned bricks send back a message of vast yet weightless space. This is the immense night sky of the cathedral, which would be transfigured into a vivid, intensely coloured Heaven if the completists had their way.

The marbles of the lower cathedral gleam in the light of the chandeliers and candles. The man charged with procuring them was William Brindley, a Derbyshire stone carver whose firm of stonemasons, Farmer & Brindley, lay just across the Thames from the cathedral site. Brindley had surmised that coloured marble was the coming thing in monumental architecture. In the 1880s and 90s he and his wife travelled all over Greece, Turkey and North Africa, following a hunch he had that there must still exist dozens of quarries that had been used by the Romans and abandoned before they were fully worked out. He negotiated concessions to work these quarries wherever he found them – in the Greek mainland and islands, and in the North African desert – and the brilliantly shaded and coloured marbles made their way by overland and sea routes to London and the stoneworks of Farmer & Brindley.

The fourteen Stations of the Cross placed at intervals along the aisles are so striking that I have to follow their via dolorosa to its sombre conclusion before I embark on a wider circuit of the cathedral. When in 1914 Eric Gill's designs for the Stations of the Cross panels were accepted, the salacious aspects of his personal life, particularly his incestuous relationships with his daughters, were unsuspected. He was

WORCESTER
Dramatic striped effect
of contrasting stonework
in the chapter house at
Worcester Cathedral,
its walls banded in pink
and green sandstones.

WORCESTER

Above: The crypt of Bishop Wulfstan's early Norman cathedral, built of beautiful Cotswold limestone carried to Worcester by barges on the River Severn.

GLOUCESTER

Below: In a stained-glass window in the north ambulatory, Charles Eamer Kempe's dreamy Mary of Bethany wipes Christ's feet with her hair – one of many sensual depictions of this episode in Britain's cathedrals.

HEREFORD

Below: Funeral finery, hidden tragedy: Alexander Denton (d. 1576) and his first wife Anne, who died in 1566 aged seventeen while giving birth to a stillborn infant.

Bottom: Goggle-eyed heads, cats and dragons, a Green Man spewing giant leaves: the remarkable work of the twelfth-century Herefordshire School of Sculpture.

GLOUCESTER

Above: Abode of 'Saint' Harry Potter and Hogwarts School of Witchcraft and Wizardry, the cloisters of Gloucester Cathedral, roofed in with intricate fan vaulting.

St Magnus

Left: South doorway whittled by nine hundred years of Orcadian weather.

Above: For whom the bell tolls: the Kirkwall hangman's double ladder.

Right: One of the slit-like passages within the walls of St Magnus Cathedral.

St Davids

Below: St Davids is unique in its positioning: rather than beckoning you afar from a high perch, the cathedral lies sunk in a hollow, invisible from the nearby sea, so that your first sight is looking down upon it.

Inset: A Green Man strange and fierce, one of the misericord carvings in the quire.

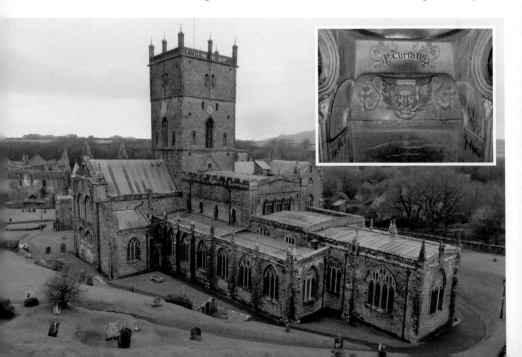

St Paul's

Left: John Wesley raises the hand of admonishment in St Paul's churchyard, a famous location for outdoor preaching and demonstration down the years.

Westminster

Above: Architect Sir Jeremy Dixon contemplates the working model made for J. F. Bentley, architect of Westminster Cathedral.

Below: A blaze of light and colour below; a dark vault above, mysterious and profound.

Armagh C of I

Above left: Dean Gregory Dunstan tests an old organ pipe in Armagh's Archbishop Robinson Public Library.

Above right: Enigmatic stone carvings in the crypt of St Patrick's C of I cathedral.

Armagh RC

Below left: The twin towers of St Patrick's RC cathedral rise from Tealach na Licci, the Sandy Hill.

Below right: Cardinals' galeros or crimson hats hang amid the flamboyant marbles and mosaics of the Roman Catholic cathedral.

LIVERPOOL ANGLICAN

Above: Monolithic aspect of Liverpool's Anglican cathedral, its north wall soaring up from the rim of St James's Gardens.

Right: Stewardess Mary Rogers, who sacrificed her own life during a shipwreck in 1899, commemorated in the Lady chapel stair windows.

Below: Wall memorial to Bishop David Sheppard, cricketer and social reformer.

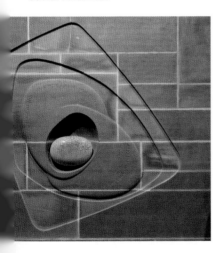

LIVERPOOL CATHOLIC

Right: The Mersey Funnel: reminiscent of Ely Cathedral's fourteenth-century Lantern, the hollow Crown of Thorns spire and colourful roof lantern fill the circular Catholic cathedral with intense light.

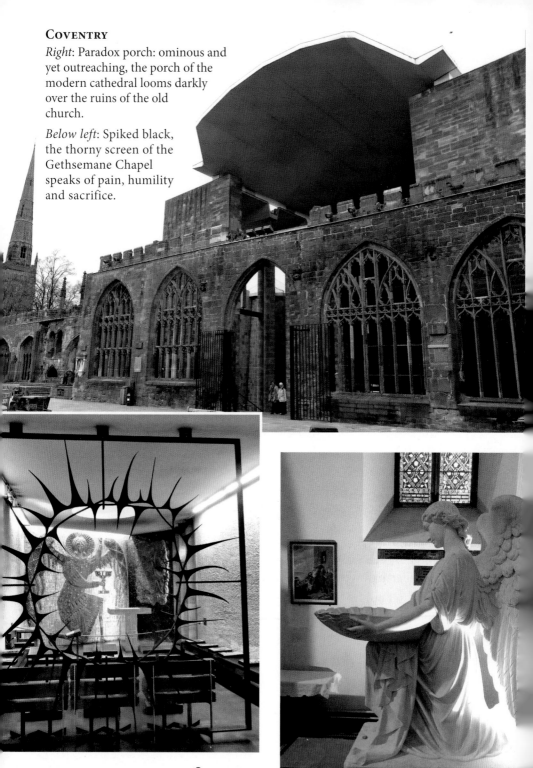

COVENTRY

Right: Paradox porch: ominous and yet outreaching, the porch of the modern cathedral looms darkly over the ruins of the old church.

Below left: Spiked black, the thorny screen of the Gethsemane Chapel speaks of pain, humility and sacrifice.

INVERNESS

Right: The angel font in Inverness Cathedral, a calm and thoughtful presence in cold white marble.

known simply as a brilliant designer and artist recently converted to Roman Catholicism – and as Gill had yet to make a reputation as a sculptor, the fee he charged was a very modest £765 for all fourteen Stations. The panels of beautiful white limestone flecked with grey, from Hopton Wood quarries in Derbyshire, were carved in low relief in Gill's Ditchling studio in Sussex, and finished off in situ in Westminster Cathedral. They feature Gill's wonderful Arts and Crafts figures, soldiers and Christ alike serene and graceful even in the worst throes of the Crucifixion saga. Panel 1 is notable for an arrogant Pilate in a tremendous flowing cloak dipping his long white fingers in a bowl of water, and Panel 10 for the figure of Jesus, bared to the waist as he is stripped of his clothes by soldiers with aggressively intrusive hands, which Gill modelled on himself. Panel 14, 'The body of Jesus is laid in the tomb', shows a corpse etiolated in death, carried by two disciples with Mary following, their expressions marrying calm acceptance and deep desolation.

After the unveiling of the first four Stations in June 1915, letter-writers to the *Universe* and the *Observer* had a field day of indignation. 'Grotesque,' they blared, 'undevotional, primitive, cold, hideous, pagan!' Others found Gill's work 'dignified, superb, restrained'. Time has been a lot kinder to the Stations, if not to Eric Gill and his private malefactions.

The chapels that open off the side aisles of the cathedral are arranged to lead a traveller through the Christian pilgrimage from Baptism to Resurrection. I set out on the journey from the baptistery in the south-west corner with its octagonal marble font, big enough to bathe a grown-up or two. In the Chapel of St Gregory and St Augustine a woman kneels rapt in prayer, a rosary entwined in her fingers, next to the floor slab under the red galero or cardinal's hat of Archbishop Basil Hume (1923–99). This tradition of hanging a cardinal's hat up over his tomb until it rots to fragments symbolizes the crumbling of all human aspirations and vanities to dust, a rather gentler version of the memento mori tomb where the effigy of the departed in full glory of armour, court dress or ecclesiastical robes is shown recumbent above the naked corpse or skeleton that lies beneath such vanities.

The marbles and mosaics in the Chapel of St Gregory and St Augustine were installed in 1916 and paid for by a Roman Catholic convert and judge, Lord Brampton, with £8,500 (about £300,000 today). He intended the chapel to be a chantry where prayers would be said for the souls of himself and his wife for evermore, a throwback to pre-Reformation practices. The mosaics are good examples of the two styles employed in the cathedral: the classic mosaic style composed of 'tesserae' or tiny squares of glass or ceramic; and the 'opus sectile' style of cutting out shapes from marble, glass or mother-of-pearl, sometimes painting them, and fitting them together like a jigsaw to form a picture. The story told in the Chapel of St Gregory and St Augustine is the conversion of heathen England. Above the altar in opus sectile is Augustine, the pioneering saint sent from Rome, in conversation with a somewhat cynical-looking King Aethelbert. Over the windows in mosaic tesserae are the saints who kept the faith alive during the Dark Ages: Benedict, Wilfrid and, notably, Cuthbert, holding the severed head of Oswald, King of the Northumbrians. The gold of the mosaics glitters warmly in the subdued light. Another opus sectile work shows the Judgement of Solomon, the mother pleading for the life of her baby with arms outstretched before the king while a flunky with a sword carelessly swings the chubby infant by its heels.

It was the firm of Clayton & Bell of Regent Street that designed the chapel decorations; John Clayton was briefed by the cathedral's architect J. F. Bentley to avoid the Gothic style to accord with the cathedral's Byzantine mode. But Clayton knew what he was good at, and did it in Gothic anyway. The mosaic designs were sent out to the Murano Glass Company in Venice, who made coloured glass tesserae and attached them to the drawings, face down, to form each design. These open sandwiches of drawing-and-tesserae were then returned to London. From December 1902 till May 1904, craftsman George Bridge and twenty-six assistant mosaicists, all of them young women, gently hammered each section of the design into the place prepared for it on the wall with mallets and flat baulks of boxwood, before stripping off the drawings to reveal the tesserae face-up below. This technique bore fruit in the glowing colours of these late-Victorian Gothic designs.

The procession of chapels continues anticlockwise. In St Patrick's Chapel the saint in bold modern mosaic holds a shamrock of pearlescent green. The mosaics in St Paul's Chapel were designed in the 1960s by Boris Anrep, a Gauloise-smoking Russian military hero nearing his eightieth year, who'd commanded a troop of Cossacks in the First World War. They show St Paul, shipwrecked off Malta, calmly swimming away from the calamity. But the reality of such wrecks hits with full force in the chapel dedicated to St Andrew, where grey-green fish and red mottled crabs inlaid in the floor continue the sea theme. The chapel's cross is no artwork of silver or gold, but something in its way more priceless. It's the simplest of all designs, a shaft crossed with a spar, square in section, of varnished and smearily painted wood. Italian carpenter Francesco Tuccio made it, and hundreds of others similar, out of the strakes of wooden refugee boats from North Africa that he found cast up on the beaches of his native island of Lampedusa from 2013 onwards, along with the bodies of people who had drowned after shipwreck as they tried with desperation to reach the promised land of Europe.

'Cardinal Manning and Cardinal Vaughan, between them,' says architect Jeremy Dixon, 'commissioned four Gothic-style cathedrals before Vaughan finally settled on this one. He went for a neo-Byzantine style, a basilica form, because he wanted a wide nave for processions and ritual, and to fit more people in.'

I have broken off from the pilgrimage route among the chapels to meet Jeremy, who with his professional's eye and sensitive understanding considers Westminster Cathedral one of his favourite buildings.

'The difference between the two styles', he explains, 'is that with

Gothic all the detail is actually carved into the fabric itself, the stone the building is made out of, as in all those medieval cathedrals. So it's time-consuming and expensive. Whereas with the Byzantine, you put up the fabric of the church and then attach the detail to it. It's much quicker and cheaper. Also, Vaughan didn't want a retro style for his cathedral that could be compared unfavourably with the real Gothic deal, Westminster Abbey, just along the road.

'The structure is essentially three square bays, end to end, each under a flat dome. The domes exert an enormous outward thrust. To counter that and support them you've got the square pillars of the nave, immense things that are really buttresses. In Gothic cathedrals the buttresses are set on the outside, but here, like all the great European basilicas, they're inside the building.'

We stand halfway up the nave, taking in the cathedral. The really bizarre aspect of this building, all light and colour below, all dark immensity aloft, strikes me anew. This is where a professional architect such as Jeremy Dixon can pinpoint magic and mystery.

'The most poetic thing for me about the place', he says after gazing around and overhead, 'is that its magical appearance, the marble below and the dark vaults above, is in fact a creative accident, one of the best examples I know, resulting from there not being enough money to cover the whole thing in mosaic. The detail just stops, halfway up the wall. It's a cathedral of halves: incredible detail in the bottom half, and plain bricks above, blackened by the smoke from incense and all those candles. You get a clear sense of two worlds – the world below, full of colour and detail and human movement, held down by the hanging lights, and then, above that, a still world of completely mysterious dark. The tremendous darkness of the whole of the upper church, the strength and simplicity of the materials, gives a degree of abstraction which you don't get in Gothic churches, and which I find very appealing.'

Jeremy leads me back to the southwest corner of the cathedral and the Chapel of St Gregory and St Augustine. From here he indicates the shiny surface of the marble sheets applied to the square nave pillars.

'I'm a great believer in these creative accidents, and an excellent example here is the effect of these sheets of marble. The main feature that catches the eye is their simplicity. They're not embellished in any way; they directly convey the essence of the material. In this respect they come quite close to the modern sensibility that's developed around minimalism. And the quality of the marble is extraordinary. A hundred and twenty different types, and each has its own individual colour and pattern.'

Jeremy indicates two slabs of marble laid side by side on the floor of the Chapel of St Gregory and St Augustine. 'See how these two panels have been bookmatched?' The twin patterns are almost, but not quite, mirror images of one another, a pair of outrushing forms, black streaks on grey, that might be wintry trees, or cold fires burning, or rather more sinisterly a brotherhood of insectoid pagan priests extending spiky arms skywards. 'The marble has been sawn to expose these adjoining faces' – Jeremy holds his palms together, then opens them out side by side like the paired pages of a book – 'then they've been smoothed and polished.' He points away east down the aisle. 'Look at the way the different marbles – grey, green, white, red – proceed into the distance in squares and rectangles and open frames, the varying shades and shapes drawing the eye on and away.

'The colour is all in the marble, not in the windows – there's no coloured glass. And the windows themselves are few and small. So actually there's not too much light coming in. It's a clever trick. You come in out of the light outside with the irises of your eyes closed down, and they gradually open in this subdued light to give the interior the monumental quality of a great Roman ruin, one of those Lateran churches, perhaps – the solemnity of something very early.'

Up on the first-floor balcony stands a glass case that holds cathedral architect J. C. Bentley's 1:48 scale wooden model of Westminster Cathedral. The choice of woods was that available to a country with a global colonial reach – Kauri pine from the Antipodes, polished to a softly gleaming chocolate brown, footed on a base of mahogany from the Americas. Jeremy and I peer in through the inch-high windows to see pillars, floors and walls all exquisitely reproduced. 'It comes to pieces,' Jeremy says. 'See this little hook and hinge? It's a practical tool, not just a pretty model. A section of tower could be taken off, or a bit of wall swung open, to demonstrate a point while Bentley was discussing the construction with the builder or the engineer.'

We lean on the balcony rail beside the model, looking down at the nave of the real church. From a far corner plainchant arises, the mournful modulations calling up echoes of a pre-Reformation world. People sit dotted around, bowed in prayer or private pain. The bag-woman with wild greasy hair mutters to herself. Above these figures the hanging lights cast their dozens of interconnecting nebulae, reflected in marble and gold.

'When you consider the richness and variety of the materials here,' muses Jeremy Dixon, 'the sheer cost of sourcing and collecting and transporting them all across the world – well, it would be impossible nowadays. It's the sort of commission that as an architect you long for, everything to be designed so as to fit together, right down to the chairs and the knives and forks, so to speak. I might dream of making a building such as this, but you just couldn't do it these days. It would be much too expensive. And that's a remarkable thought, considering that the brief for building this place not much more than a hundred years ago was to make it quick and cheap.'

Next day is gloomy and threatens rain. Inside Westminster Cathedral the upper circle of lamps on each chandelier has been lit. The coruscation of these higher bulbs throws the smoke-blackened upper works of the building into even more Stygian gloom. Under its vault I resume my pilgrimage round the chapels.

Beside the pulpit of marble as streaky as Danish blue cheese, a transept window arch carries the mosaic image of Mary Magdalene. A beautiful young woman, proud in face and body, she stands outside a little house on stilts, labelled 'Domus Pharis', the Pharisee's house. One hand keeps the ends of her long curling tresses under control, the other holds the jar of expensive oil with which she intends to anoint the feet of Christ before wiping them with that thick rope of hair. She looks at once sexy, sensual and spiritual. It's a hard trick that the artist has pulled off here.

The barrel roof of the Chapel of the Blessed Virgin Mary at the southeast corner of the cathedral is covered in tiny gold tesserae and embellished with six magnificently winged angels. In the apse roof the Tree of Life shelters Mary, with a backdrop of Tower Bridge and the Tower of London, and opposite her St Peter, patron saint of Westminster, is backed by Westminster Cathedral. The arches of the high windows are filled with mosaics of fruit, flowers and foliage, a burst of colour and fertility.

Across the nave the Chapel of St Joseph contains a wonderful mosaic, perhaps the one that speaks most clearly to my tastes. In brilliant colours it shows a group of Italian craftsmen carving the marble for the cathedral. Heavily moustachioed, with comically macho frowns, they wear biblical clothes, but sport twentieth-century hairstyles. Chisels and planes are wielded. Two men cut a streaky block of marble with a massive bow saw, while their greybeard boss measures things off with a giant pair of calipers. This mosaic, designed by Christopher Hobbs and full of humour and vigour, was installed in 2006, a good century after the cathedral was consecrated – a reminder of the ongoing intention to finish things off.

In another of the chapels on this north side of the cathedral, Cardinal Vaughan lies in marble state under his hanging galero (now faded to pink and crusted with dust) within a gilded cage of wrought railings. This Vaughan chantry doubles as a Chapel of Thomas Becket. The Friends of Westminster Cathedral raised £200,000, much of it from the USA, for Christopher Hobbs to decorate the chapel with exquisitely done flowers and roundels in the vault. A depiction of Becket's martyrdom above the cardinal's effigy shows the four murdering knights pointing their swords at the back of Becket's tonsured head, the tip of one blade already buried in the saintly skull in a scarlet stripe of blood. The assassins' noses are red with wine and choler, the wicked glint of their eyes suggested by cunningly placed tesserae of white.

Down in the northwest lies the Chapel of the Holy Souls, decorated to J. F. Bentley's orders in 'a severe and very Greek style'. George Bridge and his twenty-six 'young lady mosaicists' from the Chapel of St Gregory and St Augustine embellished this chapel, too. They made the tesserae, and inserted them directly over an eighteen-month period (June 1902–November 1903) into a putty of lime and boiled oil with which they'd prepared the walls and vault.

Bentley and his co-designer William Symons were given a free hand by the donors, Mr and Mrs Robert Walmsley. They came up with an interpretation of the doctrine of Purgatory that looks funereally Victorian rather than Byzantine: deep dark grey and green marble, a pattern of black and white lozenges in the floor. On the south wall the old Adam stands trapped against the Tree of Knowledge, wrapped around by the tail of the Evil One in the form of a great serpent that hisses into his face through a human skull held in its jaws. The foliage of the Tree is tangled in very Celtic-looking strapwork. William Symons intended the figure of Eve to stand opposite Adam on the north wall, but he was over-ruled in favour of a Jesus as romantically handsome as a film star.

On the west wall of the Chapel of the Holy Souls three fresh-faced young men in wide-brimmed floppy hats – Shadrach, Meshach and Abednego – step out of the burning fiery furnace towards a figure of Jesus with a flagon of wine and a tray of bread. On the east the Archangels Raphael and Michael, bestriding Purgatory, restrain a fearsome panther-faced, black-skinned dragon by tugging it back like a dog on a chain. The sinners in Purgatory, cloaked figures in a sea of flames, crouch and hide their faces from these avenging angels in agonies of self-abasement.

I finish my circuit of the chapels and return to the cathedral nave, my head buzzing with hues of marble and flashes of light, with images of pride brought low, of saints and the saved, of the supreme love and anger of God. Excessive emotions in glass and stone that I need to sit and unpick in a quiet corner, out of the lights and colours. But there's little respite here today. A Mass of the Good Samaritan is due to begin at half past two. It's the feast day of St John Southworth, who was executed at Tyburn in 1654, the last man to be hanged, drawn and quartered in England simply for being a priest. How fantastically brave these lonely men were, following their consciences through a hostile land, through paranoia and betrayal to a humiliating and unimaginably painful death, half-choked, emasculated, disembowelled, beheaded and chopped to pieces in public.

St John Southworth's body, its pieces sewn together, normally occupies the Chapel of St George and the English Martyrs. But today his glass sarcophagus has been brought into the nave and lies in the centre of a square of brilliant candlelight. The mummified saint wears a lace soutane and dinky black slippers. His face is nothing if not sinister and cinematic; it is a highly polished, solid silver mask, like that of a classy Carnevale clown in Venice, or some progressive 1970s band's album cover.

Catholic schoolchildren from all over the diocese pour into Westminster Cathedral for the Mass of the Good Samaritan. They are amazingly well behaved. By the time the service begins there are three hundred youngsters packed into the chairs. The Mass is celebrated by red-robed priests and a bishop in an outsize golden mitre. The choir, hidden from sight somewhere in the apse, sings gorgeously; the organ thunders fit to make the building's fabric quiver. The martyr in the silver mask lies impassive, his little slippers pointing east, lending a touch of Grand Guignol theatre of horror to proceedings. My head whirls. The dark and light of the cathedral give the impression of the deck of a glorious barge where we sit, looking up from sheltered waters into an enigmatic Heaven, a sky of the softest night, or of a gathering storm.

14

Armagh

Two Lookouts

Across the sea will come Adze-head, crazed in the head,
his cloak with hole for the head, his stick bent in the head.
He will chant impieties from a table in the front of his house;
all his people will answer: So be it, so be it.*

SO THE IRISH DRUIDS PROPHESIED the coming of Christian missionaries clothed in simple one-piece garments, their curly-headed staves in hand. Much mist has gathered around those early years of the Christian presence in Ireland, not least around the provenance of St Patrick, patron saint of the Irish, who arrived in the island around AD 432. He wasn't the first Christian in Ireland. But who was he? Scotsman, Welshman, Cumbrian? Slave, captive, apostle, hustler? What's not in doubt is that Patrick was a mighty and very brave preacher, an effective parable-spinner, and a skilled reader of men, a diplomat who knew how to negotiate with pagan leaders accustomed to giving short shrift to anyone they took against.

It was a lot more than impieties that pioneer Christians like St Patrick brought to the table. In AD 445, some thirteen years into his Irish ministry, Patrick persuaded the local king at Ardmacha (Armagh), one Daire, to let him build a stone church on a sandstone knoll called Druim Saileach, the 'ridge of sallows'. Patrick, always a canny operator, chose a place already of historical, political and spiritual importance to

* Quoted by Muirchú moccu Machtheni, seventh-century Irish monk, in his *Vita Sancti Patricii.*

the local pagan people. Just opposite Druim Saileach was the hill fort of Eamhain Mhacha (Navan hill fort), from which eminence the legendary Lords of Ulster had ruled for a thousand years. Soon the great 'Amen, amen: so be it, so be it' would travel from the little knoll of Druim Saileach into every mouth and every heart in Ireland.

A curve of pleasant but unremarkable roadway leads to the Ridge of Sallows. Armagh's present-day Church of Ireland cathedral occupies a pool of tarmac and lawns on the knoll where Patrick's original building stood. Considering its ancient pedigree, and its resonance in Ireland's religious story, this Protestant cathedral is a modest, even a self-effacing structure. It's plain, stumpy, much patched, the latest in a succession of churches on this spot. I have to remind myself that the predecessors of the cathedral on the knoll have changed their religious complexion, have been destroyed and resurrected, burned and rebuilt again and again as time, war and religious intolerance have swept across the nation. Even on its ridge top above the city, which hugs the hill as though under its protection, St Patrick's C of I Cathedral appears dogged, grey and dug in. And this defensive impression is only reinforced when one climbs the opposing hummock of Tealach na Licci, Sandy Hill, a steeply stepped knoll half a mile away. From here one can hardly see St Patrick's, so low does it crouch among its trees, as though reluctant to take a proper look across the valley at what now crowns Sandy Hill – Armagh's great Victorian Roman Catholic Cathedral of St Patrick. St Patrick's on the Ridge of Sallows occupies roughly the same footprint as the medieval Catholic cathedrals that were there before; the other St Patrick's on Sandy Hill is taller by far and half as long again as its counterpart. Its two west towers face the Protestant cathedral, their pointed spires like two fingers cheekily upraised.

'The foundation is the oldest in the British Isles, a hundred and fifty years older than Canterbury Cathedral,' Robert Somerville of the Friends of Armagh C of I Cathedral tells me over a cup of tea in Armagh

city, 'but I feel it's never been given its due. Armagh was an extraordinary wellspring of mission in those early centuries. Missionaries
went out all over Europe – literally bearing the light of Christianity
through the Dark Ages.' He gestures in the direction of Druim Saileach. 'That cathedral up there hasn't got the grandeur of an English
cathedral – we have no cloisters, no extra room. It *is* modest – definitely low church. The Friends support it as best they can, of
course – they've paid to keep the cathedral website going, for some new
stained glass, for some hangings and a new rail for the altar, for the
choir outing, music-room refurbishment, new kneelers, all that sort of
thing. But the cathedral has been forced into selling off property over
many years, usually for short-term gain. Frankly, it's a small building
with a small congregation, and money's always been tight.'

The Archdiocese of Armagh held sway over the Irish Church pretty
much undisputed until the eleventh century, when a long-drawn-out
contest for the Primacy of All Ireland began between Armagh and
Dublin. After the Anglo-Norman invasion of 1170 the English kings
began to emphasize their power, making each successive Archbishop of
Armagh humbly beg for the properties and revenues of the see. And
the primates themselves, while generally active in trying to keep the
peace between the Norman invaders/settlers and the native Irish, preferred not to live in the shabby city, so often a target for raids, but based
themselves at their luxurious palace at Drogheda fifty miles away. After
the Reformation the Roman Catholic archbishops were little more than
ciphers as far as active influence went, while the Protestant archbishops
that took their place were equally reluctant to take up residence in
Armagh itself. The city became neglected, a half-forgotten outpost of
its own see.

As for the cathedral on the Ridge of Sallows, through the turbulent
centuries it suffered plundering and burning by opposing Irish chief-
tains, by marauding Danes, by Normans, by English settlers and the
Irish opposing them. In 1641 the Irish rose against the English Crown
and the Protestant 'planters' who had been given their land. The

following year local rebel leader Sir Phelim O'Neill burned the cathedral once again, along with the whole town.

> Ardmacha was burned – the Cathedral clogas [belfry], its bells, its organ, and its glass windows, and the whole city with its white-lime houses, along with all the learned books of the English on Divinity, logic and philosophy . . . The weather was warm and the wind from the east, and the flames reached the Cathedral.*

Once more the cathedral was rebuilt, but money was so tight and rents from the impoverished tenants so low that half a century later the glass was still missing from the windows, and the churchyard gates and five out of the six cathedral bells had yet to be replaced. Towards the end of the following century Dean Hamilton had to threaten his parishioners with legal action to get them to deliver the due tithe of one-tenth of their hay and flax. But by then Archbishop Richard Robinson was at the helm, and already embarked on his mission to transform the neglected city into a seat worthy of its status as the ecclesiastical capital of Ireland.

'In 1004, when the High King of Ireland, Brian Boru, came here to acknowledge the supremacy of the Church at Armagh, he left a pile of gold weighing thirty ounces on the high altar.'

So says Gregory Dunstan, Dean of Armagh, who has been waiting to meet me by the west door of St Patrick's. Trim and gentle, English-born, he presides over a cathedral with a majestic past and an uncertain future. St Patrick's Cathedral has no parish. Most Church of Ireland people naturally gravitate to their parish churches, and those who come to the cathedral do so, Dean Dunstan says, because they like its particular style of worship.

* Quoted in the diary of Fr Tarlach O'Mellan, a chaplain in Sir Phelim O'Neill's army.

We walk inside. It's a slender building; the impression is of a nipped-in waist, and a crimson and white netting of ribs overhead in the barrel roof of the nave. Whitewashed walls bear witness to how the 'Great Scrape' of the Victorians, back to the bare stone, passed St Patrick's by. 'What we're seeing is not the ancient foundation, of course,' says the dean, 'it's what Lord John Beresford got his architect Lewis Cottingham to do to the cathedral in the 1840s.'

In a stained-glass window on the south side of the choir I spy Archbishop Richard Robinson holding a miniature of the public library he provided for Armagh, one of many splendid public edifices in the city built by this Yorkshire-born ecclesiastic, Ireland's grandest primate by a very long chalk. Richard Robinson was translated from the see of Kildare to the Archbishopric of Armagh in 1765. The Archbishops of Armagh still had their principal residence at Drogheda at that date, but Robinson – now the Primate of All Ireland, and soon to be created Baron Rokeby – set about using his riches and authority to transform the bedraggled city of Armagh.

The name of the city and county of Armagh reverberated again and again in the news while I was in my twenties and thirties, a name associated with the bombings, shootings and sectarian intolerances of Northern Ireland's Troubles. Every camera shot of the city reinforced the notion of a grim grey place. It is a shock, and a healthy slap of reality, to find a neat little town full of eighteenth-century architecture, most of its best features the legacy of Archbishop Richard Robinson and his wealth, pride and ambition.

As well as repairing the old cathedral, Archbishop Robinson built Armagh a public library and a new prison, an infirmary, and the wonderful scientific venture of Armagh Observatory. He had the Mall, a new and beautiful park, laid out on the public space where bears had been baited and horses raced. And after taking a look at the poky archbishop's residence on offer in the heart of the city on English Street, he built himself a splendid palace on the outskirts in parkland that had once been the site of the Franciscan friary.

Walking the paths of the archbishop's extensive grounds – now a public park, the Palace Demesne – on a steamy damp evening I pass under great lime and oak trees, past the walled garden and the glass-house, climbing a slope to the stables (now a classy restaurant) and the palace itself, a great foursquare block of neoclassical consequence. Standing modestly to one side are the picturesquely ruined arches of the Franciscan Abbey of St Peter and St Paul. When the stones of the friary were reshaped for use in a new Presbyterian meeting house in the city, Jonathan Swift commended the masons for 'chipping the pop-ery out of the stones'.

Archbishop Robinson intended the crest of the Ridge of Sallows to be an enclave of light and learning centred on St Patrick's Cathedral. The university that he envisaged for the hill never materialized, but the externally modest, extremely tasteful buildings abutting the cathedral are part of his legacy, notably the Archbishop Robinson Public Library that contains eight thousand of the primate's books. This quiet capsule of a library, built in 1771, is a place where I could quite happily lose my-self, day or night, in the rich fusty smell of old leather bindings and even older paper, the ordered shelves and solicitous enquiries of the librarians as they proffer white kid gloves with which to turn the pages of old records, old bibles, old diaries and journals. Here are huge mon-astic iron handbells, treasure hunts and puzzle sheets for kids, and a priceless first edition of TRAVELS *into several Remote Nations of the WORLD* by one Lemuel Gulliver, 'First a Surgeon and then a Captain of several SHIPS' – Jonathan's Swift's own copy, scribbled over with the author's notes and corrections.

Just round the curve of the hilltop at number 5 Vicar's Hill is Rob-inson's Diocesan Registry, built in 1772, a very clever amalgamation of two octagonal rooms to aid air circulation and avoid the damp that was so deadly to paper records. Nowadays it displays a tremendous timeline of the accession of the Archbishops and Abbots of Armagh, 125 of them from the first, St Patrick, in AD 444, to the current incumbent, Richard Lionel Clarke, in 2012. Archbishop Robinson's portrait in the

Registry museum doesn't do him any favours – it shows a suspicious-looking man in a full wig glancing sideways at the viewer, his little mouth pinched in. Ill-favoured or not, though, Robinson poured out funds for the benefit of Armagh as well as for his personal glory – £30,000 of his own money, about £6 million in today's terms.

When Archbishop Lord John George Beresford (Eton and Christ Church), son of the Marquess of Waterford, succeeded to the Primacy of All Ireland in 1822, he found the cathedral in a parlous state. The architect that Beresford engaged, Lewis Nockalls Cottingham, was one of the best, and Cottingham straightened up the crippled old cathedral on the Ridge of Sallows, bracing the outward-leaning arcades with heated iron rods, taking off the little stumpy spire and rebuilding the tower supports, and letting more light in by unblocking the clerestory windows. He also restored the exterior in sandstone.

'English Perpendicular windows,' comments Dean Dunstan. 'This was Cottingham's idea of what a cathedral should be like. Critics tend to say it's too clean, too neat.' William Makepeace Thackeray, visiting in 1843, found Cottingham's work 'neat and trim as a lady's drawing room'.

Marble monuments shine palely in the cathedral's subdued light. Thomas Molyneux MD (1661–1733) is a calm presence near the door, perusing a book on a five-foot pedestal. No floor in his grandson's house was strong enough to support the good doctor's tonnage in white marble. So in 1839 he was brought to the cathedral and installed in just the wrong place, blocking everyone's passage between the west door and the north aisle, a thundering nuisance too grand to be got rid of.

Just along the aisle, Archbishop William Stuart (1755–1822) kneels in high relief. The son of the 3rd Earl of Bute, Stuart was an unpopular figure who insisted that his clergy live in their parishes, but himself lived in London. On 6 May 1822, during a bout of illness, he drank a dose of physic administered by his wife. She thought she was giving her husband a draught against a stomach upset, but in fact it was an embrocation of laudanum and camphorated spirits, for external application only. The archbishop died of this mistake, not pleasantly.

Nearby, as if deliberately placed as a counterweight to the marble hagiography, the stumpy Tandragee Idol stands grinning with puffed-out cheeks. He has two vestigial horns and a little crest on top of his head, a squat figure of coarse granite that was perhaps a thousand years old when Jesus Christ was born in Palestine. The idol's right hand grasps his left shoulder, an indication that he could be Nuada of the Silver Arm, King of the fairy folk Tuatha Dé Danann who ruled in Ireland in a grand mythic past.

St Patrick's is a cathedral with strong ties to the military past. In the Regimental Chapel of the Royal Irish Fusiliers there are proud and fond memorials to those who died in the First World War. The regiment was known as the Faughs, from their war cry of 'Faugh-a-ballagh!' – 'Clear the way!' The chapel holds a simple wooden cross, brought back from France where it marked the grave of Lieutenant Colonel John Lenox Conyngham, commanding officer of the Connaught Rangers, who was killed on the Somme in September 1916. Dean Dunstan pauses in front of this humble cross, and glances across at me. 'The Sixth Connaught Rangers were raised in Catholic West Belfast. They marched away in 1914 to cheering crowds. But when they returned at the end of the war – those that did – no one wanted to know them. The Easter Rising had happened in between.'

In one sense the Easter Rising of 1916 was just another rising, one more in the long line of Irish nationalist rebellions against the Crown. It was soon snuffed out, its leaders shot, its few adherents forced on to the back foot once again. But this rising was different. Popular opinion in Ireland, outraged by a long-drawn-out series of executions of imprisoned men, began to kick back in the first wave of what became known as 'the Troubles'. A War of Independence from 1919 to 1921 saw the armed guerrilla forces of the IRA force the British Army and government to the negotiating table and a treaty guaranteeing Irish independence as a free state. Pro- and anti-Treaty factions then fought an excruciating and deeply damaging Civil War (1922–3) that ended in defeat for the IRA and confirmation of the Irish Free State.

One intransigent problem remained for the island of Ireland: the six Northern Ireland counties of Down, Antrim, Derry, Tyrone, Fermanagh and Armagh, still declared to be part of the United Kingdom and separated by an international border from the twenty-six counties of what soon became the Irish Republic. It was never as simple as: Unionists = Protestants = pro-British; Nationalists = Catholics = anti-British. Neither was the resurgence of the Troubles as time-specific as 1969 or 1970. In a country of two often antipathetic cultures, native Irish and Anglo incomers, sparks had been spurting for eight hundred years. In the Robinson Library's archives there is a letter written in 1838 by Dean Jackson to Lord John Beresford, the primate, complaining about the 12 July celebrations by Protestant crowds of the 1692 Battle of the Boyne, with 'orange flags being displayed on the cathedral tower, and the bells rung from 12 o'clock at night till 8 in the evening of the 12th. The worst people of Armagh were responsible. We shall be considered as having lent ourselves to the bad passions of the people.'

When the second wave of the Troubles engulfed Northern Ireland in the late 1960s and it seemed incumbent upon people to take sides, there was the British Army, soon to be seen on the streets of Armagh and all the other towns and cities of Northern Ireland, backing up the almost exclusively Protestant Royal Ulster Constabulary; there were the politicians, the local councillors and community figures with their avowed political and religious affiliations; and there were the ordinary shopkeepers and bar owners and taxi drivers with their Catholic or Protestant surnames and schools and churches, ready targets for anyone who needed a target. In Armagh city alone more than twenty were killed, hundreds more injured, bereaved, mentally and emotionally broken, embittered, alienated. The people of Armagh turned to the two cathedrals, symbols of the two branches of the one religion and of the political and cultural divide, for guidance and an example. If the two figureheads in the public spotlight, the Protestant and Catholic Archbishops of Armagh, had been weaker or more intransigent, far worse disasters could have unfolded. But luckily for peace in Northern Ireland, successive archbishops on both sides played it more or less right.

On the Protestant side, George Simms (Archbishop 1969–80) chaired the first ecumenical meeting between the leaders of Ireland's Protestant and Catholic Churches. His successor John Armstrong (1980–6) was ecumenically minded, too. As for the Catholic Archbishops of Armagh, Cardinal Tomás Ó Fiaich (1977–90) was a man with the common touch, born in the so-called 'bandit country' of South Armagh and often accused of being soft on Republicans, especially the Maze hunger strikers of 1981 – though he spoke out against 'men of violence' on both sides. But it was the two archbishops presiding when the Troubles were coming to an end but before the Good Friday Agreement became a reality in 1998, a ticklish period during which breakdown and chaos often seemed near, who are best remembered as symbolizing the overriding need for the two Churches to show solidarity – the Roman Catholics' Cardinal Cahal Daly (1990–6), and the Church of Ireland's Robin Eames (1986–2006), who had been Cardinal Daly's student at Queen's University. At first the former privately judged the latter a cold fish, and rather too Unionist in sympathies, but these misgivings changed to a cordial relationship. They went to the USA together to demonstrate to Republican sympathizers how Protestants and Catholics could stand united; they appeared on the iconic RTÉ *Late Late Show* together; and they spoke out together against sectarian violence and the recrimination that so often blocked progress.

'It's a long time since the Good Friday Agreement,' says Robert Somerville, looking back. 'But people haven't stopped asking: "Are you Catholics and Protestants still fighting each other?" That annoys me a lot when I hear it. It's to do with race, and politics – it's nothing to do with religion. However, I'll tell you one of the big differences the Troubles brought about. At the time my father died, in 1964, Catholics were not even allowed to enter a Protestant church. If they wanted to speak to someone inside, they had to wait outside the door. But in recent times things have changed. I was present at two services in the cathedral – the funeral of Dean Cassidy and the consecration of Patrick Rooke as Bishop of Tuam – where the cardinal and other Catholic clergy attended. So that's progress.'

'Oh, Jack O'Hare's your man,' I've been told. 'He knows the lot.' And when I meet Jack, upright, elderly, immaculately clad in suit and tie, we sit in a pew at the back of St Patrick's Roman Catholic Cathedral while this knowledgeable guide slowly and methodically unfolds the history of place and church. To Jack O'Hare the personality of every Roman Catholic archbishop since the building of the cathedral is sharp and distinct, and he paints a splendid parade in my mind of these increasingly powerful and persuasive men.

The plan for a new cathedral for Roman Catholics in Armagh was hatched very shortly after the Act of Catholic Emancipation of 1829. Now Roman Catholics could sit as MPs at Westminster, the culmination of a general abandonment of the Penal Laws that had disenfranchised Catholics. Clamour was raised at once for the building of churches and cathedrals to accommodate the overwhelmingly Roman Catholic population of Ireland. As the ancient seat of the Primate of All Ireland, Armagh had particular resonance. Since the Reformation no Roman Catholic bishop had been allowed within three miles of the city, let alone to live or build there. But things changed once William Crolly was appointed archbishop in 1835.

'Oh well,' says Jack O'Hare, 'Dr Crolly wanted to restore the Primacy of Armagh to the centre, as he saw it, of Christian worship in Ireland, and to reconnect it with its Patrician roots; he wanted the Roman Catholic archbishops to come back and live in the city; and more than that, he wanted to build a cathedral – a huge, huge statement for the times. The Earl of Dartry sympathized with the Roman Catholics, and it was he who leased the hilltop to Primate Crolly.'

Now the archbishop had tenure of Tealach na Licci, the Sandy Hill that rose so provokingly (some thought) opposite the Ridge of Sallows where the ancient St Patrick's Cathedral stood. Primate Crolly's first act was to create a Catholic cemetery at the foot of the hill. Under the Penal Laws, leases to Roman Catholics had been restricted to fourteen years, making it impossible to establish graveyards. The dead had had to be buried either formally in Protestant churchyards, or informally in 'fairy forts' (prehistoric ring forts) or other semi-superstitious places. After the cemetery, Archbishop Crolly established a seminary on Sandy Hill. Penny collections were raised among the local Catholic people, the poorest of the poor, and in 1840 the foundation stone of the cathedral – designed by architect Thomas Duff and dedicated, naturally, to St Patrick – was laid on that saint's feast day.

The foundations had been laid and the walls partially raised when the project had to be abandoned in the face of Ireland's terrible disaster of 1845-9, the Great Famine. 'Obviously with people dying of hunger and disease in their thousands, it was an untenable practice to spend the money that had been collected on continuing to build the cathedral,' says Jack. 'So the money was distributed for the relief of the starving poor. Then William Crolly himself died of cholera in 1849, and his successor Paul Cullen was translated five years later to Dublin without ever reviving the project.'

Roddy Hegarty at Armagh's Cardinal Ó Fiaich Library notes, 'Churches for Catholics were few and far between, even then. The dearly beloved Roman Catholic icon of the faithful gathered at some remote Mass rock to celebrate an illegal Mass is actually, I'm sorry to say, largely a myth fostered by nineteenth-century nationalism – although the scarcity of Catholic clergy early in that century did see the establishment of a lot of Mass houses, in barns and old dwellings. In the mid-part of the nineteenth century, of course, money and energy were in short supply following the Famine. But in the latter part of the century there was a big surge in building Roman Catholic churches. Emigrants began to send money home, and so there was more for church-building – including the cathedral.'

Archbishops came and went; construction of Armagh's Roman Catholic cathedral stuttered and stopped and started again. Joseph Dixon (archbishop 1852–66) solicited contributions from everyone who might be persuaded to feel an obligation – his ex-seminarians, priests who'd emigrated, and émigrés intending to return home. In 1854 he oversaw a grand bazaar – first prize, an ivory carving of Raphael's *Madonna di Foligno* donated by Pope Pius IX; second prize, a Sèvres vase donated by Napoleon III. (A grandfather clock, an unclaimed prize from this event, still stands in the cathedral sacristy.) There were more penny collections, not just from local Catholics, but from all over. And under a new architect, James Joseph McCarthy, the cathedral resumed its skyward creep in a Decorated Gothic style, with mock fourteenth-century upper works being added to the mock sixteenth-century walls of Duff's creation, along with those landmark twin towers at the western end.

Jack O'Hare stands up and leads me out on to the terrace outside the west end of the cathedral. We sniff the drizzly Armagh air at the top of a grand flight of steps made to lead the feet of a worshipper from Cathedral Road up to St Patrick's, high on its hillock. 'Archbishop Daniel McGettigan built these steps, all fifty-two of them,' comments Jack, and he gestures along the terrace to the two big white statues with mitres that guard the door. 'There's himself, and Dr Crolly along with him. A very tall, very dignified man, Daniel McGettigan, and very conscious of the importance of his office.'

Archbishop McGettigan (1870–77) had the interior completed with a hammerbeam roof and a Caen stone reredos across the east end. St Patrick's Roman Catholic Cathedral was opened in 1873, 'a bare church, though the walls would have been painted by that time and the ceiling stencilled. It took Michael Logue to get things completed. He finished it all off in proper style.'

The interior of St Patrick's Roman Catholic Cathedral is a bobby-dazzler, one to compete with the flamboyant impact of Westminster

Cathedral. I walk from one end to the other on echoing marble floors that writhe with Celtic interlacing. I'm sure I've seen these patterns before, but I can't think where. I put the question into the mental toaster and dial the five-minute burn. Sure enough, as I stand watching the crimson galero of Archbishop Michael Logue hanging by its slowly decomposing strings, waiting to fall in God's good time, the answer pops up. Those intertwined patterns are from the margins of the Book of Kells, that fabulous early-ninth-century Gospel compilation, the most famous and beautiful book in Ireland. The last time I saw the Book of Kells, under low light in the Old Library of Trinity College, Dublin, must be twenty years ago now. But I haven't forgotten the magnetic power of that 1,200-year-old devotional artwork. It was reproduced here in the cathedral on Sandy Hill to sound a summons from the Golden Age of the deep religious past, and the romantic and nationalist Gaelic Revival of the late nineteenth century.

Arts and Crafts foliage entwines with the ceramic mosaics on the walls. Gold-leaf inlay sparkles in the arches. In the east window an olive-skinned Jesus is crucified between two swarthy robbers, the rogue on the left looking heavenward with a sly half-smile, his colleague on the right scowling earthwards. Dozens of floral bosses and many shamrocks spatter the fan vaulting of the aisles. Roundels in the ceiling show scenes from Irish religious history – baptisms, conversions, miraculous cures and raisings from the dead. The weight and significance of the pre-Reformation past, the pure Irishness of the atmosphere, speak of the new-found confidence of those nineteenth-century Roman Catholics with the yoke of the Penal Laws and of disenfranchisement lifted at last.

In 1887 Michael Logue succeeded Daniel McGettigan as archbishop. 'Small in stature, Michael Logue,' Jack O'Hare says, 'but a giant of a man in personality, and academically.' In 1893 Archbishop Logue was appointed a cardinal, the first of Armagh's archbishops to have that honour. Born in Donegal, he was no son of privilege. In contrast to his contemporary counterpart Robert Knox, Protestant Bishop of Armagh (LLD Cantab., son of the Hon. Charles Knox, grandson of

Viscount Northland of Dungannon Park), Michael Logue's father was a coach driver and blacksmith. At eleven years old Logue learned Latin; at fourteen, Greek; at sixteen he entered Maynooth seminary and gained first place in all his studies. In 1866, aged twenty-five, he accepted the Chair of Theology at the Irish College in Paris, and was ordained priest in December that year.

After being made cardinal in 1893, Archbishop Logue built a cloister and a sacristy at Armagh Cathedral. From there he upgraded the bare, plain interior of the Roman Catholic cathedral into a feast for the eyes. In 1900 he closed the cathedral while he went to Italy and selected the best examples of Carrera and Bologna marble. German glaziers made the stained glass; Italian craftsmen installed the Irish-designed mosaics from floor to ceiling. The Italian artist Oreste Amici hand-painted the ceiling in roundels with portraits of Irish saints. Primate Logue had five marble altars made in Carrera, the pieces numbered, dismantled, brought back to Armagh and reassembled by Italian craftsmen. The aisles were fan-vaulted in Bath stone. A wonderful marble pulpit and cover was installed, along with electric lights. 'Hmm,' remarks Jack O'Hare, 'the electrolier has to be lowered on a rope by someone in the roof if a light bulb needs to be renewed. Some wanted to change that, but the traditionalists said no!'

A striking crucifix on the sanctuary pillar, *The Tree of Life*, has Christ rising from a Y-shaped cross. This bold modern design by Imogen Stuart reflects the renewal and the changes from old practices that took place after the Second Vatican Council of 1962. What a seismic shock that shake-up proved to be. It challenged the unquestioned, and unquestionable, attitude of the priest to his flock, of which his stance at Mass, clerical back turned on the faithful, face hidden as he mumbled to the altar in Latin, was one powerful symbol. From now on the Church was to be less exclusive and more accessible. Mass was to be celebrated in the vernacular rather than in Latin, with the celebrant facing the congregation rather than with his back turned as hitherto.

Cardinal William Conway, Archbishop of Armagh 1963–77, initiated a competition to reorganize Armagh Cathedral accordingly. To accommodate the celebrant in this new stance the altars had to be moved forward, and all the Italian marble at the crossing had to be repositioned or removed. Under Cardinal Tomás Ó Fiaich the light and colourful marble gave way to grim grey granite, a style not to everyone's taste. Neither was the wholesale disposal of the beautiful furnishings, the altar and pulpit of marble cut as delicately as lace, which were broken up and either dumped or sold off, to continue their diminished lives as garden statuary or mantelpiece ornaments.

Nothing lasts too long in the ever-morphing body of a cathedral. By AD 2000, damp was causing the mosaics to crumble off the walls. The window leads needed mending. In the cathedral roof the copper nails were disintegrating in the slates, the wooden rafters rotting under them. The radiators were leaking so much water it could be seen running away at the foot of the hill. Repairs fixed these problems, the dour Wicklow granite of the Ó Fiaich era was swept away in yet another refurbishment in 2003, and St Patrick's hunkered down to await the next in its never-ending procession of changes, somewhere along the line.

Great brass gates stand at the east end of the cathedral. At the other end, a massive organ fills the west gallery with its 3,500 pipes, including a 'trompeta real', a fabulous noise-maker whose pipes stick far out at one side like a Hell's Angel's fantasy exhaust. The cathedral is lucky to have had the services of Baron Georges Minne, a Belgian maestro, as organist and also carillonneur since 1959. The spire above the organ contains the carillon of thirty-nine bells, from fourteen pounds to a monster weighing over two tons. The other spire holds the Great Bell, even weightier at three and a half tons, embossed with Irish symbols: a round tower, an oak tree, a harp. 'I am the sign of Patrick,' it is inscribed, 'sounding the name of Christ.' It is only tolled on the death of an archbishop. 'I was on the golf course when I heard it toll the death of Cardinal Ó Fiaich,' says Jack O'Hare as we part by the statues of Archbishops Crolly and McGettigan, 'and I was very sorry indeed to hear it.'

Today the two Archbishops of Armagh – the Church of Ireland's

Richard Clarke and the Roman Catholic Eamon Martin – are personal friends. The two cathedrals of Armagh and their respective communities live as neighbours in a harmony inconceivable only thirty years ago. But old contrary tides are never far beneath the surface. In April 2018, just before the referendum in which the Republic of Ireland voted for abortion to be legalized, Protestant objectors brought pink and red aerosols to spray their anger over the walls and doors of the Catholic cathedral. 'Sin Fein (sic) Irish BABY Killers . . . Jeremiah I verse 5: "Before I formed thee in the womb I knew thee" . . . Revelations 3: "He that hath an ear, let him hear what the Spirit saith unto the churches" . . . The new Reformation is here.'

It's a quiet evening on the Ridge of Sallows. Dean Gregory Dunstan leads the way along the north side of St Patrick's Church of Ireland Cathedral. The summit of Druim Saileach slopes abruptly away to the east, and so does the north wall, dipping down several feet by the time it turns the corner of the east end with its small door that leads into the crypt. The dean unlocks it, and we enter the cool damp-scented basement, its vaulted ceiling held up by thick octagonal pillars, a space that has survived unchanged since 1268 while above it a succession of cathedrals has risen, fallen, blazed, crumbled, risen anew, burned again, and risen phoenix-like once more.

Dozens of eyes stare up at me, some baleful, others inscrutable, from little dark caverns and crannies at ankle height. They belong to disembodied stone heads, a sinister little army scattered here and there among the pillars, cousins once and twice removed of the Tandragee Idol in the cathedral over our heads. The rumour persists that they were unearthed from a pagan temple site discovered beneath the cathedral. In fact they were gathered over the decades from private collections, from niches in garden walls, summerhouses and ornamental borders.

Prelates, primates and princelings reside in this underworld, too, slotted neatly into shelves in the walls, their snug berths reminiscent of a Japanese capsule hotel. The Caulfields, Viscounts Charlemont, are here; Archbishop Richard Robinson, too, and his brother William. And Captain Ralph MacGeough Bond Shelton, buried in 1916, the last survivor of a famous troopship wreck on an uncharted rock off Danger Point near Cape Town on 26 February 1852, a bona fide hero who gallantly saved women and children, swam two miles through shark-infested waters, and had to fight his way free from entangling seaweed before he finally made it ashore.

The crypt with these great men and heroes would be a resonant place anyway, but a strong blast of the arcane and atavistic emanates from the homunculi that stare so blankly from the shadows. Some have mouths disapprovingly turned down at the corners. A little stumpy figure with whorled nipples and heavily marked eyebrows wears a segmented belt around its waist, its arms raised and pulling at a pair of donkey-like ears. A couple of heads sport extravagant, back-combed quiffs; others wear what look like close-fitting ribbed caps. Two long-fingered beasts hug the rocks beneath them like seals hauled out. A bas-relief carving, like a child's representation of a human figure, holds its arms stiffly by its sides, its head surrounded by rays that radiate like those of the sun.

It is as though the Christian time capsule of the cathedral, the solemn burden of the great and good, are weighted and balanced by these little sullen pagan figures that pre-date St Patrick and all his hardly believable works. The inextinguishable power of the Green Man and the idol, a secret place at the heart of belief.

15

Liverpool

'We'll haul away together'

UP ON THE TOWER OF LIVERPOOL's Anglican cathedral, five hundred feet above sea level, I walk a slow circuit, staring out as evening falls. South and west across the River Mersey to the distant Clwydian Hills and the mountain peaks of Snowdonia, all dim with evening rain. Below, a smart new housing estate, elliptical in shape, crescents and closes, leading out over Toxteth, this cathedral's parish bailiwick, towards the few cranes and many museums and restaurants of the old dock area. South-east round a long bend of the Mersey at low tide, all vast flats of sands and muds in the muted light. North to the mouth of the Mersey and a row of scarlet cranes bowing towards the Wirral peninsula, Birkenhead docks insinuating fleets of closed water among the closely packed houses. It's extraordinary to catch this panorama over the twice-rich, twice-wrecked city, as the dark closes in and the night lights come on.

Liverpool's Anglican cathedral is big, solid, heavily masculine in outward appearance, everything you imagine an end-of-Empire church to be. It's a massive block of a building, made of hard-textured sandstone, dominating the knoll of St James's Mount that overlooks Toxteth and the Liverpool docks – the district of Liverpool 8, still one of the most deprived parts of the inner city. Seen from the west there's no elaboration to the cathedral's severe façade; it all soars upwards, the tall west end, the great arches north and south, the foursquare stump of the tower behind. A nineteenth-century style of cathedral built in a twentieth-century city, a great statement of tradition, of mercantile pride and circumstance, the saga of its construction mirrors the story of the city and the nation, a stop-start progress drawn out through two World Wars and the Great Depression.

Half a mile north on the scarcely perceptible swell of Brownlow Hill stands the ultra-modernist Roman Catholic Metropolitan Cathedral of Christ the King, umbilically joined to its conservatively styled Anglican counterpart by the straight thoroughfare of Hope Street – aptly named, as I'll quickly come to learn. The Catholic cathedral dominates its own hilltop, too, but there the resemblance between the two great churches ends. It's as though the city were trying to express opposing forces – yin and yang, perhaps. The Metropolitan Cathedral is as boldly and bravely modern as the city of Merseybeat and the 1960s could make it – drum-shaped, aerial, light on its feet, a rocket to the sky crowned with a spiky nose cone of thorns. Seven flights of steps ascend to the door, a grand stairway to a Heaven of abstract shapes and colours in glass, in concrete, bronze and aluminium.

Strolling south from this Catholic end of Hope Street the following afternoon, I see the monolithic red tower of the Anglican cathedral slowly grow, then seem to twist away, until I'm suddenly standing on the paving stones outside its west door. Here I get a shock. With no warning the ground drops away precipitously, right under the feet of the cathedral's northern wall. All looks black – weather-blackened sandstone rock below the building, and a black-mouthed tunnel lined with blackened tombstones worming downwards through it. I descend between the ranks of sentinel grave slabs into the sunken pit, an ancient quarry, half city park, half superannuated graveyard, called St James's Gardens.

Cathedral and gardens are separate entities, but each enhances the Gothic quality of the other. From down here the cathedral stands dominant. You look straight up the cliff face of its northern wall. I walk in its shadow through the old cemetery until I come on a chalybeate spring falling from a curved niche into a stone basin. A faded inscription can just be made out:

Christian reader, view in me
An emblem of true charity,
Who freely what I have bestow,
Though neither heard nor seen to flow,
And I have full returns from Heaven
For every cup of water given.

I take a sip in my cupped hands. It's bitter, iron-flavoured, sucking dry every drop of saliva in the mouth.

Towards twilight, solitaries drift through the sunken park. The sunlight fades on the lawns, the shadows of the obelisks lengthen. There's a dark tinge, a psychedelic hyper-realistic atmosphere to the old quarry-turned-cemetery. I walk back up through the tunnel, and in the Anglican cathedral the first question I ask of John Baker on the welcome desk is a naïve one. Was the sandstone for the building quarried right alongside? 'Oh, no,' says John, with the monumental patience of one who deals with a thousand fools daily, 'that quarry's been closed since the 1820s. No' – he sweeps his hand around the cavernous interior – 'this stone came from Woolton.'

The construction of the Anglican cathedral began in 1904, and continued in stop-start fashion for the next seventy-four years, the red sandstone building blocks being harvested from the cliff-like quarries at the back of Woolton. In the morning I drive out there and find a quiet and predominantly middle-class Liverpool suburb with its own fine church and houses. John Lennon grew up in the semi-detached respectability of Woolton. Short straight terraces of quarrymen's cottages terminate in the overgrown workings, or the haphazard sheds and informal woodlands that have grown up there. I turn down Quarry Street as a likely conduit, and there I find quarry faces fifty feet tall, terminating in snub buttresses of sandstone. Pressed back against the inner cliffs of the quarry are modern executive houses, built as close as the architect could manage. Their back gardens enjoy sunless but spectacular views directly on to the vertical rock faces that tower high above.

I stand and listen to my heart thump. Woolton Quarry is a quiet, dark place of thinly echoing birdsong, very still in the middle of the working day. It's hard to believe that, over the course of three-quarters of a century, tens of thousands of tons of hard, durable red sandstone were cut and blasted here, dressed and loaded, and hauled the five miles to build the great cathedral on St James's Mount.

'I lived in Liverpool 8 as a child,' says John Baker. 'The ground sloped down from our house, then rose again to the cathedral on the hill. So looking out of our back bedroom window I could see it slowly being built. The tower always had a crane on top against the sky, and us kids used to wonder how the crane could stay in the same place if the tower was supposed to be growing in height all the time. We didn't under-stand how slow the building process was.

'The tower and the east end were more or less there, but the nave and the west end hadn't been completed. The place we're standing now was all rubble, a scene of tremendous bomb damage from the war. Sixty-six thousand bombs hit the docks, I've been told, and a lot of the city I grew up in was bombsites. You'll find that's true of all the fellas of my age.'

This morning the floor of the Anglican cathedral's nave is bare and uncluttered. The seating was cleared away yesterday in order to accom-modate eight hundred guests at a Barclays Bank dinner party in the cathedral. It costs £8,000 a day to maintain this particular temple, and who better to contribute to that than a gathering of bankers?

The interior, as with the exterior, is all about leading the eye and mind upwards. The tall Gothic arches, the rib vaulting and the tight clusters of the columns all point skywards. A dusky light exudes from the unadorned rose-coloured sandstone, and little daylight comes in through the windows with their thick leading and their small diamond panes in oyster-shell greys and blues. Even the Tree of Life depiction in the east window has the effect of smog-muddied glass, with greys and blacks the dominant colours. It's as though an industrial pall still hangs like a miasma, inside and out.

The parish of Toxteth butts up to the cathedral on its southern flank. 'Toxteth is one of the most deprived city areas in Britain,' says Stuart Haynes, the cathedral's Director of Communications. 'The Church is a significant employer for local people. We have our "Volition" programme in partnership with local hotels and shops where long-term unemployed people – half of them men, half women, aged eighteen to sixty, from ethnic to white – can volunteer for ten weeks' training and work experience. Together with the RC cathedral we run a food bank. There are lots of casual workers in the area, some of them trafficked people. The cathedral's a big building, an obvious focus, and we have to help the people round us. And draw people in, too, with arts projects of all sorts. Arts and crafts markets in December, modern art installations, music festivals like "Cream Classics" where the Liverpool Philharmonic Orchestra perform dance music classics from Cream nightclub – we got two thousand along to that, and almost all were under thirty. We have to keep innovating – if you keep doing things, daring things, most people come round to seeing that it's OK.

'This cathedral exists at the centre of the life of Liverpool. The city of Liverpool is more important than Catholic Liverpool or Protestant Liverpool. It's a family thing, and we genuinely do all feel part of the same family.'

In the aisles on either side of the altar hang two large parable paintings by Glaswegian artist Adrian Wiszniewski, *The Good Samaritan* and *The House Built on Rock*. You can't escape their bright colours and challenging styles. The cathedral authorities certainly don't want to – their self-proclaimed brief is to offer the cathedral as 'a safe place to do risky things in Christ's service'. *The Good Samaritan*, painted in 1995, is particularly striking. It's a bold picture: the robbery victim, bleeding, naked and full frontal, is tended by a young woman in a blue catsuit. She kneels and offers him a golden goblet – to catch his blood, or to give him a drink? Nearby, Wiszniewski shows a gaggle of young hipster men in old school ties and trendy suits going about their business unconcernedly.

The Anglican cathedral at first sight is all red-faced, upstanding and macho. But as I wander the twilight interior, its distaff aspect becomes clearer. Initially the Lady chapel, a crypt-like space forward of the altar, seems highly traditional. It was the first part of the cathedral to be built. It is dedicated to the Blessed Virgin Mary. But the females depicted here are far from the soft, pliant and doe-eyed stereotypes you might expect. Instead, here are women in stone and stained glass, some stern-faced, some stubborn-looking – real people with real, gritty lives and strengths to celebrate.

A memorial commemorates twenty nurses with Liverpool connections – Scots, Irish, Welsh, English – who died during the First World War on home soil or in faraway places, in battle or from flu and malaria. In the atrium and on the stair leading up from the Lady chapel, glass panels depict women who had a major influence on Victorian society. Installed between 1904 and 1910, the panels were paid for by the Girls' Friendly Society, set up in 1875 as a non-sectarian means of empowering young women, and also of promoting 'self-control', i.e. maintenance of virginity, among young working-class girls. The idea was to find, for every such girl of 'unblemished character', a friend in a class above her own, thus helping to bridge the yawning gulf between the social classes.

I linger on the stair, mesmerized by these striking portraits and their little tags of tribute. Elizabeth Barrett Browning, who has seen 'the infinite in things', is the only one posed like a film star, pouting amid a cloud of loose hair. Cotton merchant's daughter Anne Clough (1820–92), a 'true teacher', suffragist and first Principal of Newnham College, Cambridge, possesses a pair of piercing eyes under quizzically raised brows.

Josephine Butler (1828–1906), feminist and social reformer, was a tireless worker in the cause of abolishing child prostitution, sexual trafficking and the sex trade in young children (the age of consent being twelve) from the UK to the continent. 'A champion of purity' proclaims her tag, a claim that sounds mealy-mouthed today. But Josephine Butler was anything but prissy. She was a vehement campaigner for women's rights, women's votes and education for women. With Elizabeth Wolstenholme she formed a pressure group to force Parliament to bring in an Act (1882) to acknowledge married women's right to property – until then they had none, legally. She faced plenty of hostile opposition, especially in public meetings; she had cow dung thrown at her by a gang of pimps, her hotel windows were smashed, she was physically threatened and her meetings disrupted by the smoke from burning straw and the spraying of cayenne pepper.

Prostitutes had no voice in society back then, but Josephine Butler gave them one. In a public letter she quoted an anguished, and angry, cry from a prostitute of her acquaintance:

> It is men, only men, from the first to the last that we have to do with! To please a man I did wrong, then I was flung about from man to man. Men police lay hands on us. By men we are handled, examined, doctored. We never get out of the hands of men till we die!

In 1903 Giles Gilbert Scott, grandson of the celebrated Victorian designer Sir George Gilbert Scott, won the competition to design an Anglican cathedral for Liverpool. Scott was a 22-year-old trainee architect who by his own admission had never designed anything more elaborate than a pipe rack. Even more likely to disqualify the young man was his Roman Catholicism. Nevertheless, it was Scott's Gothic Revival design, modified as it progressed, that went ahead the following year.

In the southwest corner of the cathedral I scan the stained-glass panels of the 'Laymen's Window' like a puzzle to find the men – and they are all men; not one woman among them – who are shown bringing the improbable edifice into being during its long gestation before completion in 1978. Here they are in beautiful tints of rose and royal blue, gold and green: a grey-bearded man turning the first sod, the organ builder and the engineer, the Clerk of Works sporting a shiny green hat as he unfolds his plans, the quarryman in a red cloth cap with his pneumatic drill. A bricklayer, a scaffolder, a bearded wood carver creating a panel, a besmocked sculptor, glaziers in the stained-glass workshop. A pair of cloth-capped masons setting the arch stone. A metalworker cradling an elaborately wrought cross. Foundrymen tuning the gleaming cathedral bells. And alongside these craftsmen and labourers, the men who drove the project, grouped round a model of the cathedral with its original twin towers – benefactors the Earl of Derby and Sir William Forwood, supervising architect George Bodley, and his colleague the young shaver Giles Gilbert Scott, a youth in a rounded close-front collar, his face fresh and open in comparison to the other three heavily bearded, heavily self-confident men.

Scott designed the great red edifice to be a mighty cathedral in a city that had none, and his is a cathedral of superlatives – the longest purpose-built Anglican cathedral in the world, with the highest Gothic arches, the biggest stained-glass windows and the largest organ in England. This triumphant 'bigger, taller, heavier, longer' theme, appropriate enough for the end of the Victorian era in which it was conceived, ran counter to the tenor of the times in which the cathedral was actually built. The British Empire and its great west coast port were beginning a long decline. The disastrous global wars and economic slumps of the twentieth century, the mass deaths and destruction, slowed the building of the cathedral to snail's pace, picking up and slacking off as the economic or world situation dictated. They also consumed the old world of confident superlatives.

'I was born in the Dingle,' says Alan Matthews, Chairman of the Friends of Liverpool Cathedral. 'Lived there as a boy all through the war. There was tremendous bombing, but I wasn't afraid. There were bombsites to explore and plenty of shrapnel to collect, you know!

'Toxteth, the next district to the Dingle, was very poor in the early twentieth century, and it sat right at the feet of the site. There was a bit of opposition to building the cathedral. Why not use the money to feed and clothe the poor, heal them and house them? In fact, though most of the money was given by shipping firms and big businesses, there was also an appeal for contributions from ordinary people. The intention was for it to be built by the people of Liverpool, for the people.

'The fact is that Liverpool was a very sectarian city, Catholics versus Protestants, something brought into focus during the Irish famine and immigration. When I was young, Protestants wouldn't turn up to vote if the polling station was in an RC church hall – they'd rather lose their chance to vote than set foot in a place like that! That overlooks rather conveniently the fact that the architect of this cathedral, Giles Gilbert Scott, was a Roman Catholic. On Whit Sunday we'd have ecumenical marches with the Catholics along Hope Street, and protesters would stand there with banners, yelling "No Popery!" When the Pope came to pray here in the Anglican cathedral in 1982, Ian Paisley came over from Northern Ireland and led a protest outside.

'For many years now we've been committed to an ecumenical approach between the two cathedrals and communities. It didn't go down too well with everyone at first. If we had a Roman Catholic priest at a service, there'd often be protests. People would get up and shout in the middle of the service. The organist was primed to play very loudly if that happened! But it's all going now, that sectarian feeling. Both cathedrals are looked upon by Liverpudlians as "our cathedrals", rather than "my" cathedral and "theirs". And that's largely thanks to the work of the two bishops, our own David Sheppard, and Derek Worlock across at the RC cathedral.'

In the south aisle, near the east end of the cathedral, the memorial to David Sheppard, Bishop of Liverpool from 1975 to 1997, forms part of the wall. A white, water-smoothed Portland-stone cobble is set in the red sandstone wall, the centrepiece of a swirl of elliptical shapes – 'breaking boundaries', an allusion to Sheppard's eminence as a cricketer. He played for Sussex and England after the Second World War, a career interspersed with time out for him to pursue his ecclesiastical calling. He made 113 runs against the Australians in Melbourne in 1962, but dropped some vital catches. 'Just pretend it's Sunday, Rev,' fast bowler Fiery Fred Trueman told him, 'and keep your bloody hands together.'

When he was installed as Bishop of Liverpool in 1975, Sheppard, at forty-six, was the youngest diocesan bishop in England. He was a social reformer, an evangelical Christian and a campaigner against apartheid, and he was an outspoken critic of Margaret Thatcher's Tory government in the 1980s, beating the drum for action on poverty in the cities. But maybe his most notable achievement was the productive partnership and friendship he created with his counterpart Derek Worlock, Roman Catholic Archbishop of Liverpool from 1976 to 1996.

The cordial and exemplary relationship between the two men is celebrated in sculptor Stephen Broadbent's Sheppard–Worlock statue, halfway along Hope Street. You can see both cathedrals from the memorial, which consists of a pair of bronze doors. On one is a relief sculpture of Derek Worlock in his many-buttoned surplice, his bespectacled gaze modestly downcast, his high brow thoughtfully furrowed. David Sheppard on the other door wears Geneva bands. His hair brushed back, he holds your gaze with a half-smile.

'Completing the cathedral in the 1970s was itself a contentious issue,' says Alan Matthews. 'Bishop Sheppard wrestled with his conscience when he was appointed in 1975 – should the money not be spent on improving conditions in the immediate area surrounding the cathedral? As a result of this kind of thinking, the cathedral has been very involved in the regeneration of the area, in outreach, and in rebuilding – especially when Derrick Walters was dean here at the same time as David Sheppard. Walters lobbied and argued and used all his influence to get regeneration projects going, commissioning public housing nearby and so on. You've never seen so many politicians in one place as there were at his memorial service here!

'The people who planned Liverpool Cathedral never envisaged a regular congregation. The cathedral was intended for big religious and civic occasions rather than day-by-day worship. But in fact the congregation has established itself, and has increased. And not necessarily with the kind of worshippers you might imagine. A lot of Iranian refugees have been relocated to Liverpool, and they're quite a significant part of the city now – they have their own service on Sunday, in Farsi, with their own curate, Mohammad Edghtedarian. Chinese Christians too – our Chinatown is the oldest Chinese community in Europe. At Christmas there's a congregation of about two and a half thousand, and we see a huge number of Chinese in that. Sometimes it feels as though the whole of Chinatown has turned up.'

And what about Hillsborough, the great shadow across the psyche of the city?

'Oh, Hillsborough ... well, we kept the Eternal Flame here for twelve months while renovations were going on at Anfield. We toll our big bell, Great George, on the anniversary. We still get people coming in, still hurt and angry. There's always someone on duty who's detailed to look out for those.'

At the north end of Hope Street I climb the seven flights of steps and enter the splendid tent – 'Paddy's Wigwam' to one and all – of the Metropolitan Cathedral of Christ the King, Liverpool. It's an enormous drum, is my first impression; a great cartwheel of blue light, its rim made up of shapes and colours as disparate as can be, unified as segments in an all-encompassing circle. The heart and mind lift, not pushed upwards in forceful sandstone hands as they are on entering the Anglican cathedral, but expanding outwards in a swirl before being sucked upwards towards the central funnel of the spire. A remarkably strong sensation, and one I wasn't in the least expecting.

'Oh, the circular shape of the cathedral works pretty well,' says Canon Tony O'Brien, Dean of the Metropolitan Cathedral. 'You can get two thousand five hundred people in at one time, though I must admit there actually are places where you can't see the altar properly. And the acoustics have been a bit of a problem. We used to have speakers hanging from the corona over the altar, and the sound would distort and bounce all around the cathedral. Thankfully with modern technology these acoustic problems have now been resolved. And it works. Our congregation numbers have increased over the years. Cathedrals are felt to guarantee a certain standard, I think – good singing by a choir, good music, better preaching and preparation.

'In some ways ours is a traditional working-class congregation. But things are changing. Now we have a separate Polish service on Sundays; we have Filipinos, Middle Easterners, Indonesians, people from various African nations, as more and more refugees and displaced persons arrive in Liverpool. It's the same in the Anglican community. The two cathedrals, I'd say, very actively represent the life of this city. The difference between them, though . . . well, I suppose the main difference is in the style of the two buildings themselves, and what that says. The Anglican cathedral seems to say, "Look how important the city was." The Catholic one gives the impression of a church moving with the times, with no pillars blocking the view, nothing in the way – saying, "Look how the city is now." But,' Tony O'Brien stresses, 'relationships between the Roman Catholic and Anglican cathedrals are very cordial. We attend each other's services. Our cathedral guides have the same function. We work together to organize a food bank, work experience, social interaction and so on. We get on, and we complement each other.'

The dean, a Liverpool boy, casts his mind back. 'I was born in the Anfield district, on the edge of an Orange area. There were big divisions between communities back then, not long after the war. There were one or two areas you'd stay out of, as a Catholic boy. The tenement flats at Thomas White Gardens, that was a very Orange housing estate.

289

If your mum sent you on a message, you'd run through there as quick as you could!

'On the Whit Walk at Pentecost between the two cathedrals there'd be knots of people shouting and chanting, with banners: "No Popery Here!" This would have gone on right up until the 1980s. And there's no doubt that David Sheppard and Derek Worlock did a huge amount by their personal example to dispel that sectarianism.'

It's a strange turn of events that Giles Gilbert Scott, architect of the Anglican cathedral, was a Roman Catholic, and Frederick Gibberd, architect of the Roman Catholic Metropolitan Cathedral, was a Non-conformist. Gibberd's cathedral as it was built is a masterful marriage of practical economy and modernity. But the plans drawn up in 1929 by Britain's pre-eminent twentieth-century architect, Sir Edwin Lutyens, were for the greatest cathedral in Christendom. Speculative drawings show a fantasy temple dwarfing the tiny human figures around it, a vast dome and towers soaring over the city, outdoing even the Gothic Revival monster then slowly rising at the Anglican end of Hope Street. A giant scale model of the 'greatest building never built', about twice man height, is on display in the Liverpool Museum at the Pier Head, a construction to make one gasp and stretch one's eyes like Hilaire Belloc's Matilda.

Like Tothill Fields and Westminster Cathedral, the land chosen for the new Roman Catholic cathedral, Brownlow Hill, was unhappy ground. On it stood Brownlow Hill Institution, a vast workhouse nick-named 'the Hospital of Ireland'. The stones of Brownlow Hill were full of Irish bones and pain. The archbishop on whose watch the new cath-edral was to be built was Richard Downey. A photograph of him in the crypt shows a full-fleshed, bushy-browed, portly cleric with a double chin and large, liquid, soulful eyes, by all accounts a man of charm and guile, skilful with people. He decided to buy the Brownlow Hill site after the workhouse closed its doors in the late 1920s. There was sect-arian rage to contend with, particularly from one Revd Harry Longbottom, who was vocal in his implacable opposition to the site being sold to 'this Prince-Bishop'. Downey got his way, and the site, and had the wit to wisecrack: 'Though I won by a short nose, that's better than being beaten by a Long Bottom!'

Contemplating the planning of the new cathedral, Archbishop Downey declared: 'It must be a vast one, a challenge to the mediocrity of the age.' Lutyens's proposal certainly was vast, but actually quite mediocre in its overbearing colonial style. Three million pounds was raised initially, with contributions great and humble. World-famous Irish tenor John McCormack made a record, the proceeds of which went to the fund. Cathedral Tea and Cathedral Cigarettes were branded and sold. There were lotteries. Wills were made. Work began on Lutyens's mighty crypt, the foundation stone being laid on Whit Monday, 1933, in the presence of thirty thousand onlookers.

Then came the Second World War. Workers went away to war duties. The workforce dwindled. In 1941 Archbishop Downey was moved to declare, 'The greatest cathedral of modern times is being built by one boy – an apprentice bricklayer.' In 1944 Lutyens died. His unfinished crypt proved useful as an air raid shelter, provided with beds, central heating and a canteen.

Downey died in 1953, his slogan 'A cathedral in our time' as yet unfulfilled. The crypt was still unfinished, and the design costs for the whole Lutyens project had risen to £27 million. The crypt was finally finished in 1958, but it was obvious that the whole massive project was never going to come to fruition. When John Heenan was appointed Archbishop of Liverpool in 1957 he abandoned the grand Lutyens cathedral. A new competition for a new design was announced. To be incorporated along with the existing crypt were eight chapels, a car park, and seating for two thousand with an uninterrupted view of the altar. It amounted to a fundamental restatement of purpose, simple and profound, and daringly modern, too. Back to basics, and the timeless purpose of a cathedral, to enshrine the altar sacrifice and to serve its people.

The ultra-modern design of architect Frederick Gibberd was selected, and construction began in October 1962. The brief stipulated a five-year deadline for completion and a maximum spend of £1 million – a modest outlay that chimed with the austere post-war economic climate.

The people of the diocese, however poor, did what they could to help finance the project. They contributed their savings, their small change, their melted-down wedding rings. Archbishop Heenan acknowledged this generosity of spirit at the consecration of the cathedral on the Feast of Pentecost in May 1967. 'Cathedrals are not usually built by rich men,' he remarked in his address. 'They are built by the self-denial of the poor.' It was Heenan who articulated exactly why it was not a self-indulgent waste of money to build the cathedral: 'If it were wrong to build churches, it would be equally wrong to build theatres, youth clubs, radio stations and concert halls.' He saw the cathedral as one more essential service provider to the community – and not just the Roman Catholic community, either. 'It is significant', he told city dignitaries at a banquet, 'that the architect of the Metropolitan Cathedral was a non-Catholic. I don't regard the Metropolitan Cathedral of Christ the King as Catholic property, but as belonging to you all.' This, admittedly, was said in the liberal after-glow of the Second Vatican Council, but it was a pretty bold statement for the times, all the same.

The focal point of the cathedral, outside and in, is the roof lantern with its spiky thorn-like pinnacles. In the *Catholic Herald* of 12 May 1967 Cardinal Heenan described the thinking:

> 'The cathedral is lit by a tremendous lantern which supports the Crown of Christ the King. This lantern contains more coloured glass than any cathedral in Christendom. Yet it manages to be unobtrusive. It commands without dominating the cathedral space. At night this lantern will glow warmly and protectively over the city, and will be seen from the ships coming into harbour. This is fitting because in the ages of faith when seamen turned their faces towards the port of Liverpool, they thought of the Mother of God whose shrine would welcome them home.'

The elegant roof spire with its coloured lantern (John Piper the artist, his much younger acolyte Patrick Reyntiens the craftsman) soon saw the cathedral dubbed the 'Mersey Funnel'. And the Funnel soon began to fill with the finest modern artworks that could be devised.

A guitarist is sitting on the altar steps in front of a horseshoe of elderly listeners, playing 'Jesu, Joy of Man's Desiring', as I plunge into the under-world. Edwin Lutyens's grand crypt is reminiscent of the interior of Westminster Cathedral, a huge dusky hall of dark brick vaulting. Ro-manesque arches march away, turning left and right into further shadowy tunnels of brick. It feels like what it is, the foundation for a massive edi-fice that was never completed. Save for the twinkle of gold and silver in the treasury, a subterranean brown light, cut with bars of sun through high windows, pervades all these tunnels, the concert rooms and chapels and pontifical hall. Ascending from the crypt into the coloured light and open space of the main body of the cathedral is like being propelled from past to present – or even future – at warp speed.

I walk a circuit of the circular cathedral. In the Chapel of Reconcili-ation, a crucified Christ sails in a cubist sea of repentant and reconciling couples, while Liverpool's two cathedrals, Anglican and Roman Cath-olic, float like ghostly sister ships in the background.

The Children's Chapel holds a figure of Christ in a gritty sandstone finish, with children at his knee – the whole sculpture the gift of Kwok Fong and Elizabeth his wife, members of Liverpool's Chinese commun-ity. Also here is a very poignant Babies' Memorial Book full of little beribboned tickets inscribed with poems and shreds of words by be-reaved parents and grandparents of babies who 'have no known grave', or who have died soon after birth. 'I will always listen for the song of your soul' is the cry of one young mother of two stillborn children. On the wall is a tapestry of the 'Sea of Galilee' inspired by the Sefton coast just north of Liverpool, unmistakeable with sparkling sandhills and thorny black bushes under a restless northern sky of grey and pink.

I pass spiky, angular, highly physical Stations of the Cross. Faceless men load Christ with his cross; murderous villains nail an outsize Christ's sinewy limbs to the cross; Christ on the cross screams in anguish to the sky.

The Chapel of Abraham displays a striking life-size sculpture of Abraham by Sean Rice (1931–97), the patriarch shown as an Old Man of the Sea figure, his hair and beard in flying tendrils, a look of pain and of pride on his face. He's vigorous, bare-chested, his bronze breeches ragged in a semblance of the goatish thighs of the great god Pan. With one hand he pushes aside the thorns of the thicket where a ram is trapped, while a sharp knife in his other hand betrays his intentions towards his son Isaac.

In St Joseph's Chapel lies the massively simple, grey-slate-slab tomb of ecumenical peacemaker Archbishop Derek Worlock. A big wedge-shaped Lady chapel is filled with pale cinnamon light, and further round in a glass-fronted altar three great golden jorums each contain a year's supply of holy oils. And finally, in the clean white space of the baptistery, thin black lines radiate inwards across the floor, drawing one's eye to the font on the far wall.

There is also a Chapel of Remembrance with a big book containing ninety-six names in gold letters, an alphabetical progression from John Alfred Anderson to Graham John Wright. It is inscribed simply 'Hillsborough, 15 April 1989'.

Hillsborough. The word falls across the city like a sword. It cut deep at the time, and still does. The bare facts are terrible enough. On 15 April 1989, ninety-six Liverpool Football Club supporters were crushed and asphyxiated to death at Sheffield Wednesday's Hillsborough football ground while attending an FA Cup semi-final match between Liverpool and Nottingham Forest. More than 750 were injured. It was a horrific scene, relayed live to BBC's *Grandstand* show.

The cause of the disaster remained a matter of debate for decades afterwards. The behaviour of some of the Liverpool fans was called into question. They were said to have turned up to the match late and drunk, to have pushed their way recklessly into the ground, to have been fighting and out of control. In fact it wasn't Liverpool fans who caused the Hillsborough disaster, but the panicky actions of the police who let more fans into the ground than it could hold. But at the time of the tragedy the city of Liverpool was going through hard times, with docks and factories closing, Trotskyist politics on the city council, strikes, and slum estates which hard drugs were beginning to ravage. The city's public image was appalling, and a rush to judgement took place over Hillsborough.

It took years for the truth to begin to emerge, decades for the fans to be exonerated. These were years in the wilderness for the Hillsborough families. But they were not left alone with their pain and anger. Under the leadership of Archbishop Derek Worlock and Bishop David Sheppard, the two cathedrals presented a united front right from the start.

While the disaster was still unfolding, the two bishops hurried over to Sheffield to comfort the survivors in the hospitals. Both bishops officiated at the special Mass in the Roman Catholic cathedral next day, along with Revd Dr John Newton, Chairman of Liverpool Methodists, and the Moderator of the Merseyside Free Church. 'You will not want much sermonizing from me,' said Archbishop Worlock. 'Even if you had ears for it, I do not think I would have the heart for it. It has been as if the rest of this country, and perhaps of Europe itself, have combined to sing to us in chorus that, especially in these dark days, we shall never walk alone.'

At that Mass a drift of Liverpool Football Club scarves was left behind on the altar that had been set up outside on the piazza. In the Metropolitan Cathedral's archive room I open a cardboard box. Inside, carefully wrapped in tissue paper, are some of these scarves. They are like holy relics, like icons, special to touch once you know the emotion with which they were laid down outside the cathedral. 'You shouldn't underestimate the effect that Hillsborough still has in the city,' says archivist Neil Sayer.

Clergy at both cathedrals are well used to seeing people coming in or sitting in pain, still working out their trauma. Cathedral staff are briefed in recognizing and handling the stages of such grief – from stunned and lost bewilderment through anger and rejection of help, from euphoria at having survived through feelings of desolation and isolation when the focus of attention has moved away. Debts for funeral costs, financial difficulties, organizing visits to Hillsborough and the hospitals – these problems still involve the cathedral staff.

Dean Tony O'Brien has to cut short our talk. He needs to prepare himself for this afternoon's occasion in the crypt under the Metropolitan Cathedral, a gathering intended to express formally the outrage that the families of the exonerated fans feel at the way they have been treated and their loved ones stigmatized. Bishop James Jones, former Anglican Bishop of Liverpool, is presenting, in front of the families and the press, a report entitled 'The Patronising Disposition of Unaccountable Power'. It details all the abuse and indignities those ordinary people suffered because of the patronizing attitude displayed to them by police, press, government and the wider public. It is a report commissioned by the current government, and it calls for more candour, accountability, sensitivity and inclusion on the part of these organizations, which are so inclined to close ranks in the face of ordinary individuals and their demands for justice. The fact that it is an Anglican bishop delivering this report in a Roman Catholic cathedral seems right and fitting in a city that has done so much to combat its own ingrained sectarianism.

'There was an abiding desire to clear the names of those who died,' says Tony O'Brien to me afterwards. 'And now they have been exonerated, there's a feeling among the families not to maintain the same scale of demonstration of grief. But the fact is,' he concludes, 'at times of grief and trouble, we stand together. That's Liverpool's default position.'

16

Coventry

Shipbuilding

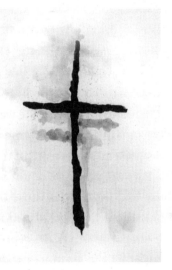

'I WAS SIX YEARS OLD,' says Barry Gittins, the Blitz tour guide, in his strong, singsong Coventry accent. 'I hid under the stairs with my mum. She said, "If the Lord wants me, he knows where to find me."'

It was 14 November 1940, and the Luftwaffe had come to Coventry. 'I couldn't distinguish the noise of the bombs exploding from the noise the AA guns made. I can remember my dad coming in and saying, "Don't worry, them guns will knock all the bombers down. They're so good, the gunners, they've just shot a chunk out of the moon, look!"'

It was a frosty moonlit night. A fire guard of four was standing watch at Coventry Cathedral: Provost Howard (fifty-six), the cathedral stonemason Jock Forbes (sixty-five), and two youngsters in their early twenties. The building they were guarding had been constructed between 1373 and 1433 as St Michael's parish church; it had only been playing the role of cathedral since 1918, after Coventry had undergone a huge expansion. Before its elevation in status St Michael's had been reckoned one of the largest and most beautiful parish churches in England, and Coventry was proud of its red sandstone cathedral in the heart of the city.

Shortly after 7 p.m. the first sirens were heard, and within five minutes there was the sound of planes overhead. High-explosive and incendiary bombs began to fall. Soon the city was burning. The plan was to create chaos and rip open buildings with the high-explosive bombs, then follow up with incendiaries to burn everything out.

Within an hour the cathedral was hit by incendiaries, wicked little things the size of a policeman's truncheon. They fell on the chancel roof, the nave roof and the south aisle above the organ. The fire guard extinguished these first bombs with buckets of sand and water. Then more fell on a side chapel, and four on the roof of the Girdlers' or Children's Chapel. Fire took hold in the dry, centuries-old wood of the ceiling, and the cathedral watchers couldn't put it out. The fire brigade was fully occupied elsewhere in the city, with roads blocked and fire engines trapped by craters caused by the high-explosive bombs. Solihull Fire Brigade did eventually arrive, but the water supply failed – the water main had been shattered by the bombing.

The four men of the fire guard realized that they couldn't save the cathedral. Instead they rushed to retrieve as many of its treasures as they could – armfuls of candlesticks, the altar cross, ancient communion vessels, prayerbooks, the colours of the Royal Warwickshire Regiment.

The flat oak ceiling burned; so did the oak screen and misericords, the wooden memorials and the interior woodwork, the organ that Handel had played. Victorian repairers had inserted steel girders into the medieval oak beams of the roof to strengthen their tying properties. These girders buckled in the heat. The roof fell. Relieved of the 500-year-old stresses of holding up the roof, the stone pillars of the arcades tottered. Then pillars, clerestories and chancel arches all crumbled and fell.

By morning, the interior of the cathedral was nothing but rubble and charred beams. The exterior walls of the chapels that ringed the church were still standing, though; also the walls of the sanctuary and the south side of the apse. The south porch, too, and the tower and spire at the west end, had survived the inferno. The Revd A. P. Wales, wandering among the rubble, picked up three of the large hand-forged medieval nails that were lying in the ruins where they'd fallen out of the beams. He formed them into a cross, tied it with wire, and presented it to the bishop – the first Cross of Nails, original of hundreds offered down the years in token of peace and reconciliation to individuals and congregations all over the world.

*

Coventry was always going to be a target; its car factories had been turned over to production of munitions. The city was bombed several times. But the cathedral raid was different.

Cathedrals are packed with symbols. And people reach for symbols at such times. Symbols were vitally important in maintaining morale in wartime. Winston Churchill and other opinion-makers saw the opportunity for some effective propaganda. Coventry was not the first or the worst raid on Britain, but the image of the cathedral tower and spire defiantly standing over the ruins was as perfect a symbol of Nazi barbarity and British defiance as was Herbert Mason's photograph, taken less than two months later, of the dome of St Paul's Cathedral rising above the fires of the London Blitz. The Coventry images went round the world, along with the provost's words to a reporter from the *Coventry Standard* as they stood in the smoking ruins at ten o'clock next morning: 'We shall build it again.' The BBC was directed not to hold back in reporting the death and destruction. Around six hundred citizens had been killed, and two-thirds of the city was damaged or ruined. King George VI visited two days after the raid, and a pillar was set up to show the spot from which he had first viewed the ruins.

The Wyley Crypt underground was undamaged, and by the Sunday after the raid a temporary chapel had been formed there, leaky and cold. Holy Communion was celebrated in the chapel at 8 a.m., a tradition that continued all through the war and for years afterwards. On Christmas Day 1940 the Empire Broadcast was transmitted to the world from the ruins. A few boys, a few men and a fragment of the cathedral choir were present. Provost Howard said: 'What we are trying to tell the world is this: that with Christ born again in our hearts today, we are trying, hard as it may be, to banish all thoughts of revenge; we are bracing ourselves to finish the tremendous job of saving the world from tyranny and cruelty; we are going to try to make a kinder, simpler, a more Christ-Child-like sort of world in the days beyond this strife.'

Those words, too, went round the world – the start of those themes, all-pervasive at Coventry Cathedral then and now, of reconciliation and forgiveness.

In January 1941 an altar of rubble stones and a cross of charred beams from the wreckage were set up by cathedral stonemason Jock Forbes in the ruins of the sanctuary. On Good Friday, with Coventry reeling from a fresh series of bombing raids, an open-air service in the sanctuary was attended by a small congregation and a Salvation Army band. The theme: 'It doesn't matter when you die; it only matters how you die.'

Eventually the question of what to do next came up. Leave the ruins as a Garden of Remembrance? Or rebuild? Had the interior pillars not collapsed, the medieval Cathedral Church of St Michael would probably have been rebuilt on its own footprint after the war. As it was, the cost and trouble were reckoned too great for a country exhausted and drained of money and manpower. Anyway, here was a chance for a new phoenix to rise, a bolder one, a place of worship more relevant to the city and the times.

Sir Giles Gilbert Scott, designer of Liverpool's neo-Gothic Anglican cathedral, was invited to submit plans in 1942. His design was initially accepted, but then rejected by the Royal Fine Arts Commission in 1947. Scott resigned, and the search was on for a new architect. The brief was 'not to conceive a building and place in it an altar, but to conceive the altar and create the building'. The altar was to be at the east end, as tradition dictated, but everyone should be able to get a clear view of it. This was a new sensibility echoed in Archbishop Heenan's brief ten years later for architects competing to design Liverpool's new Roman Catholic cathedral: 'The High Altar is not an ornament to embellish the cathedral building. The cathedral, on the contrary, is built to enshrine the altar sacrifice. The attention of all who view should be arrested and held by the altar.'

Wartime restrictions on the use of labour meant that the rubble of the old cathedral had lain uncleared till 1948. At first the intention was to demolish all the ruins except the medieval crypts and the tower with its spire. But Basil Spence's design, chosen in 1951, retained the ruins complete and made them an integral part of the plan, by setting his cathedral at right angles to the old one so that the new building's main door, at its south end, opened directly on to the ruins. This ninety-degree twist from the conventional east–west orientation of a church, with the new cathedral's altar now placed at the north end, caused a huge amount of harrumphing, as did the hulking shape of the building, at first sight more like a municipal library or city hall than a house of God.

There were conscience struggles on the city council, a post-war moral dilemma – would the money be better spent on housing, schools and hospitals for Coventry, where bomb damage had left ten thousand homeless, than on this project? Eventually Basil Spence's plans were approved. Work began in 1955; Her Majesty the young Queen Elizabeth laid the foundation stone in 1956, and she returned for the cathedral's consecration on 25 May 1962.

Coventry suffered, not only from wartime bombing, but from brutalist planning in the aftermath. At the same time as the cathedral was being built, a tight circle of ring road with endless back-to-back junctions was constructed around the largely ruined city centre. Along with much utilitarian post-war building, Coventry's cathedrals, old and new, are caught inside this concrete ring of underpasses and flyovers.

The new cathedral lies at right angles to the old, the light red sandstone of Basil Spence's conception linked forever to its own darker shadow. A striking image guards the new cathedral: Jacob Epstein's bronze sculpture of St Michael and the Devil, fixed to the wall near the entrance. Epstein pulls no punches. Michael is lean and vigorous. He grasps a spear, his muscular arms tensed for action, great wings outspread, Byzantine eyes wide. His attitude is grimly determined, a fighter who has gained the victory but remains alert for trouble. At his feet sprawls the Devil, newly ejected from Heaven. He is stark naked, his penis flaccid between his thighs, his stubby horns erect like those on a jester's hood. He looks up at his conqueror with hollow eyes, apparently impotent, abject and terrified. But it's an illusion. He's a trickster and a charlatan, quite undefeated in spite of appearances. The chains are slipping away from his waist and ankles; the wrists behind his back are unbound. He could leap up at any moment, as full of devilry as ever. It's only the stern will and undying vigilance of Michael that's holding him down.

On a cloudy morning in Holy Week I enter the ruins through a tall arched doorway in the north wall, and find a hollow box of stone open to the sky, paved with smooth flags, the whole effect far lighter than the fire-scorched old sandstone might suggest. The windows with their elaborate tracery, the tower and spire, all are miraculously intact. I walk a circuit via Jock Forbes's rubble altar and a replica of his charred cross, round the shells of medieval side chapels with weather-blurred corbel heads and fragments of stained glass half melted in the fires of 1940.

The ruins hold sculptures in wildly differing styles. Epstein's *Ecce Homo* shows a blunt-faced and blocky Christ in the style of a primitive idol or an Aztec god, grim-faced and intransigent before an unseen Pontius Pilate. Also here is Helmut Heinze's powerful bronze *Chor der Überlebenden*, the *Choir of Survivors*. The figures of the survivors cluster together, their heads and faces unblemished, but their bodies melted like candle wax in a fire. On the fiftieth anniversary of the new cathedral's foundation the sculpture was presented as a gift from the Frauenkirche cathedral in Dresden, itself rebuilt after being destroyed by the RAF's Bomber Command in the notorious air raid of February 1945.

On the north side of the old cathedral looms the new, the bulk and weight of its windowless wall feeling ominous, even threatening. I can't rationalize this sense until I take note of the modern porch that projects from the new cathedral out over the old, connecting the two buildings. The porch is disturbingly dark and light-excluding. It could be the underside of a bomber flying at roof height across the ruins.

I go in under the belly of the machine, climb a flight of shallow steps and enter the new cathedral at its 'west' end. Hmm . . . I'm going to have to rethink my preconceptions about what goes where. The old cathedral ruins follow the traditional orientation of churches – an elongated nave lying east–west, with the altar at the east end and tower at the west. But since the new cathedral sits at right angles to the old, the two buildings form a reversed L-shape. So the nave of the new cathedral runs north–south, with the altar at the north end and the 'tower' – a radio mast – at the south where the main entrance lies. Well – I'll think of it as traditionally laid out, since that's how the guidebook deals with it. Altar in the 'east', entrance in the 'west', then.

The 'west' wall is a screen of glass, floor to ceiling, engraved with ranks of saints and angels, conceived by Basil Spence and designed by John Hutton. Seen from inside the cathedral, the strong pale light of the cloudy spring morning backlights the figures to translucency. The saints are upright and stern, hooded or crowned, elongated skeletal figures with long hands folded in attitudes of prayer, or cradling miniature churches. Their ordered rows are interspersed with ranks of musical angels blowing trumpets as long as alpenhorns, gracefully bending and playfully leaping in ecstatic dance as though the music they are making and the windy sky behind them are blowing them about like thistledown. One's glance passes outside through their light transparency to the dark complications of the ruined medieval windows beyond.

First impressions inside the new cathedral are of clean lines, bareness and simplicity. It's more of a hive than a ship, really, with the roof in diamond-shaped cells. The nave pillars are slender, smooth concrete. The nave is a dark tunnel leading 'east' to the bright but subtle greens and greys of Graham Sutherland's enormous tapestry behind the high altar.

In 1944 the recently enthroned Bishop of Coventry, Dr Neville Gordon, envisaged a Chapel of Unity to be shared between the Anglican and the Free Churches.

> Wave after wave of immigration over twenty years has almost overwhelmed the community sense of Coventry. War has brought into it a flood of strangers from the entire British Isles.

The returning fighting man will hardly know its people . . . The problem of transition back to peace will be overwhelming for this unformed community unless we can set up some centre of leadership. It is the church's great chance.

The Chapel of Unity stands offset on the 'north' side. On a piece of plain sackcloth at the entrance lies a parched Good Friday garden of dry cacti. It sets the theme for the day and the tone for the whole cathedral, one of a journey through pain and penance to atonement and reconciliation. The chapel is lit by tall, thin windows with thick slabs of cast glass faceted like jewels, a gift from the German Evangelical Churches. The marble floor, by Swedish designer Einar Forseth, carries a jagged pattern out of which the eyes of the Four Evangelists stare, wide and penetrating. The five continents of the world encompass St John, an eagle with Aztec beak and wings and a blazing, all-seeing eye; St Mark, a more or less benign lion; St Luke, a mad, trampling bull; and St Matthew, a wild, blue-eyed seer. Here is the uncontrolled force of apocalypse; the Gospel message as challenging, disturbing and strong; and a reminder that all the artists who came together to create Coventry Cathedral had one experience at least in common – the horror of a whole world at war.

On either side of the nave hangs a mesh of vertical and horizontal tubes: the pipes of the organ, ascending upwards from tiny tubes the size of a tin whistle to cylinders as fat as water pipes. In contrast to this ultra-modernist assembly, six casements have been filled with medieval stained glass, stored in safety before the war began: tonsured monks, women sporting curly coiffures, monstrous villains with warped lips and noses. Such works are normally tucked away so high up in a cathedral that you can't appreciate the detail unless you've brought a pair of binoculars. Here every stroke of the artist's brush, every accidental smear shows at eye-level how sparks of artistic brilliance and the ageless impulse to humour can leap the gap between then and now.

I zigzag from side to side of the nave, starting beside the cathedral door in the baptistery. Here a great rugged ball of rock scooped from a Bethlehem hillside does duty as the font, its top carved into a scalloped bowl, all cradled in a tall concavity of glass that rises to a tremendous sunburst of gold and silver. The journey culminates at the 'east' end beside the high altar in the Chapel of Christ in Gethsemane, guarded by a screen that's a viciously spiked crown of thorns, made by men of the Royal Engineers to Basil Spence's design. Inside, a glinting mosaic shows Christ in doubt and pain, his eyes on the cup of suffering offered by an angel with enormous, threatening wings.

Opposite in the 'northeast' corner of the cathedral I notice a panel of beaten bronze bearing a figure bent in shame and distress, its arms outstretched towards a cross. It was made by Berlin artist Fritz Kuhn and given by Aktion Sühnezeichen Friedensdienste, Action Reconciliation Service for Peace, a German organization founded in 1958 to help young Germans face, and make amends for, the evil that members of their parents' generation unleashed on the world. The first work they carried out was here in Coventry, founding the International Centre for Reconciliation in the ruins. During the Cold War the ICR was most closely involved in reconciliation with Iron Curtain countries. In 1965 its work led to youngsters from Coventry going out to Dresden in Communist East Germany to help rebuild the Deaconess Hospital, half destroyed by the RAF in the Dresden Raid. Gradually, since the fall of the Iron Curtain, the focus has shifted to reconciliation between Christians, Muslims and Jews – a busy enough agenda, in all conscience.

Beyond, pinned to a wall halfway down the stairs, hangs a timeless symbol, the charred cross that stonemason Jock Forbes erected in the ruins of the old cathedral in the New Year of 1941, two twists of scorched timber from the bombed-out roof, lashed together with a hank of wire. Black, lumpy and asymmetric, it's no smoothly realized work of art. Gazing up at it, I get a shock of recognition. My mind flies back fifty-odd years, and I see myself as a reluctant teenager, trudging round the newly opened Coventry Cathedral with my parents. How they had thrilled to see this phoenix risen from the ashes of their war. How patient they had been with a son too immature and self-absorbed to appreciate the dazzling modern works of art, and with no inkling of what the birth of the new cathedral symbolized to them and their whole generation. And now I recall how struck I had been, even then, by the simple sadness of this burned cross when I found it standing in its weakness and desolation on the rough rubble altar in the black shell of the ruins. A pure remembrance of a time and a self long past, never resurfaced until this moment.

The light in the nave, by clever design, has been growing darker the nearer the 'east' end I come. Now I arrive at the high altar, a plain slab, enormous and low-built. On it stands the original Cross of Nails fashioned the morning after the Coventry raid, now silver-gilt, sheltered below a twisted crown of thorns.

The Lady chapel beyond is barred off by black railings shaped like spear tips or nails ten feet tall. They don't offer a welcome, but a warning: you can't pass through here lightly or easily. Above looms Graham Sutherland's great work, *Christ in Glory in the Tetramorph*. It was a controversial decision to hang this giant tapestry at the 'east' end, instead of inserting a conventional great window letting in light. East windows are the pride and glory of most cathedrals, the natural focus of a gaze sliding past the high altar. But a worshipper's attention should be fixed on the altar and on Christ, so went the reasoning, not distracted and bedazzled by the light show beyond – which being north-facing, would in any case have had a greatly diminished effect.

The tapestry was woven at Felletin in France by Pinton Frères, at twenty-three by twelve metres the largest tapestry in the world at that time. A golden mandorla frames Christ, who sits with rounded knees, his bloodied hands upraised in a gesture of blessing and welcome. His sparsely bearded face is that of a young man, the beginnings of a thoughtful frown drawing his brows together; he is a presence that exudes a gentle, strong authority. Circling round him is the Tetramorph, the four figures of the Evangelists, every bit as powerful and odd as those in the Chapel of Unity. Actually these are the four beasts from the Book of Revelation, and as I remember the end-of-the-world terrors depicted in John Thornton's great Apocalypse window at York Minster, the shadow of war seems to fall across them. Mark's rather comic lion appears to be strangling in a halter. John's proud eagle stands open-beaked, its wings raised, ready to strike. Matthew's man, bearing a flaming burden on his back, crawls down a flight of stairs towards Christ, his arms bent in a bow before him, fingers interlocked in a spasm of fear and awe. Only Luke's bull shows any playfulness as he capers on disjointed legs.

I've almost turned away from this mighty and remarkable work when I notice that there's a tiny figure between Christ's nail-torn feet. It's a naked man, overwhelmed by the scale and drama of all that's going on around him, but still standing bravely to attention, staring right back over my head and down the nave.

Now, after walking 'east' into gloomier and gloomier light with only that lambent figure of Christ as an aiming point, there's a Big Reveal as I, too, turn 'west' to look down the full length of the nave. The dark is banished in an instant, and the whole cathedral is ablaze with light from the slender side windows. Unseen till now, they rise from floor to roof in pairs, their blocks of glass in glowing colours – fresh spring green for birth and creation, red for fiery youth, a tumbled mass of contrasting shades for struggle and growth, sombre purple for suffering and ageing, gold for Heaven at the end of the pilgrimage. You can only understand your life, this revelation says, when you've come through the gathering dark to Christ at the end, and can turn and look back on it.

Nowhere in my journey round the Ships of Heaven, not even at Salisbury with its silver and gold wash of light, has there been a moment to compare to this.

'Look out for them peregrines,' says Barry Gittins as he shakes my hand in the ruined shell of the old cathedral. 'What a bloody racket they make!' And as if on cue, a raptor's squeaking and creaking echoes sharply from the top of the tower. It's overlain almost immediately by the tolling of a bell for the midday Service of Reconciliation in the ruins. The Dean of Coventry and one acolyte come into view, processing from the new to the old cathedral, carrying a rod tipped with a silvered Cross of Nails. In the sanctuary by the rubble altar with its charred cross, against a backdrop of empty window tracery, a semicircle forms, half a dozen people – worshippers, onlookers, penitents or voyeurs, it's hard to say.

With the cold wind whipping his stole the dean gives a short résumé – the raid, with five hundred bombers dropping high explosives and incendiaries as they crisscrossed the city for eleven hours; dawn revealing a mountain of smoking rubble where the cathedral had stood; Provost Howard's vow in the ruins, 'We will rebuild in the spirit of forgiveness.'

'On this day of all days, Good Friday, it's appropriate that we should be standing here in the ruins,' says the dean. His words resonate. News has broken of an attack carried out yesterday by the US Air Force on a tunnel complex in Afghanistan, killing unknown numbers of Islamic State militants. The twenty-thousand-pound bomb dropped by the USAF is the most powerful ever deployed, a weapon named MOAB (Massive Ordnance Air Blast, immediately nicknamed 'Mother Of All Bombs'), never before used in combat. Although a non-nuclear weapon, reports of its size (it had to be dropped from a cargo plane) and terrifying effectiveness send Hiroshima shudders up my spine.

The present Coventry Cathedral is a house of atonement and of reconciliation. Is its sister ruin alongside, sitting so low and empty, always to be a dark reminder, a shadow forever dogging the footsteps of the future? 'Father Forgive' says the inscription behind the rubble altar – not 'Forgive Them', but just 'Forgive'. A spatter of cold spring rain blows through the roofless sanctuary. 'Father, forgive,' prays the dean, intoning the Liturgy of Reconciliation, 'forgive the hatred which divides nation from nation, race from race, class from class; forgive the covetous desires of people and nations to possess what is not their own; forgive the greed which exploits the work of human hands and lays waste the earth . . .'

A melody plays in my mind, the sound of a haunted voice. I grasp for it, then catch it: Robert Wyatt singing 'Shipbuilding':

> *Within weeks they'll be reopening the shipyard*
> *And notifying the next of kin*
> *Once again.*
> *It's all we're skilled in –*
> *We will be shipbuilding.*

Other singing sounds far off. In the new cathedral a choir is piled up in tiers, forty strong, practising for this afternoon's Good Friday performance of St John Passion. A cross hangs above them, its arms draped in blood-red cloth. Out here in the ruins we have our own cross, a black one that falls from the rainclouds in a rushing swoop.

Here is the heartbeat moment I have been dreaming of. The peregrine circles round the spire, screaming thinly. There's an answering call, a rapid burst of screeches. Another peregrine emerges from the arch at the tower top and throws itself into the air. For an instant the two birds meld into one; then, as the invisible choir laments and the dean makes the sign of the cross, they go chasing and calling above the ruins, away down the sky and out of sight.

17

Inverness

Launching Lucy

THE CATHEDRAL OF ST ANDREW at Inverness is no bigger than one of those high Victorian churches in some industrial parish in the north of England. It stands square and solid in red sandstone on the west bank of the River Ness just upstream of the city centre.

A modest cathedral for a notably modest Scottish town, you might think. But what St Andrew's lacks in pomp and circumstance, it makes up for in consequence. When Essex country rector Robert Eden was elected Bishop of Moray and Ross in 1851, the enormous diocese of nearly five thousand square miles contained only ten Episcopalian churches and about five hundred churchgoers. No cathedrals had been built in Scotland since the Scottish Reformation, and the Presbyterian Church held sway. Nevertheless, Bishop Eden dreamed of building a cathedral for the Highlands of Scotland in the region's capital, Inverness. He was a forceful character, and got his way after a fifteen-year campaign.

The grand cathedral plans of the young architect, Alexander Ross, had to be cut back, thanks to lack of funds. The Cathedral of St Andrew that was opened on 1 September 1869 had the size and aspect of a large parish church, though it was furnished with twin towers 'to give it more of a cathedral character and to relieve its appearing only as a local church'.* As the sole cathedral in the Highlands, though, the status of St Andrew's belied its stature.

On a cold and snowy December afternoon the light inside the cathedral falls grey and sombre through the Victorian glass. There's a faint

* Quotation from the cathedral's minute book.

sparkle in the pale sandstone of the arcade footings, and a cold gleam from the pink and grey granite of the pillars, polished to a glassy sheen. The icons given to Bishop Eden by Tsar Alexander II, when the bishop made a 'pastoral visitation' to Russia back in 1866, exude the chilly bloom of old gold.

The only thing in St Andrew's not subdued by the cold Caledonian light is the white marble font, the cathedral's most striking treasure. An outsize angel kneels barefoot, proffering a huge scallop shell for the baptismal water. Large wings are half unfolded at the seraph's back. The pensive and androgynous Pre-Raphaelite face with its centre-parted hair was modelled by the sculptor as a likeness of Charlotte Learmonth, wife of Colonel Alexander Learmonth of Dean near Edinburgh – they jointly gave the font to the cathedral in 1871. The angel's expression is massively calm, a mature and thoughtful accept-ance of what was and what will be.

I sit in the pew nearest the font and stare at the angel. An ancient notice gummed to the hymnbook shelf of the pew exhorts visitors to be mind-ful of the cathedral's small endowment and to 'contribute liberally to the collection'. I am feeling neither mindful nor liberal. In fact I am steaming mad. I'm bitterly disappointed. I dislike myself for it; the sulky body chemicals taste strange and bad. But I can't get rid of them.

In Orkney, a couple of hundred miles north of here, St Magnus Cathedral at Kirkwall is gearing up for the Festival of St Lucy, so seduc-tively outlined by Fran Flett Hollinrake. 'That's the one,' Fran had said. 'That's our great day.'

I should be there. I have plotted and planned for months, just to be there. To see the young girls processing with lights in their hair, to hear the speeches of the visiting dignitaries from Norway, to see the annual gift of a great Christmas tree ritually lit in snowy Kirkwall. To follow my Ships of Heaven voyage through the wintry dark of the north to its conclusion in an Orkney ship of lights.

Now Storm Caroline has put paid to those best-laid plans. Caroline has leaped over northwest Scotland like a lioness, and has gone out like one, roaring off into the North Sea. The hills and roads round Inverness are blanketed with snow. The pavements are slippery. The wind along the River Ness is icy, piling up lumps of black water through the city. At Inverness and Kirkwall airports Caroline has iced the runways and the wings of the aeroplanes. She has strewn the land with snow and left a trail of severe gales and a string of cancelled flights – mine included – in her wake.

I sit in the cold cathedral, unable to let go of my cherished notion, sulking like a child denied a lollipop. A woman glances at me as she walks out and her expression tells me all I need to know about mine. I dredge up a watery grin for her, and perhaps it's this poor attempt at a smile that brings a stranger to my side. He's one of those shadow folk who haunt cathedrals, restless souls carrying a burden of unease, drawn to the big empty space, the quiet and calm, the clergy or steward ear that's usually ready to be bent. But this afternoon in Inverness Cathedral there is only me, stuck like a stone where I don't want to be.

The man hovers, fixing me with large, dog-like eyes. He holds out a flimsy strip of yellow paper. 'I b-bought these raffle tickets this m-morning. And I don't, I d-don't know if I won. I might have – I might have won. And I don't know what to do . . .'

Where did he buy them – was it here at the cathedral? 'I th-think so. I might, I might have won something. But there's no one to ask. And I've got to go home, go to England t-t-tomorrow. I don't know what to do.'

Could he come back this evening when there'll be a concert and lots of people there? 'Could I . . . ? But I haven't got a ticket for the concert. And will, will the raffle lady be here? What if sh-she isn't? I might have won something. I might have to c-collect it. I don't know . . . I don't know what to do.'

He stares at me hopelessly, the strip of tickets trembling in his fingers, his dream of winning floating just beyond his grasp. A bottle of sherry, a packet of shortbread: it doesn't matter. I can't help him. No one can help him. At last he shuffles away, head down, and parks himself somewhere out of sight to wait in ambush for the next stranger.

Brothers in hope, brothers in disappointment. The shadow man has held up a mirror to me. I crack a bitter smile at myself. Now comes a soft *ting* from my mobile. It's a message from Minister David McNeish in Orkney. He's sad not to be seeing me in St Magnus Cathedral. But he'll send me an account of the goings-on. Better still, someone's filming the whole event. He'll be in touch. Cheers!

They will all be going into the cathedral just now, packing into the narrow nave, the visiting dignitaries from Norway, the locals, the little children in their choir. Fran Flett Hollinrake fills in the gaps for me by email. There are speeches, and a jolly carol. Now the lights go dim. Everything dials down to darkness and silence. A movement at the west end. The children's choir quietly sings the Hymn to St Lucy as a small group of local youngsters comes slowly down the aisle. The cathedral is full of darkness, of anonymous rustling noises. St Lucy leads the procession, wearing a gown of stars and crowned with a coronet of glowing candles. The modest light from her crown shines on her shadowy companions, a bobbing river of red felt elven caps and sparkly cloaks.

The congregation keeps silence as the procession moves down the nave. Behind St Lucy, the faint glimmer of coloured lights starts to grow brighter. The song ends and St Lucy climbs the pulpit. She stands high and faces the congregation, a little girl in a pink cloak of sparkles, exhorting the heavens to shine forth 'one thousand Christmas lights, to make the darkness BRIGHT!' St Lucy and her elven court throw their arms wide, and the interior of St Magnus is suddenly a blaze of light as switches are pulled behind the scenes. It's a homely *coup de théâtre*, and all the more effective for that.

The St Lucy service is over. Everyone crowds out of the cathedral into the darkened square. The children carry old-fashioned lanterns. 'One, two, three!' they shout uninhibitedly in their out-of-church voices, and the Hordaland tree springs into frosty, starry life.

David McNeish and Fran Hollinrake have thrown me a little life-line from the islands across the stormy Pentland Firth. It's a taste, a tantalizing one, of the ceremony of light in the weathered old sand-stone cathedral under the wind and snow. I can't be there. But then I can't be in Lincoln Cathedral tonight for carols by candlelight, or at Ely to watch the children carry their Christingle oranges and candles up the aisle. I can't be in the Anglican cathedral in Liverpool, at another St Lucy service with its candlelit procession and its traditional songs in Swedish. All over Britain at this moment there's bustle and activity in side chapels and sanctuaries. There are practice scales being tried out in cathedral corridors I've walked this year, and candles being lit on carved choir stalls I've sat in for evensong at nightfall.

I sit and picture them, those fragile Ships of Heaven I've come to know, service vessels and showboats all. What rough seas the flotilla has met and breasted, what tactical manoeuvres to port and starboard, what mad swerves of direction. What heroes, what villains the ships have swept up in their voyage to who knows where. From the seed of the new religion planted in a cast-off Roman building in Kent, through Norman militarism and 'power and presence', through Gothic flowering and souring, Reformation, iconoclasm and a turning away from old forms of worship. Through doldrums of poverty and neglect, through the smooth waves of the Victorian revival, through colonial and evangelical certainties, to ground themselves on the bitter disillusion of the war-torn twentieth century. Groping through the fog of pain, penance and penitence to a harbour of atonement and reconciliation. And then away again into the Twitterstorms, the cyber tempests, the whirlpools of many faiths and none, still puzzling out the course to follow, still caught between floating and sinking on the voyage to those blessed isles forever just beyond the horizon, just above the clouds.

Paul Ellis's 'dog's bollocks' hounds race in and out of his limestone undergrowth at Ely. Candlelight winks in the gold filigree of the Broderers' altar cloth at Durham, and glows on the red stained-glass cloak of Mad Henry of Fordwich in the ambulatory at Canterbury

Cathedral, where they have swept up slips of gift wrapping and some strands of Santa's beard after the St Nicholas Parade. Handel's *Messiah* in York Minster. 'The Snowman' at Coventry Cathedral. People and places, sandstone and limestone, murder and miracle. I picture them all as I sit here alone in the one and only cathedral in all the land, it seems, to be dark and empty at this hour of Advent.

I get up and go out into the dark. Snow falls, gently and thickly. Street lights shine in the slate-black water of the River Ness as it hurries north towards the North Sea. On an impulse I open my notebook. There is one blank page left. I tear it out and fold it, longways and sideways, to make a little paper boat. I have no candle to sanctify it with. The lamp glints on the river will have to serve. I sidestep down the slippery bank of snow until the swollen river races just beyond my boots. Here's a bent twig about two feet long – it will do. I impale the paper boat on the tip of the twig and lean out over the black rushing water as far as I dare. I christen the little craft *Lucy* in a private murmur, and with a flick of the wrist I launch her into the tideway.

Miraculously she flutters down keel first into the water. She bobs away towards the town and the sea, upright among the tumbling river waves. I try to keep alongside her, stumbling and sliding on the pavement snow, but she draws ahead.

'Passe avant,' whispers Mappa Mundi's huntsman at the edge of the world. 'Go forward.'

I stop and watch as she sails away, afloat against all the odds, at first among the lights and then on round a bend in the river and out of sight. Maybe to sink in the darkness, maybe to speed like a bird on the wing over the sea beyond, where stones endure and saints live on and little children wear crowns of light.

Acknowledgements

Very many thanks for contacts, introductions and reading suggestions are owed to Dave and Lucy Richardson, Judy Hurst, Philip Dixon, the Ven. Dick Acworth, Howie Firth and Anne Hughes. I'm very grateful to Elizabeth Archibald and Barbara Harrison for accommodation, good cheer and general encouragement.

Cruising among the Ships of Heaven, I met with a tremendous amount of help. For sharing so much of their valuable time and expertise I'd like to thank these people:

Wells: Right Revd Peter Hancock, Bishop of Bath & Wells; Very Revd John Davies, Dean of Wells; Caroline Thornborough, Marketing & Events Officer.

Lincoln: Paul Ellis, stone carver; Patrick Deeming, External Communications Officer; Neville Birch, guide.

Salisbury: Emily Naish, archivist; Sam Kelly and Vicky Burton, glaziers; Canon Treasurer Robert Titley; Lee Andrews, head mason; Luke Kingston, David Vanstone, stonemasons; Pam Barton, PA to the Dean; Acting Dean Edward Probert; Dudley Heather, guide; John Singleton, Visitors' Chaplain.

Canterbury: Canon Christopher Irvine; Canon Max Kramer; Léonie Seliger, Director of the Stained Glass Conservation Department; Joy Bunclark, conservator; Nathalie Cohen, archaeologist.

York: John David, stonemason; Vicky Harrison, Head of Collections; Minnie Triggs, Collections Assistant; Geoff Green and Sandra, guides; Stacey Healey, Marketing.

Durham: Cheryl Penna and Tracy A. Franklin, Broderers; Lilian Groves and Margaret Tindle, guides; Norman Emery, archaeologist; Rob Matthews, former Clerk of Works; Scott Richardson, stonemason; Catherine Hodgson, Marketing Officer; Canon Librarian Rosalind Brown; Maya Polenz, Head of Property; Ruth Robson, Head of Marketing; Marie-Thérèse Mayne, Open Treasure.

Ely: Michael White, Mark Bradford and Will Schenck, guides; Barbara McGowan, guide; Residentiary Canon Vicky Johnson; Canon Stephen Bourne, Administrator and Chapter Clerk.

Worcester: Andy Harrison, geologist.

Gloucester: Pascal Mychalysin, head mason.

Kirkwall: Beatrice Searle, sculptor; Minister David McNeish; Minister Fraser Macnaughton; Fran Flett Hollinrake, Custodian of St Magnus Cathedral; Ross Flett, guide; Dave Flanagan, Tourism Officer.

St Davids: Bishop Wyn Evans; Des Harries, stonemason; Catherine Marks, Deanery Office; Mari James, Development Officer.

Westminster: Jeremy Dixon, architect.

Armagh C of I Cathedral: Very Revd Gregory Dunstan, Dean of Armagh; Robert Somerville and David Hamilton, Friends of Armagh Cathedral; Lee Vage, Cathedral Steward; Lorraine Grattan, Administrative Officer; Carol Conlon, Armagh Robinson Library.

Armagh RC Cathedral: Jack O'Hare, guide; Roddy Hegarty, Cardinal Tomás Ó Fiaich Memorial Library and Archive.

Liverpool Anglican Cathedral: Alan Mathews, Chairman, Friends of Liverpool Cathedral; Clare Kerrigan, Executive Assistant to the Dean of Liverpool; Val Jackson, archivist; Stuart Haynes, Director of Communications; Jenny Moran, Visitor Services Manager; John Baker, guide.

Liverpool RC Cathedral: Claire Hanlon, Executive Assistant to the Dean; Canon Tony O'Brien, Dean of the Metropolitan Cathedral; Neil Sayer, archivist.

Coventry: Very Revd John Witcombe, Dean of Coventry; Barry Gittins, Blitz tour guide.

And most of all, loving thanks to my wife and collaborator, Jane, who was with me the whole way.

Bibliography

Individual Cathedrals

Armagh (St Patrick's C of I)
Curl, James Stevens, *Funerary Monuments & Memorials* (Historical Publications, 2013)
Fleming, Revd W. E. C., *On the Hill of Armagh* (Dundalgan Press, 2016)
'Primate J. G. Beresford's Correspondence' (in Bishop Robinson Library, Armagh)
Rennison, Henry West, 'Manuscript Notes on St Patrick's Cathedral, Armagh' (in Bishop Robinson Library, Armagh)

Armagh (St Patrick's RC)
Gates, Revd Fr John and O'Hare, Jack (eds), *St Patrick's Cathedral* (available in the cathedral)

Canterbury
Culmer, Richard, 'Cathedral Newes from Canterbury' (1644) (http://www.durobrivis.net/library/1644-culmer.pdf)
Eliot, T. S., *Murder in the Cathedral* (Faber & Faber, 1935)

Chichester
Bernstein, Leonard (composer and conductor), *Chichester Psalms*, sung by the Poznan Nightingales (https://www.youtube.com/watch?v=7Yhnml4DW9g)

Coventry
Campbell, Louise, *Coventry Cathedral: Art and Architecture in Post-war Britain* (Clarendon Press, 1996)
Howard, R. T., *Ruined and Rebuilt* (The Council of Coventry Cathedral, 1962)
Schuegraf, Oliver, *Cross of Nails* (Canterbury Press, 2012)

Durham
Venerable Bede, *The Life and Miracles of St Cuthbert, Bishop of Lindisfarne* (https://sourcebooks.fordham.edu/basis/bede-cuthbert.asp)

BIBLIOGRAPHY

Ely
White, Michael, *A Promise of Beauty: The Octagon Tower and Lantern at Ely Cathedral* (FrameCharge Press, 2007)

Hereford
Arrowsmith, Sarah, *Mappa Mundi: Hereford's Curious Map* (Logaston Press, 2015)
Harvey, P. D. A., *Mappa Mundi: The Hereford World Map* (Hereford Cathedral, 2010)

Kirkwall
Rendall, Jocelyn, *Steering the Stone Ships* (St Andrew Press, 2009)

Liverpool (Anglican Cathedral)
Redman, Roy, *Liverpool Cathedral Chronicles* (Liverpool Cathedral, 2015)
Woolton Society (compiler and publisher), *Woolton Stone and Liverpool Cathedral* (2016)

St Davids
Evans, J. Wyn, *St Davids Cathedral* (Pitkin Publishing, 2015)
Evans, J. Wyn and Turner, Rick, *St Davids Bishop's Palace* (Cadw Welsh Historic Monuments, 1991)
Morgan, Hugh et al., *The Hallowed Hole in the Wall* (available in the cathedral)

Westminster
Rogers, Patrick, *Westminster Cathedral: An Illustrated History* (Oremus, 2012)

Worcester
Barker, Philip, Romain, Christopher and Guy, Christopher, *Worcester Cathedral: A Short History* (Logaston Press, 2007)
Explore Worcester Cathedral: Building Stones Trail (Herefordshire & Worcestershire Earth Heritage Trust)

Fiction

Follett, Ken, *Pillars of the Earth* (Macmillan, 1989)
Golding, William, *The Spire* (Faber & Faber, 1964)
Trollope, Anthony, *The Barchester Chronicles* (Penguin Classics)

General Guidebook

Jenkins, Simon, *England's Cathedrals* (Little, Brown, 2016)

History and Architecture

Barron, Robert, *Heaven in Stone and Glass: Experiencing the Spirituality of the Great Cathedrals* (Crossroad Publishing Company, 2002)

Cannon, Jon, *Cathedral: The English Cathedrals and the World that Made Them* (Constable, 2007)

Davis, Jenni, *Cathedral Architecture* (Jarrold Publishing, 2001)

Duby, Georges, *The Age of the Cathedrals: Art and Society, 980–1420* (University of Chicago Press, 1981)

Erlande-Brandenburg, Alain, *The Cathedral Builders of the Middle Ages* (Thames and Hudson, 1995)

Hislop, Malcolm, *How to Build a Cathedral* (A & C Black, 2012)

Macaulay, David, *Cathedral: The Story of its Construction* (Sandpiper, 1981)

Marlow, Peter, *The English Cathedral* (Merrell, 2012)

Platten, Stephen (ed.), *Holy Ground: Cathedrals in the 21st Century* (Sacristy Press, 2017)

Ramirez, Janina, *The Private Lives of the Saints: Power, Passion and Politics in Anglo-Saxon England* (WH Allen, 2015)

Tatton-Brown, T. W. T., *The English Cathedral* (New Holland, 2002)

Social Aspects

Barrett, Philip, *Barchester: English Cathedral Life in the Nineteenth Century* (SPCK, 1993)

Graves, C. Pamela, 'From an Archaeology of Iconoclasm to an Anthropology of the Body: Images, Punishment, and Personhood in England, 1500–1660' (*Current Anthropology* Vol. 49, No. 1, February 2008, pp. 35–60)

Religion and Society (www.religionandsociety.org.uk)

Theos Think Tank, *'Spiritual Capital': The Present and Future of English Cathedrals*, 2012 Report (https://www.theosthinktank.co.uk/research/2012/10/12/spiritual-capital-the-present-and-future-of-english-cathedrals)

Pilgrimage

University of York, *Pilgrims and Pilgrimage* (www.york.ac.uk/projects/pilgrimage)

Must-See Items

Out of the thousands of treasures that each cathedral contains, this round-up of must-see items is a ragbag of the author's personal favourites, intended for visitors in a hurry who want to cut to the chase.

Wells

Medieval clock, jousting knights and Jack Blandiver the quarter-jack, north transept

Bishop's Palace (south of cathedral), with swans on the moat ringing for their food

Magnificent west front

Pillar carvings, transept capitals – grape stealers, toothache man

Unique scissor arches under the central tower

Jumble windows of the Lady chapel

Lincoln

Views – from afar; over castle and town from west front; interior from west end gallery

West front carvings – fate of sinners

Humorous modern-day carvings by Paul Ellis, exterior

Fire and earthquake windows in the chapter house

Rose windows – Bishop's Eye (south transept) and Dean's Eye (north transept)

Roofers' shoe graffiti (tower tour)

Salisbury

Spire, inside (tower tour) and outside

William Pye's infinity font, central nave

Monuments – elaborate Seymour monument (east end, south choir aisle); graffiti'd tomb of John, Lord Cheney (c. 1442–99), 6 foot 8 inches tall, chief henchman or squire to three English kings (north side of nave)

New Sarum cathedral model by James Mogford (northwest aisle)

Original Magna Carta copy, chapter house

Peregrine nestcam (tower tour)

Chichester

Holy Trinity tapestry (John Piper) behind the high altar
Joyful Psalm 150 window by Marc Chagall, northeast corner
Noli Me Tangere painting (Graham Sutherland) in Chapel of St Mary Magdalene
Twelfth-century raising-of-Lazarus carving, south quire aisle
War memorial panels, Royal Sussex Regiment, St George's Chapel
Epitaph memorial to melancholy poet William Collins, baptistery

Canterbury

Monastic ruins, museum and grave of St Augustine, east of cathedral
Graffiti in the crypt, including the witch's trap (pillar at east end)
The Martyrdom, where Archbishop Thomas Becket was murdered
Stone slabs hollowed by pilgrims' knees at Becket's shrine
Superb stained-glass windows in the ambulatory
Becket and Henry II graffito on south wall near Becket's shrine

York Minster

Beginning and end of the world in the Great East Window
Chapter house – 700-year-old carvings of monkeys, pigs, lions, priests, nuns and a great quantity of grotesques
Tour of mason's loft, roof and chapter house timbers
The Doomstone in the crypt – what happens to sinners!
Roman foundations and 'Revealing York Minster' exhibition in the undercroft
Rose window, south transept, brilliantly mended after 1984 lightning strike

Durham

View from afar (especially from west, down beside River Wear and from railway viaduct)
External walls weirdly sculpted by weather
Twelfth-century sanctuary knocker, north door
Galilee Chapel and tomb of the Venerable Bede, west end
Miners' Memorial, south aisle
Embroidery in Chapel of the Nine Altars, east end
The College – Durham's monastic range, south and east of the cathedral
'Open Treasure' exhibition and St Cuthbert's relics in the monks' dormitory and kitchen
Monks' prison in the chapter house, south side
St Cuthbert's shrine, east end

Ely

Views – the Ship of the Fens from afar, the wonky view from the west
The Octagon and Lantern tour
Tour of roof and Stone Store
Lady chapel, northeast end
Tunnell Bros – wartime graffiti in the Lantern
Beautiful monument to fen drainer Humphry Smith (1743), south porch
First World War memorial panels, Chapel of St George
Remarkably complete monastic range, south side

Worcester

Cloisters – Green Men carvings
Many varieties of colourful stone
Early Norman crypt

Gloucester

Cloisters – home of Harry Potter and Hogwarts School of Witchcraft and Wizardry
Crypt (remains of ancient church) and undercroft (Roman remains)
Renovated Lady chapel, east end
Royal tombs – King Edward II (north of presbytery) and Robert Curthose, Duke
    of Normandy (south of presbytery)
Misericord carvings (quire) – elephant, donkey, goat, birds, pigs, squirrel

Hereford

John Maine's 'Ascension' window and monument to the SAS (south aisle)
Herefordshire School of Sculpture – pile of wild carvings of Green Men, etc., cloisters
Historic thirteenth-century Mappa Mundi map of the world (off cloisters)

Kirkwall

'Gollum' monsters on west front
Monument to John Rae, Arctic explorer (southeast corner)
Upper levels tour – hangman's ladder; oyster-shell spacers; 'last gasp' gravestone;
    roof view
Bishop's Palace and Earl's Palace, across road to south

St Davids

View from above of the cathedral in the hollow
Massive Bishop's Palace, west of cathedral
Beautiful carved sixteenth-century nave roof

Wonky aspect – crooked arches, crumbly stone, sloping floor
Caer Bwdy, the cathedral's coastal quarry, one mile southeast
Contrast of sandstone and limestone, exterior
Misericord carvings, quire – eels, dragons, puking boat traveller, shipwrights on their lunch break, clowns playing bump-arse, pigs devouring a dog

St Paul's
Galleries – Whispering Gallery, Stone Gallery, Golden Gallery
The huge, impressive crypt
Martial monuments – General Charles George Gordon (north aisle), Sir William Ponsonby (crypt), Sir John Moore (south transept), Sir Duncan MacDougall (crypt)
Odd monumental touches – Ponsonby's sinking horse, Admiral Lord Howe's lion (south transept), Moore's cherub
Frederick, Lord Leighton monument with sensual attendants (north aisle)
Memorial to war correspondents who died in 1880s Sudan campaign (crypt)
Monolithic tombs of Admiral Lord Nelson and Duke of Wellington (crypt)
Four Evangelists – G. F. Watts mosaics above the crossing

Westminster
View over London from tower
Fabulous, flashy marble and mosaic below, contrasted with the dark vault above
Eric Gill's Stations of the Cross (north and south aisles)
Galero hats of Cardinals Basil Hume (Chapel of St Gregory and St Augustine, south side) and Herbert Vaughan (Chapel of St Thomas of Canterbury, north side) hanging above their tombs
Lampedusa Cross refugees' memorial (Chapel of St Andrew, south side)
Feretory (portable shrine) of St John Southworth, priest and martyr, hung, drawn and quartered in 1654 (Chapel of St George and the English Martyrs, north side)

Armagh C of I
Clumsy, impressive Molyneux monument, northwest aisle
Tandragee idol, a pagan presence (north aisle)
Regimental Chapel of the Royal Irish Fusiliers, south side
Crypt and its pagan stone carvings

Armagh RC
Twin towers high on the hill
Organ with a splendiferous trompeta real
Arts and Crafts interior

Liverpool Anglican
View from the tower
Adrian Wiszniewski paintings, in aisles either side of altar
Lady chapel, east end – women celebrated in memorials, carvings and stained glass
'Laymen's Window' showing all the crafts and trades employed in building the cathedral (southwest corner)
Bishop David Sheppard memorial (south aisle, east end)

Liverpool RC
View from below
Massive, haunting crypt by Sir Edwyn Lutyens
Brilliant conception and colours of the roof spire and Lantern
Angry, agonized Stations of the Cross between the chapels
Goatish Abraham statue by Sean Rice, west apse
Chapel of Remembrance with the Hillsborough tragedy Book of Remembrance

Coventry
Ruins
Jacob Epstein's 'St Michael and the Devil' sculpture, 'south' wall
'West' wall glass engravings
Graham Sutherland's tapestry, 'Christ in Glory in the Tetramorph'
Big Reveal view 'west' from altar
Chapel of Unity floor mosaic ('northwest' aisle)
Chapel of Christ in Gethsemane, screen and mosaic ('southeast' aisle)
Charred Cross from the bombing ruins ('northeast', above steps to café and St Michael's Gallery)

Inverness
Angel font (southwest corner)

Picture Acknowledgements

Colour plates, Section One
Page 1: Cathedral interior, Wells Cathedral: author's photograph with kind permission of Wells Cathedral. **Page 2:** (*above*) Cathedral exterior, Wells Cathedral: author's photograph with kind permission of Wells Cathedral, (*left*) Bishop Peter Hancock, Wells Cathedral: author's photograph with kind permission of the Rt Revd Peter Hancock, (*below*) Paul Ellis's 'greedy skull' carving: author's photograph with kind permission of Lincoln Cathedral. **Page 3:** (*above*) View of Lincoln Castle, Lincoln Cathedral: author's photograph with kind permission of Lincoln Cathedral, (*left*) Paul Ellis, Lincoln Cathedral: author's photograph with kind permission of Paul Ellis, (*below*) William Pye font, consecrated 28 September 2008, Salisbury Cathedral: by kind permission of the Chapter of Salisbury Cathedral. **Page 4:** (*above*) Mogford model (1985), Salisbury Cathedral: by kind permission of the Chapter of Salisbury Cathedral, (*above*) Léonie Seliger, Canterbury Cathedral: author's photograph with kind permission of Léonie Seliger, (*above*) collapsed steeple, Chichester Cathedral: image reproduced with the kind permission of Chichester Cathedral, (*right*) Chagall window, Chichester Cathedral: author photo with kind permission of Chagall ® / © ADAGP, Paris and DACS, London 2018. **Page 5:** (*above*) Cathedral exterior, Canterbury Cathedral: Author's photograph with kind permission of Canterbury Cathedral, (*Left*) Great East Window, York Minster: author's photograph © Chapter of York: reproduced by kind permission, (*below*) chapter house roof, York Minster: author's photograph © Chapter of York: reproduced by kind permission. **Page 6:** (*above*) Cathedral interior, York Minster: author's photograph © Chapter of York: reproduced by kind permission, (*top right*) door knocker, Durham Cathedral: author's photograph with kind permission of Durham Cathedral, (*right*) Saint Aidan tapestry, Durham Cathedral: author's photograph with kind permission of Durham Cathedral, (*below*) sandstone wall, Durham Cathedral: author's photograph with kind permission of Durham Cathedral. **Page 7:** (*above*) Fourteenth-century lantern, Ely Cathedral: author's photograph with kind permission of Ely Cathedral, (*right*) nave roof paintings, Ely Cathedral: author's photograph with kind permission of Ely Cathedral, (*below*) Christ's Apostles, Ely Cathedral: author's photograph with kind permission of Ely Cathedral. **Page 8:** Cathedral exterior, Ely Cathedral: author's photograph with kind permission of Ely Cathedral

PICTURE ACKNOWLEDGEMENTS

Colour Plates, Section Two

Page 1: Chapter house, Worcester Cathedral: author's photograph with kind permission of Worcester Cathedral. Page 2: (*above*) The crypt, Worcester Cathedral: author's photograph with kind permission of Worcester Cathedral, (*below*) Charles Eamer Kempe's stained glass, Gloucester Cathedral: author's photograph with kind permission of Gloucester Cathedral. Page 3: (*above*) Cloisters, Gloucester Cathedral: author's photograph with kind permission of Gloucester Cathedral, (*below*) tomb effigies, Hereford Cathedral: author's photograph with kind permission of Hereford Cathedral, (*bottom*) twelfth-century sculptures, Hereford Cathedral: author's photograph with kind permission of Hereford Cathedral. Page 4: (*left*) South doorway, St Magnus Cathedral: author's photograph with kind permission of St Magnus Cathedral, (*above*) hangman's ladder, St Magnus Cathedral: author's photograph with kind permission of St Magnus Cathedral, (*right*) passageway, St Magnus Cathedral: author's photograph with kind permission of St Magnus Cathedral, (*below*) Cathedral exterior, St Davids Cathedral: by kind permission of the Dean and Chapter of St Davids Cathedral, (*inset*) Misericord carving, St Davids Cathedral: by kind permission of the Dean and Chapter of St Davids Cathedral. Page 5: (*left*) Statue of John Wesley, St Paul's Cathedral: author's photograph with kind permission of St Paul's Cathedral, (*above*) Cathedral model, Westminster Cathedral: author's photograph with kind permission of Westminster Cathedral and Jeremy Dixon, (*below*) Cathedral interior: photographed by Marcin Mazur and reproduced by kind permission of Marcin Mazur and the Catholic Bishops Conference of England and Wales. Page 6: (*above left*) Dean Gregory Dunstan, St Patrick's C of I Cathedral: author's photograph with kind permission of the Very Revd Gregory Dunstan, (*above right*) stone carvings, St Patrick's C of I Cathedral: author's photograph with kind permission of St Patrick's C of I Cathedral, (*below left*) Cathedral exterior, St Patrick's RC: author's photograph with kind permission of St Patrick's RC Cathedral, (*below right*) cardinals' hats, St Patrick's RC Cathedral: by kind permission of Fr Peter McAnenly, administrator of St Patrick's Cathedral, Armagh. Page 7: (*above*) Cathedral exterior, Liverpool Anglican Cathedral: author's photograph with kind permission of Liverpool Anglican Cathedral, (*right*) Lady chapel stair window, Liverpool Anglican Cathedral: author's photograph with kind permission of Liverpool Anglican Cathedral, (*below*) memorial for Bishop David Sheppard, Liverpool Anglican Cathedral: author's photograph with kind permission of Liverpool Anglican Cathedral, (*right*) Cathedral interior, Liverpool Catholic Cathedral: author's photograph with thanks to the Dean, Rev Canon Tony O'Brien. Page 8: (*right*) Cathedral exterior, Coventry Cathedral: author's photograph with kind permission of Coventry Cathedral, (*below*) Gethsemane Chapel, Coventry Cathedral: author's photograph with kind permission of Coventry Cathedral, (*right*) Angel font, Inverness Cathedral: author's photograph with kind permission of Inverness Cathedral.

Index

Christopher Somerville is the walking correspondent of *The Times*. He is one of Britain's most respected and prolific travel writers, with forty-two books, hundreds of newspaper articles and many TV and radio appearances to his name. He lives in Bristol.

If you have been
inspired by these walks,
you can follow Christopher's
footsteps by downloading a free
walking guide from his website

christophersomerville.co.uk / walkingguide